POEM
A DAY

POEM A DAY

Volume 2

~

*A wide range of classic
and modern poems*

~

edited by

LAURIE SHECK

STEERFORTH PRESS
SOUTH ROYALTON, VERMONT

For information about permission to
reproduce selections from this book, write to:
Steerforth Press L.C., P.O. Box 70,
South Royalton, Vermont 05068

ISBN 1-58642-031-3
LCCN 96-32784

Library of Congress cataloging-in-publication data is available from the publisher

FIRST EDITION

For my parents

Introduction

It is the morning of September 11, 2001. I'm sitting at my desk reading Emily Dickinson, whose work I plan to teach the next day. Hidden and self-banished, this outlaw of the soul wrought from intense solitude her bold volatile poems, capturing with such vividness the ways the mind thinks: its stutterings, yearnings, disruptions, slippages, awe. "I felt a Funeral, in my Brain." "Pain — has an Element of Blank —." Her letters, too, are radical, exploratory, slant, often wrestling with the threat of desolation, wringing out of it a fierce energy and eruptive beauty: "I always ran home to Awe when a child, if anything befell me. He was an awful Mother, but I liked him better than none." And to Thomas Wentworth Higginson's criticism of her poems, Dickinson replied, "You think my gait 'spasmodic' — I am in danger — Sir —."

In the words of Emerson: "People want to be settled. Only insofar as they are unsettled is there any hope for them." Within her small room, all was unsettled, charged with risk.

Though I'm only about a mile away, I don't hear the planes hit the towers. When the phone call comes, I leave the book open on my desk, and run.

I'm running to my daughter's school. On Broadway hundreds of people, some covered in dust and white ash, some wounded, limping, are all heading uptown. There are no subways for getting home; cell phones are disabled. People stand patiently in long lines to use the pay phones. When my daughter and I return to our building, we can see, and will see for days after, a strangely luminous white cloud of smoke billowing and billowing. For several days there's not a single car on Broadway. The sky is completely quiet except for fighter planes, the sidewalks mostly empty; businesses are closed, mail delivery suspended. The air smells like burning computers. A few baffled looking people wander around our neighborhood, holding maps, searching out the nearest hospital, hoping to find a loved one alive. Faces of the missing are plastered on store fronts and walls.

When classes resume two weeks later, I wonder how we'll concentrate. How will we talk about poems? But the poems of this woman who knew that "experiment escorts us" allow our minds to move again, to break through the stunned haze we've been in for so many days. What she wrote in one poem can apply to all fine poetry, I think, "It keeps the nerves progressive / Conjecture flourishing." And such flourishing is redemptive.

There is much talk these days about the relevance of poetry. But must poetry be relevant in any direct sense? I don't think so. As William Carlos Williams wrote, "the objective of writing is to reveal. It is not to teach, not to advertise, not to sell." What it gives us is the texture of words put side by side. As Gertrude Stein phrased it: "the mind writes what it is." Poetry embodies the human love of language, its music and movement through time, keeping alive what Williams so wished for — the ability to free the word and dynamize it at the same time.

I have collected here 366 poems, one for every day of the year. There are poems from the canon, contemporary poems, and poems in translation. No poem that appeared in Volume 1 is included here. In having to bypass Christopher Smart's glorious "For I Will Consider My Cat Jeoffry" from his *Jubilate Agno,* for example, I used instead a much less read but very fine section that focuses on flowers: "For flowers are good both for the living and for the dead. / For there is a language of flowers. / For there is a sound reasoning upon all flowers." Length was also a necessary consideration in selecting poems, as was cost.

Even now, I sometimes catch myself looking down the street, half-expecting to see the towers that were once there: "There is a pain — so utter — / It swallows substance up —." But there is also another line Dickinson wrote: "The privilege to scrutinize," which says much about the poet's vocation. Here, then, 366 moments of scrutiny, moments of creation, and awe.

January 2002

POEM
A DAY

A Mistake

I thought: all this is only preparation
For learning, at last, how to die.
Mornings and dusks, in the grass under a maple
Laura sleeping without pants, on a headrest of raspberries,
While Filon, happy, washes himself in the stream.
Mornings and years. Every glass of wine,
Laura, and the sea, land, and archipelago
Bring us nearer, I believed, to one aim
And should be used with a thought to that aim.

But a paraplegic in my street
Whom they move together with his chair
From shade into sunlight, sunlight into shade,
Looks at a cat, a leaf, the chrome steel on an auto,
And mumbles to himself, *"Beau temps, beau temps."*

It is true. We have a beautiful time
As long as time is time at all.

CZESLAW MILOSZ
(1911–)

Born in Lithuania, Czeslaw Milosz grew up in Poland and as a young man cofounded the Polish avant-garde literary group Zagary. He served as a diplomat of communist Poland, first to the United States and later to France, where he requested and received political asylum. He returned to the United States and became a citizen in 1970. His work was banned in Poland until 1980, when he received the Nobel Prize. He is Professor Emeritus of Slavic Languages and Literature at the University of California at Berkeley.

#657

I dwell in Possibility —
A fairer House than Prose —
More numerous of Windows —
Superior — for Doors —

Of Chambers as the Cedars —
Impregnable of Eye —
And for an Everlasting Roof
The Gambrels of the Sky —

Of Visitors — the fairest —
For Occupation — This —
The spreading wide my narrow Hands
To gather Paradise —

EMILY DICKINSON
(1830–1886)

Extremely prolific, but famously reclusive, Emily Dickinson wrote almost 1700 poems, many of which she sewed into packets and secreted in a locked box. She once defined poetry in a letter to a friend, writing, "If I read a book [and] it makes my whole body so cold no fire ever can warm me, I know that is poetry. If I feel physically as if the top of my head were taken off, I know that is poetry." Along with her contemporary Walt Whitman, she is considered a progenitor of an authentic American poetry.

Danse Russe

If I when my wife is sleeping
and the baby and Kathleen
are sleeping
and the sun is a flame-white disc
in silken mists
above shining trees,—
if I in my north room
dance naked, grotesquely
before my mirror
waving my shirt round my head
and singing softly to myself:
"I am lonely, lonely.
I was born to be lonely,
I am best so!"
If I admire my arms, my face,
my shoulders, flanks, buttocks
against the yellow drawn shades,—

Who shall say I am not
the happy genius of my household?

WILLIAM CARLOS WILLIAMS
(1883–1963)

One of the leading American poets of the 20th century, William Carlos Williams made his living practicing medicine in Rutherford, New Jersey, the same city where he was born and where he died. He produced a large, innovative body of work during his long career, often writing at night and between patients; it was not uncommon for him to jot down lines and notes for poems on his prescription pads. This poem is from an early book, *Al Que Quiere!* In 1913, Williams wrote, "Now life is above all things at any moment subversive of life as it was the moment before— always new, irregular. Verse to be alive must have infused into it something of the same order . . . something in the nature of an implacable revolution." Williams was awarded the Pulitzer Prize shortly after his death in 1963.

And shame on all involved!

Ode on Solitude

Happy the man, whose wish and care
    A few paternal acres bound,
Content to breathe his native air,
        In his own ground.

Whose herds with milk, whose fields with bread,
    Whose flocks supply him with attire,
Whose trees in summer yield him shade,
        In winter fire.

Blest, who can unconcern'dly find
    Hours, days, and years slide soft away,
In health of body, peace of mind,
        Quiet by day,

Sound sleep by night, study and ease,
    Together mixed; sweet recreation;
And innocence, which most does please
        With meditation.

Thus let me live, unseen, unknown,
    Thus unlamented let me die,
Steal from the world, and not a stone
        Tell where I lie.

ALEXANDER POPE
(1688–1744)

Because he suffered from tuberculosis of the spine, Alexander Pope never grew taller than four foot six. His literary stature was such, however, that he is credited with being the first English literary figure to support himself by his writing alone. As a Roman Catholic, he was barred from public school and university, but managed to teach himself Greek and Latin. The composition of "Ode on Solitude" has been estimated to have been written about 1700, when Pope was not quite twelve.

The Grammar School Angels

None of us understood the night secret of the blackboards
nor why the armillary sphere got excited only when we looked at it.
We only knew that a circumference doesn't have to be round
and that a lunar eclipse confuses flowers
and sets the birds' clock ahead.

None of us understood anything:
not why our fingers were of India ink
nor why the evening closed compasses to open books at dawn.
We only knew that something straight, if it wants, can be curved
           or broken
and that the wandering stars are children who don't know arithmetic.

RAFAEL ALBERTI
(1902–1999)
Translated by Christopher Sawyer-Lauçanno

Andalusian poet Rafael Alberti was a member of Spain's so-called "Generation of 1927." He began his artistic career as a painter and numbered Federico García Lorca, Juan Gris, Salvador Dali, and Pablo Picasso among his friends and contemporaries. Also known as a playwright with a strongly anti-fascist bent, Alberti was compelled in 1939 to flee to Argentina, and then to Italy, to escape Franco's dictatorship. In 1977 he returned to Spain, where he died of a lung ailment in 1999. He has been honored with the Spanish National Prize for Literature and the Cervantes Prize, and along with García Lorca he is one of Spain's most renowned poets.

The Negro Speaks of Rivers

I've known rivers:
I've known rivers ancient as the world and older than the
      flow of human blood in human veins.

My soul has grown deep like the rivers.

I bathed in the Euphrates when dawns were young.
I built my hut near the Congo and it lulled me to sleep.
I looked upon the Nile and raised the pyramids above it.
I heard the singing of the Mississippi when Abe Lincoln
      went down to New Orleans, and I've seen its muddy
      bosom turn all golden in the sunset.

I've known rivers:
Ancient, dusky rivers.

My soul has grown deep like the rivers.

LANGSTON HUGHES
(1902–1967)

According to his biographer Arnold Rampersad, Hughes wrote this poem in a matter of minutes on the back of an envelope as he crossed the Mississippi River by train on his way to Missouri. Hughes made his national debut at the age of nineteen when "The Negro Speaks of Rivers" appeared in W. E. B. Dubois' *Crisis* magazine. The most important figure of the 1920s' Harlem Renaissance, Hughes was honored by the New York City Preservation Committee, which conferred landmark status on his former home and renamed its stretch of E. 127th street "Langston Hughes Place."

The Banishment (from *Paradise Lost*)

So spake our mother Eve, and Adam heard
Well pleased, but answered not; for now too nigh
The Archangel stood, and from the other hill
To their fixed station, all in bright array
The Cherubim descended; on the ground
Gliding metéorous, as evening mist
Risen from a river o'er the marish glides,
And gathers ground fast at the labourer's heel
Homeward returning. High in front advanced,
The brandished sword of God before them blazed
Fierce as a comet; which with torrid heat,
And vapour as the Libyan air adust,
Began to parch that temperate clime; whereat
In either hand the hastening Angel caught
Our lingering parents, and to the eastern gate
Led them direct, and down the cliff as fast
To the subjected plain; then disappeared.
They, looking back, all the eastern side beheld
Of Paradise, so late their happy seat,
Waved over by that flaming brand, the gate
With dreadful faces thronged and fiery arms.
Some natural tears they dropped, but wiped them soon,
The world was all before them, where to choose
Their place of rest, and Providence their guide:
They hand in hand, with wandering steps and slow,
Through Eden took their solitary way.

JOHN MILTON
(1608–1674)

This is the final stanza of Milton's epic poem, *Paradise Lost*, wherein he describes the expulsion of Adam and Eve from Paradise. Certainly best known for this work, Milton began writing at the age of fifteen, composing poems in Latin and Italian, as well as English. During the English Civil War, Milton publicly supported Oliver Cromwell and later served as Cromwell's Secretary for Foreign Languages. After the restoration of the monarchy in 1660, Milton was threatened with execution, but was spared thanks to the efforts of Andrew Marvell and others.

Evening Star
(Georgia O'Keeffe in Canyon, Texas, 1917)

She was just a schoolteacher then
Walking away from the town
                                    in the late-afternoon sunset,
A young woman in love
                        with a treeless place,
The scattered windmills and pounding winds
Of the whole prairie sliding toward dusk,
Something unfenced and wild
                                about the world without roads,
Miles and miles of land
                        rolling like waves into nowhere,
The light settling down in the open country.

She had nothing to do but walk away
From the churches and banks, the college buildings
Of knowledge, the filling stations
                                of the habitable world,
And then she was alone
                        with what she believed—
The shuddering iridescence of heat lightning,
Cattle moving like black lace in the distance,
Wildflowers growing out of bleached skulls,
The searing oranges and yellows of the evening star
Rising in daylight,
                    commanding the empty spaces.

EDWARD HIRSCH
(1950–)

Born in Chicago, Edward Hirsch taught for many years at the University of Houston. He is currently the President of the Guggenheim Foundation. As the epigraph indicates, this poem takes its title from the paintings in Georgia O'Keeffe's "Evening Star Series," created in 1916 and 1917 in Canyon, Texas.

January 9

Riddle #68 (from the *Exeter Book*)

The wave, over the wave, a weird thing I saw,
thorough-wrought, and wonderfully ornate:
a wonder on the wave — water become bone.

ANONYMOUS
translated by Michael Alexander

"Riddle #68" is one of a series of ninety-five riddles preserved in the *Exeter Book,* one of the largest and most important collections of Anglo-Saxon writing. (See also: May 20 and July 8.) If not for this volume, all but one example of this Old English genre would have been lost. Gifted to the Exeter Cathedral by its first bishop Leofric, the *Exeter Book* has been dated circa 940. Other familiar Old English poems contained in the book include "The Seafarer," "The Wanderer," and "The Wife's Lament." The answer to "Riddle #68" is: *ice.*

from *As You Like It*
Act II, Scene vii

Blow, blow, thou winter wind,
Thou art not so unkind
As man's ingratitude;
Thy tooth is not so keen,
Because thou art not seen,
Although thy breath be rude.
Heigh-ho! sing, heigh-ho! unto the green holly:
Most friendship is feigning, most loving mere folly.
Then heigh-ho! the holly!
This life is most jolly.

Freeze, freeze, thou bitter sky,
That dost not bite so nigh
As benefits forgot:
Though thou the waters warp,
Thy sting is not so sharp
As friend remember'd not.
Heigh-ho! sing, heigh-ho! unto the green holly:
Most friendship is feigning, most loving mere folly.
Then heigh-ho! the holly!
This life is most jolly.

WILLIAM SHAKESPEARE
(1564–1616)

The character Amiens sings this poem for the entertainment of Orlando and Adam, whom the duke has welcomed to his table. During the song, Orlando reveals that he is the son of Sir Rowland, a longtime friend to the banished duke. Holly is a traditional emblem of mirth.

Early in the Morning

While the long grain is softening
in the water, gurgling
over a low stove flame, before
the salted Winter Vegetable is sliced
for breakfast, before the birds,
my mother glides an ivory comb
through her hair, heavy
and black as calligrapher's ink.

She sits at the foot of the bed.
My father watches, listens for
the music of comb
against hair.

My mother combs,
pulls her hair back
tight, rolls it
around two fingers, pins it
in a bun to the back of her head.
For half a hundred years she has done this.
My father likes to see it like this.
He says it is kempt.

But I know
it is because of the way
my mother's hair falls
when he pulls the pins out.
Easily, like the curtains
when they untie them in the evening.

LI-YOUNG LEE
(1957–)

Born in Jakarta, Indonesia, to Chinese parents, Li-Young Lee was just a child when his
family fled to Hong Kong, Macao, Japan, and finally the United States to escape anti-
Chinese sentiment and political persecution. "Early in the Morning" is from Lee's first
book, *Rose*, which won the Delmore Schwartz Memorial Poetry Award in 1986.

The Signal Light

Silent is the house: all are laid asleep:
One alone looks out o'er the snow-wreaths deep,
Watching every cloud, dreading every breeze
That whirls the 'wildering drift, and bends the groaning trees.

The little lamp burns straight, its rays shoot strong and far:
I trim it well, to be the wanderer's guiding-star.

Frown, my haughty sire! chide, my angry dame;
Set your slaves to spy; threaten me with shame!
But neither sire nor dame, nor prying serf shall know
What angel nightly tracks that waste of frozen snow.

What I love shall come like visitant of air,
Safe in secret power from lurking human snare;
What loves me, no word of mine shall e'er betray,
Though for faith unstained my life must forfeit pay.

Burn, then, little lamp; glimmer straight and clear —
Hush! a rustling wing stirs, methinks, the air:
He for whom I wait, thus ever comes to me;
Strange Power! I trust thy might; trust thou my constancy!

EMILY BRONTË
(1818–1848)

"The Signal Light" is thought to be one of Emily Brontë's "Gondal Poems," which narrate the imaginary adventures of Queen Augusta G. Almeda and King Julius Brenzaida in the invented lands of Gondal and Gaaldine. Emily collaborated with Anne Brontë in these fantasies as a child, and continued to write her Gondal poems well into adulthood. Charlotte Brontë later destroyed many of the Gondal texts after her sisters' deaths, but preserved this poem to be printed with an 1850 edition of *Wuthering Heights and Agnes Grey*. As with Emily Brontë's other works, the poem was first published under the pseudonym Ellis Bell. Brontë died of tuberculosis at the age of thirty.

In the Microscope

Here too are dreaming landscapes,
lunar, derelict.
Here too are the masses,
tillers of the soil.
And cells, fighters
who lay down their lives
for a song.

Here too are cemeteries,
fame and snow.
And I hear murmuring,
the revolt of immense estates.

MIROSLAV HOLUB
(1923–1998)
translated by Ian Milner

Miroslav Holub was born in Pilsen, Czechoslovakia, and received an M.D. as well as a Ph.D. in immunology at the Czechoslovak Academy of Sciences, Institute of Microbiology. Holub considered science his vocation and poetry a pastime, but often combined the two, as in this poem. In addition to his poetry, he authored more than 150 scientific papers and once remarked to an interviewer, "I'm afraid that if I had all the time in the world to write my poems, I would write nothing at all." After the communist invasion of Czechoslovakia in 1968, Holub was declared a nonperson, but he was never jailed. His work was banned there until the government's collapse in 1998, the same year he died.

Smoke in Winter

The sluggish smoke curls up from some deep dell,
The stiffened air exploring in the dawn,
And making slow acquaintance with the day;
Delaying now upon its heavenward course,
In wreathéd loiterings dallying with itself,
With as uncertain purpose and slow deed,
As its half-wakened master by the hearth,
Whose mind still slumbering and sluggish thoughts
Have not yet swept into the onward current
Of the new day; — and now it streams afar,
The while the chopper goes with step direct,
And mind intent to swing the early axe.
    First in the dusky dawn he sends abroad
His early scout, his emissary, smoke,
The earliest, latest pilgrim from the roof,
To feel the frosty air, inform the day;
And while he crouches still beside the hearth,
Nor musters courage to unbar the door,
It has gone down the glen with the light wind,
And o'er the plain unfurled its venturous wreath,
Draped the tree tops, loitered upon the hill,
And warmed the pinions of the early bird;
And now, perchance, high in the crispy air,
Has caught sight of the day o'er the earth's edge,
And greets its master's eye at his low door,
As some refulgent cloud in the upper sky.

HENRY DAVID THOREAU
(1817–1862)

Most famous for his prose work, *Walden,* Thoreau wrote poems in the early stages of his career until he concluded that verse was too confining and destroyed most of his poems in a deliberately set fire. His first collection of poems was published posthumously in 1865. Thoreau never married. His only romantic prospect was a woman named Ellen Sewall. Her father forbade her to associate with the odd fellow who lived in a rustic cabin and who stubbornly refused to take over the Thoreau family's prosperous pencil business.

January 15

Blank Paper
from "Memories of the Atomic Age"

He brought home paper from work, marked CONFIDENTIAL,
a briefcase full, now stamped DECLASSIFIED,
for us to draw on, mysteriously dull
but blank as snow on the other side.

Hoping we'd be quiet after work?
We played with the badge with his picture on it,
grew bored, and fought to be the dime-store clerk
you bought arms from, who wanted more than a chit.

Did my father dread the Saturdays it snowed?
Where was the hush of a world brought to a halt
at the reactor's gate, the badge you showed?
He made the sidewalk safe for us with salt.

My mother forced a paperwhite to bloom,
pure as the snow's irradiated room.

DEBORA GREGER
(1949–)

"Blank Paper" is a section of the long poem "Memories of the Atomic Age" in Debora Greger's book *Desert Fathers, Uranium Daughters.* Greger grew up in Richland, Washington, near the Hanford Atomic Plant. Like most men in the area, her father worked for the plant, which was later revealed to have manufactured the plutonium used in the bomb dropped on Nagasaki. "The high school team was named the bombers," she explains. "The school ring had a mushroom cloud on it." Greger teaches at the University of Florida. A visual artist as well as a poet, she has designed her own book jackets.

Chaucer's Complaint to His Purse

To you, my purse, you whom I will not slight
For any other, you my lady dear,
Bitterly I complain. You are so light
That certainly you give me heavy cheer.
I had as lief be laid upon my bier,
And hoping for your mercy, thus I cry:
Be heavy again, for if not I shall die.

Grant me this very day, before the night,
Your blissful jingle once again to hear,
Or like the sun to see your hue flash bright
That for its golden brilliance has no peer.
Rudder by which I teach my heart to steer,
Queen of good company, to whom I fly,
Be heavy again, for if not I shall die.

Now purse, you are my solace, life, and light,
My savior, down here in this earthly scene!
If you won't be my treasurer, ease my plight
By helping me away at least, my queen,
Out of this town, for I am shaved as clean
As any friar! yet still your grace I'll try:
Be heavy again, for if not I shall die.

GEOFFREY CHAUCER
(1343–1400)

Should be 1336

At the age of fifteen, Geoffrey Chaucer became page to the countess of Ulster, beginning a career of court service that would extend through the positions of Diplomat, Controller of Export Taxes, Justice of the Peace, Member of Parliament, and Deputy Forester. In 1936, he married a relation of King Richard II (the sister-in-law of his uncle) and was granted a royal annuity. However, when Henry IV ascended the throne in 1399, there was some doubt as to whether Chaucer would continue to enjoy royal patronage, a situation that doubtless inspired this poem written in 1400. At some point after its original composition, Chaucer added an obsequious "Envoy to Henry IV" and his annuity was reconfirmed. Nevertheless, his debt continued to be a problem until he moved to Westminster Abbey and was officially absolved of all financial responsibility. He is best known for his *Canterbury Tales*.

Who Makes These Changes?

Who makes these changes?
I shoot an arrow right.
It lands left.
I ride after a deer and find myself
chased by a hog.
I plot to get what I want
and end up in prison.
I dig pits to trap others
and fall in.

I should be suspicious
of what I want.

RUMI

(1207–1273)

translated by Coleman Barks

Jelalludin Rumi was born in 1207 near the city of Balkh (located in what is now Afghanistan). While still a young man, he and his family were forced to flee their home to escape the advancing troops of Genghis Khan. The family eventually settled in Konya (located in what is now Turkey), where Rumi's father became the head of the Sufi dervish community, a sect of mystic Muslims. Rumi succeeded his father as leader of the community and composed his poems spontaneously while circling around a pole, as a scribe took them down. The whirling of the Mevlevi whirling dervishes derives from this practice. Rumi spent the last twelve years of his life on his masterwork, a six-volume poem known as the *Masnevi*, or *Mathnavi*. Poetry, along with song, meditation, and fasting, is essential to the practice of Sufism.

The Flea

Mark but this flea, and mark in this,
How little that which thou deniest me is;
It sucked me first, and now sucks thee,
And in this flea our two bloods mingled be.
Thou know'st that this cannot be said
A sin, nor shame, nor loss of maidenhead;
   Yet this enjoys before it woo,
    And pampered swells with one blood made of two;
    And this, alas! is more than we would do.

Oh stay, three lives in one flea spare,
Where we almost, yea, more than married are.
This flea is you and I, and this
Our marriage bed, and marriage temple is.
Though parents grudge, and you, we're met,
And cloistered in these living walls of jet.
   Though use make you apt to kill me,
    Let not to that self-murder added be,
    And sacrilege, three sins in killing three.

Cruel and sudden, hast thou since
Purpled thy nail in blood of innocence?
Wherein could this flea guilty be,
Except in that drop which it sucked from thee?
Yet thou triumph'st, and sayest that thou
Find'st not thyself nor me the weaker now.
   'Tis true; then learn how false fears be;
    Just so much honor, when thou yieldest to me,
    Will waste, as this flea's death took life from thee.

JOHN DONNE
(1572–1631)

Now recognized as one of the greatest English poets, John Donne remained relatively obscure during his lifetime, publishing very few poems and drawing the disapproval of luminaries such as Ben Jonson. His poems circulated widely in manuscript, however, and were appreciated by many who were privileged to read them. Donne took Anglican orders in 1615 and proved to be a talented clergyman, giving well-attended sermons at St. Paul's Cathedral in London until his death in 1631. As unusual as it may seem to readers today, the flea — and its unhindered access to the flesh — was a popular motif in Renaissance poetry. Donne borrowed and elaborated on the conventional conceit in this poem.

There is also "The Song of the Gnat"
in Mussorgsky's "Boris Godunov"

Blonde Bombshell

Love is boring and passé, all the old baggage,
the bloody bric-a-brac, the bad, the gothic,
retrograde, obscurantist hum and drum of it
needs to be swept away. So, night after night,
we sit in the dark of the Roxy beside grandmothers
with their shanks tied up in the tourniquets
of rolled stockings and open ourselves, like earth
to rain, to the blue fire of the movie screen
where love surrenders suddenly to gangsters
and their cuties. There in the narrow,
mote-filled finger of light, is a blonde
so blond, so blinding, she is a blizzard, a huge
spook, and lights up like the sun the audience
in its galoshes. She bulges like a deuce coupe.
When we see her we say good-bye to Kansas.
She is everything spare, cool, and clean,
like a gas station on a dark night or the cold
dependable light of rage coming in on schedule like a bus.

LYNN EMANUEL
(1949–)

Lynn Emanuel was born in Mt. Kisco, New York. She holds degrees from Bennington College, the City College of New York, and the University of Iowa. She is a professor of English and the director of the Writing Program at the University of Pittsburg. "In English in a Poem" from Emanuel's book *Then Suddenly* also takes the movies as a theme: "Gertrude Stein said America / was a *space filled with moving,* but I hate being moving. / If you want to *feel,* go to the movies, because poetry / has no intention of being moving; it is perhaps one / of the few things left in America that is not moving."

We know this much

Death is an evil;
we have the gods'
word for it; they too
would die if death
were a good thing

SAPPHO
(CA. 610–580 B.C.)
translated by Mary Barnard

Not much can be confirmed about the life of Sappho, except that she was born to a wealthy family on the Greek island of Lesbos and spent most of her life in the city of Mytilene. She married and had a daughter and ran an academy for young women devoted to the cult of Aphrodite. Plato referred to Sappho as "the tenth Muse," and she was a literary celebrity even in antiquity, depicted on coins and in civic statuary. Most of her extant poems consist of fragments collected from various papyri or culled from quotations by other authors.

Snow

The room was suddenly rich and the great bay-window was
Spawning snow and pink roses against it
Soundlessly collateral and incompatible:
World is suddener than we fancy it.

World is crazier and more of it than we think,
Incorrigibly plural. I peel and portion
A tangerine and spit the pips and feel
The drunkenness of things being various.

And the fire flames with a bubbling sound for world
Is more spiteful and gay than one supposes—
On the tongue on the eyes on the ears in the palms of one's
    hands—
There is more than glass between the snow and the huge roses.

LOUIS MACNEICE
(1907–1963)

Born in Belfast, Ireland, Louis MacNeice was among the Oxford Poets, a group that
included W. H. Auden, Stephen Spender, and Cecil Day Lewis. He also wrote radio
plays, stage plays, and a novel (as Louis Malone) and worked as a producer for the
British Broadcasting Company. He and Auden remained close after leaving Oxford
and cowrote *Letters from Iceland* after a journey to that country in 1936. In 1963,
MacNeice caught pneumonia following a BBC recording session in a damp mine and
died shortly thereafter. Auden dedicated a section of his long poem "Thanksgiving for
a Habitat" to MacNeice's memory, lamenting the loss of his lifelong friend: "I wish
you hadn't / caught that cold, but the dead we miss are easier / to talk to."

Homage to the Empress of the Blues

Because there was a man somewhere in a candystripe silk shirt,
gracile and dangerous as a jaguar and because a woman moaned
for him in sixty-watt gloom and mourned him Faithless Love
Twotiming Love Oh Love Oh Careless Aggravating Love,

    She came out on the stage in yards of pearls, emerging like
    a favorite scenic view, flashed her golden smile and sang.

Because grey laths began somewhere to show from underneath
torn hurdygurdy lithographs of dollfaced heaven;
and because there were those who feared alarming fists of snow
on the door and those who feared the riot-squad of statistics,

    She came out on the stage in ostrich feathers, beaded satin,
    and shone that smile on us and sang.

ROBERT HAYDEN
(1913–1980)

Born Asa Bundy Sheffey in Detroit, Michigan, Robert Hayden was raised by foster
parents who changed his name. At the University of Michigan, Hayden studied with
W. H. Auden, who recognized Hayden's talent on the first day of class and con-
tinued to mentor him for several years. The winner of two Hopwood Awards and a
fellow of the Academy of American Poets, Hayden became the first African-
American to hold the office of Poetry Consultant to the Library of Congress (a posi-
tion later retitled Poet Laureate) in 1967. "Homage to the Empress of the Blues" was
included in Hayden's first book, *A Ballad of Remembrance,* and is a tribute to the leg-
endary blues singer Bessie Smith.

Of All Works

Of all works I prefer
Those used and worn.
Copper vessels with dents and with flattened rims
Knives and forks whose wooden handles
Many hands have grooved: such shapes
Seemed the noblest to me. So too the flagstones around
Old houses, trodden by many feet and ground down,
With clumps of grass in the cracks, these too
Are happy works.

Absorbed into the use of the many
Frequently changed, they improve their appearance, growing enjoyable
Because often enjoyed.
Even the remnants of broken sculptures
With lopped-off hands I love. They also
Lived with me. If they were dropped at least they must have been carried.
If men knocked them over they cannot have stood too high up.
Buildings half dilapidated
Revert to the look of buildings not yet completed
Generously designed: their fine proportions
Can already be guessed; yet they still make demands
On our understanding. At the same time
They have served already, indeed have been left behind. All this
Makes me glad.

BERTOLT BRECHT
(1898–1956)
translated by Michael Hamburger

A playwright, poet, theater director, and prose writer, Bertolt Brecht was born in Augsburg, Germany. He published his first piece, a play about the Bible, in his school newspaper at the age of fifteen, but was later threatened with expulsion from school for a controversial essay. Such turmoil became a frequent feature of his later career. Among his best-known plays are *The Threepenny Opera, Mother Courage and Her Children,* and *The Caucasion Chalk Circle.* Brecht is considered one of the most influential playwrights of the twentieth century. Brecht invested many of his plays with Marxist and anti-Capitalist messages, was blacklisted by the Nazis, and fled Germany after Hitler's rise to power, after which he spent time in several countries, landing eventually in the United States, until his return to Germany in 1949.

Her Face	Her Tongue	Her Wytt
Her face	Her tongue	Her wytt
So faier	So sweete	So sharpe
first bent	then drewe	then hitt
myne eye	myne eare	my harte
Myne eye	Myne eare	My harte
to lyke	to learne	to love
her face	her tongue	her wytt
doth leade	doth teache	doth move
Her face	Her tongue	Her wytt
with beames	with sounde	with arte
doth blynd	doth charm	doth knitt
myne eye	myne eare	my harte
Myne eye	Myne eare	My harte
with lyfe	with hope	with skill
her face	her tongue	her wytt
doth feede	doth feaste	doth fyll
O face	O tongue	O wytt
with frownes	with cheeks	with smarte
wronge not	vex nott	wounde not
myne eye	myne eare	my harte
This eye	This eare	This harte
shall Joye	shall yeald	shall swear
her face	her tongue	her wytt

ARTHUR GORGES
(1557–1625)

Sir Arthur Gorges was a poet and translator who happened to be first cousin to the better-known poet Sir Walter Ralegh. He fought for England against the Spanish Armada, commanding a ship on the Island Voyage with Ralegh as Vice-Admiral. "Her Face Her Tongue Her Wytt" exists in various versions, at least one of which has been credited to Ralegh. Some critics think the poem may have been a joint effort between the two men.

Ralegh, whose name others have since found cause to spell "Raleigh" or "Raliegh"

Language Lesson 1976

When Americans say a man
takes liberties, they mean

he's gone too far. In Philadelphia today I saw
a kid on a leash look mom-ward

and announce his fondest wish: one
bicentennial burger, hold

the relish. Hold is forget,
in American.

On the courts of Philadelphia
the rich prepare

to serve, to fault. The language is a game as well,
in which love can mean nothing,

doubletalk mean lie. I'm saying
doubletalk with me. I'm saying

go so far the customs are untold.
Make nothing without words,

and let me be
the one you never hold.

HEATHER MCHUGH
(1948–)

Heather McHugh was born in San Diego, California, and grew up in Virginia. She was educated at Harvard and has taught at the Iowa Writers' Workshop and the M.F.A. program at Warren Wilson College. She is also on the Creative Writing faculty at the University of Washington in Seattle. The Academy of American Poets elected her Chancellor in 1999. With her husband, the translator Nikolai Popov, she is also known for translating the poems of Paul Celan. "Language Lesson 1976" is set in Philadelphia, during the bicentennial celebration of the Declaration of Independence.

The Chimney Sweeper (from *Songs of Innocence*)

When my mother died I was very young,
And my father sold me while yet my tongue,
Could scarcely cry weep weep weep weep.
So your chimneys I sweep & in soot I sleep.

Theres little Tom Dacre, who cried when his head
That curl'd like a lambs back, was shav'd, so I said.
Hush Tom never mind it, for when your head's bare,
You know that the soot cannot spoil your white hair.

And so he was quiet, & that very night,
As Tom was a sleeping he had such a sight,
That thousands of sweepers Dick, Joe Ned & Jack
Were all of them lock'd up in coffins of black

And by came an Angel who had a bright key,
And he open'd the coffins & set them all free.
Then down a green plain leaping laughing they run
And wash in a river and shine in the Sun.

Then naked & white, all their bags left behind,
They rise upon clouds, and sport in the wind.
And the Angel told Tom if he'd be a good boy,
He'd have God for his father & never want joy.

And so Tom awoke and we rose in the dark
And got with our bags & our brushes to work.
Tho' the morning was cold, Tom was happy & warm,
So if all do their duty, they need not fear harm.

WILLIAM BLAKE
(1757–1827)

William Blake's parents recognized their son as an unusual child early on and never sent him to conventional school. From the age of four Blake experienced visions, claiming to see God at the windows or angels in the trees. He learned to read and write at home, though later he did attend art school for a brief period. At the age of fourteen, he was apprenticed to an engraver from whom he learned the trade by which he would make his living. This poem is from an early collection of Blake's poetry, *Songs of Innocence*. Like many of his later books, it was illustrated with engravings and watercolored by hand. Blake used a technique involving copper plates for these illustrations. He credited the invention of this method to a visit from his deceased brother's spirit.

The Sleepwalker

The sleepwalker
circling upon his star
is awakened by
the white feather of morning —
the bloodstain on it reminds him —
startled, he drops
the moon —
the snowberry breaks
against the black agate of night
sullied with dream —

No spotless white on this earth —.

NELLY SACHS
(1891–1970)
translated by Michael Hamburger

Nelly Sachs was born to Jewish parents in Berlin, Germany, and began to write poetry at an early age. She also studied music and dance and at one time hoped to become a professional dancer. At the age of fifteen she struck up a correspondence with the Swedish novelist Selma Langerlöt that lasted for thirty-five years. In 1940 Langerlöt helped arrange sanctuary for Sachs and her mother, who fled to Sweden to escape persecution by the Nazis. Sachs settled in Stockholm in a one-room apartment, in circumstances quite different from her privileged upbringing. She lived the remainder of her life in this same residence, writing poems and verse plays and translating Swedish poetry into German. She received the Nobel Prize for Literature in 1966.

The Chimney Sweeper (from *Songs of Experience*)

A little black thing among the snow:
Crying weep, weep, in notes of woe!
Where are thy father & mother? say?
They are both gone up to the church to pray.

Because I was happy upon the heath,
And smil'd among the winters snow:
They clothed me in the clothes of death,
And taught me to sing the notes of woe.

And because I am happy, & dance & sing,
They think they have done me no injury:
And are gone to praise God & his priest & King
Who make up a heaven of our misery.

WILLIAM BLAKE
(1757–1827)

Blake's *Songs of Experience* followed *Songs of Innocence* in 1794. The two collections were published together with the descriptive subtitle "Shewing the Two Contrary States of the Human Soul." Like *Songs of Innocence, Songs of Experience* was illustrated and hand-colored using the copper-plate technique invented by Blake. Many readers, including William Wordsworth and Robert Southey, considered Blake to be insane, but Blake never wavered from his commitment to his inner vision in creating his drawings and poems. His rare double genius was unfortunately not widely recognized during his lifetime and he died in poverty in 1827.

A Noiseless Patient Spider

A noiseless patient spider,
I mark'd where on a little promontory it stood isolated,
Mark'd how to explore the vacant vast surrounding,
It launched forth filament, filament, filament, out of itself,
Ever unreeling them, ever tirelessly speeding them.
And you O my soul where you stand,
Surrounded, detached, in measureless oceans of space,
Ceaselessly musing, venturing, throwing, seeking the spheres to
    connect them,
Till the bridge you will need be form'd, till the ductile anchor hold,
Till the gossamer thread you fling catch somewhere, O my soul.

WALT WHITMAN
(1819–1892)

Born on Long Island, New York, in 1819, Walt Whitman is considered the father of American poetry. Like his visionary predecessor William Blake, Whitman was largely self-taught and fascinated with the printer's trade. He turned from printing to journalism, writing for and editing several New York newspapers and founding both the *Long Islander* and the *Brooklyn Freeman*. His controversial and strikingly original first edition of *Leaves of Grass* in 1855 did not contain "A Noiseless Patient Spider," which was added to the repeatedly revised and updated volume in 1868. The so-called death-bed edition of *Leaves of Grass* was published in January 1892.

English Lessons

When it was Desdemona's time to sing,
and so little life was left to her,
she wept, not over love, her star,
but over willow, willow, willow.

When it was Desdemona's time to sing
and her murmuring softened the stones
around the black day, her blacker demon
prepared a psalm of weeping streams.

When it was Ophelia's time to sing,
and so little life was left to her,
the dryness of her soul was swept away
like straws from haystacks in a storm.

When it was Ophelia's time to sing,
and the bitterness of tears was more
than she could bear, what trophies
did she hold? Willow, and columbine.

Stepping out of all that grief,
they entered, with faint hearts
the pool of the universe and quenched
their bodies with other worlds.

BORIS PASTERNAK
(1890–1960)
translated by Mark Rudman with Bohden Boychuk

The son of a painter and a pianist, Boris Pasternak grew up in a home frequented by many of the writers, artists, and intellectuals of the day, including Rainer Maria Rilke. Pasternak's earliest interests included botany and music, and it was assumed for a time that he would become a professional musician. Instead he turned to academia and philosophy and eventually to poetry. His first several collections made little impression, but he ultimately became so popular that audience members at his readings could prompt him from memory if he forgot a line. In 1958 he was awarded the Nobel Prize for Literature, which he at first accepted but was later forced to decline due to pressure from the Soviet government. "English Lessons" features Shakespeare's heroines Desdemona and Ophelia, from *Othello* and *Hamlet* respectively. Pasternak translated both plays, along with other Shakespearean works, into Russian.

The Mock Turtle's Song

"Will you walk a little faster?" said a whiting to a snail.
"There's a porpoise close behind us, and he's treading on my tail.
See how eagerly the lobsters and the turtles all advance!
They are waiting on the shingle — will you come and join the
    dance?
  Will you, won't you, will you, won't you, will you join the
    dance?
  Will you, won't you, will you, won't you, won't you join the
    dance?

"You can really have no notion how delightful it will be,
When they take us up and throw us, with the lobsters, out to sea!"
But the snail replied "Too far, too far!" and gave a look askance —
Said he thanked the whiting kindly, but he would not join the
    dance.
  Would not, could not, would not, could not, would not join the
    dance.
  Would not, could not, would not, could not, could not join the
    dance.

"What matters it how far we go?" his scaly friend replied.
"There is another shore, you know, upon the other side.
The further off from England the nearer is to France —
Then turn not pale, beloved snail, but come and join the dance.
  Will you, won't you, will you, won't you, will you join the
    dance?
  Will you, won't you, will you, won't you, won't you join the
    dance?"

LEWIS CARROLL
(1832–1898)

Lewis Carroll is the pseudonym of Charles Lutwidge Dodgson, a mathematician, photographer, clergyman, and famed author of *Alice's Adventures in Wonderland* and its sequel *Through the Looking Glass & What Alice Found There.* These books were based on a series of tales told by Carroll to his young friend Alice Liddell and her siblings, the children of Henry Liddell, Dean of Christ Church, Oxford. In *Alice's Adventures in Wonderland,* the Mock Turtle sings this fanciful song to accompany the performance of the Lobster Quadrille.

February in Sydney

Dexter Gordon's tenor sax
plays "April in Paris"
inside my head all the way back
on the bus from Double Bay.
Round Midnight, the '50s,
cool cobblestone streets
resound footsteps of Bebop
musicians with whiskey-laced voices
from a boundless dream in French.
Bud, Prez, Webster, & The Hawk,
their names run together riffs.
Painful gods jive talk through
bloodstained reeds & shiny brass
where music is an anesthetic.
Unreadable faces from the human void
float like torn pages across the bus
windows. An old anger drips into my throat,
& I try thinking something good,
letting the precious bad
settle to the salty bottom.
Another scene keeps repeating itself:
I emerge from the dark theatre,
passing a woman who grabs her red purse
& hugs it to her like a heart attack.
Tremolo. Dexter comes back to rest
behind my eyelids. A loneliness
lingers like a silver needle
under my black skin,
as I try to feel how it is
to scream for help through a horn.

YUSEF KOMUNYAKAA

(1947–)

Born in Bogalusa, Louisiana, Yusef Komunyakaa won the Pulitzer Prize and the Kingsley Tufts Poetry Award in 1994 for *Neon Vernacular*. He was also awarded the Bronze Star for his service in Vietnam. The Academy of American Poets elected him a Chancellor in 1999. He is Professor of the Council of the Humanities and Creative Writing at Princeton University.

Things

My cane, my pocket change, this ring of keys,
The obedient lock, the belated notes
The few days left to me will not find time
To read, the deck of cards, the tabletop,
A book, and crushed in its pages the withered
Violet, monument to an afternoon
Undoubtedly unforgettable, now forgotten,
The mirror in the west where a red sunrise
Blazes its illusion. How many things,
Files, doorsills, atlases, wine glasses, nails,
Serve us like slaves who never say a word,
Blind and so mysteriously reserved.
They will endure beyond our vanishing;
And they will never know that we have gone.

JORGE LUIS BORGES
(1899–1986)
translated by Stephen Kessler

Jorge Luis Borges was born in Buenos Aires and educated in Europe. He published his first poem at the age of twenty in 1919. Known internationally for the short stories in his collection *Ficciones*, Borges received honorary Doctorates of Letters from both Columbia and Oxford and was honored with the International Publishers' Prize (shared with Samuel Beckett), the Jerusalem Prize, and the Alfonso Reyes Prize, among other awards. "Things" is from his fifth book of poems, *In Praise of Darkness*. In that book's introduction Borges wrote, "Poetry is no less serious than the other elements making up our earth."

Preludes

I

The winter evening settles down
With smell of steaks in passageways.
Six o'clock.
The burnt-out ends of smoky days.
And now a gusty shower wraps
The grimy scraps
Of withered leaves about your feet
And newspapers from vacant lots;
The showers beat
On broken blinds and chimney-pots,
And at the corner of the street
A lonely cab-horse steams and stamps.
And then the lighting of the lamps.

II

The morning comes to consciousness
Of faint stale smells of beer
From the sawdust-trampled street
With all its muddy feet that press
To early coffee-stands.
With the other masquerades
That time resumes,
One thinks of all the hands
That are raising dingy shades
In a thousand furnished rooms.

III

You tossed a blanket from the bed,
You lay upon your back, and waited;
You dozed, and watched the night revealing
The thousand sordid images
Of which your soul was constituted;
They flickered against the ceiling.
And when all the world came back
And the light crept up between the shutters

And you heard the sparrows in the gutters,
You had such a vision of the street
As the street hardly understands;
Sitting along the bed's edge, where
You curled the papers from your hair,
Or clasped the yellow soles of feet
In the palms of both soiled hands.

IV

His soul stretched tight across the skies
That fade behind a city block,
Or trampled by insistent feet
At four and five and six o'clock;
And short square fingers stuffing pipes,
And evening newspapers, and eyes
Assured of certain certainties,
The conscience of a blackened street
Impatient to assume the world.

I am moved by fancies that are curled
Around these images, and cling:
The notion of some infinitely gentle
Infinitely suffering thing.

Wipe your hand across your mouth, and laugh;
The worlds revolve like ancient women
Gathering fuel in vacant lots.

T. S. ELIOT
(1888–1965)

Thomas Stearns Eliot was born in St. Louis, Missouri. After college he moved to England where he lived for the rest of his life, becoming a British citizen in 1927. His major and groundbreaking poem, "The Waste Land," is one of the seminal works of English-language poetry in the twentieth century. After working in a bank, Eliot became an editor at Faber & Faber, publishing the books of W. H. Auden, Stephen Spender, Louis MacNeice, and others. He received the Nobel Prize for Literature in 1948. "Preludes" is an early poem that first appeared in *Prufrock and Other Observations,* published in 1917.

The Windows

Lord, how can man preach thy eternall word?
   He is a brittle crazie glasse:
Yet in thy temple thou dost him afford
    This glorious and transcendent place,
    To be a window, through thy grace.

But when thou dost anneal in glasse thy storie,
   Making thy life to shine within
The holy Preachers; then the light and glorie
    More rev'rend grows, & more doth win:
    Which else shows watrish, bleak, & thin.

Doctrine and life, colours and light, in one
   When they combine and mingle, bring
A strong regard and aw: but speech alone
    Doth vanish like a flaring thing,
    And in the eare, not conscience ring.

GEORGE HERBERT
(1593–1633)

George Herbert was born to a prominent family in Wales. Herbert's mother was among the patrons of John Donne and the person to whom Donne dedicated his "Holy Sonnets." At the age of sixteen, George Herbert informed his mother in a letter that he would henceforward dedicate all of his poetic efforts to the service of God. In 1630 he took Holy Orders in the Church of England and spent the rest of his life as a rector. As he was dying from consumption at the age of forty, Herbert sent the manuscript containing "The Windows" to his friend Nicholas Ferrar with instructions to publish the poems or burn them as he saw fit. The book was posthumously published as *The Temple: Sacred Poems and Private Ejaculations* in 1633 and soon became enormously popular. *The Temple* also included Herbert's shaped poems "The Altar" and "Easter Wings."

Tenuous and Precarious

Tenuous and Precarious
Were my guardians,
Precarious and Tenuous,
Two Romans.

My father was Hazardous,
Hazardous,
Dear old man,
Three Romans.

There was my brother Spurious,
Spurious Posthumous,
Spurious was spurious
Was four Romans.

My husband was Perfidious,
He was perfidious,
Five Romans.

Surreptitious, our son,
Was surreptitious,
He was six Romans.

Our cat Tedious
Still lives,
Count not Tedious
Yet.

My name is Finis,
Finis, Finis,
I am Finis,
Six, five, four, three, two,
One Roman,
Finis.

STEVIE SMITH
(1902–1971)

Stevie Smith was born Florence Margaret Smith in Yorkshire, England. From the age of three until her death, Smith lived in the same house with an aunt. She worked for nearly thirty years as a secretary at Newnes, Pearson, Ltd., a publishing house. Following a severe breakdown in 1953, Smith left her job and devoted herself solely to her writing. She often illustrated her poems with sketches and doodles, which like many of her poems are both dark and playful at once. Smith received the Queen's Gold Medal for Poetry in 1969. She died of a brain tumor in 1971.

The Snow Man

One must have a mind of winter
To regard the frost and the boughs
Of the pine-trees crusted with snow;

And have been cold a long time
To behold the junipers shagged with ice,
The spruces rough in the distant glitter

Of the January sun; and not to think
Of any misery in the sound of the wind,
In the sound of a few leaves,

Which is the sound of the land
Full of the same wind
That is blowing in the same bare place

For the listener, who listens in the snow,
And, nothing himself, beholds
Nothing that is not there and the nothing that is.

WALLACE STEVENS
(1879–1955)

Wallace Stevens was born in Reading, Pennsylvania. He earned his B.A. at Harvard and his law degree at New York Law School and was admitted to the Bar in 1904. An insurance lawyer and company vice president for almost four decades, Stevens often composed his poems while walking to his office at the Hartford Accident and Indemnity Company. He would then dictate them to his secretary who typed them up for him. Even so, many of his colleagues did not realize he was a poet until the publication of his *Collected Poems* in 1954. As Stevens explained in a letter in 1944, "The Snow Man" is "an example of the necessity of identifying oneself with reality in order to understand it and enjoy it."

Sonnet 19

Devouring Time, blunt thou the lion's paws,
And make the earth devour her own sweet brood;
Pluck the keen teeth from the fierce tiger's jaws,
And burn the long-lived phoenix in her blood;
Make glad and sorry seasons as thou fleet'st,
And do whate'er thou wilt, swift-footed Time,
To the wide world and all her fading sweets;
But I forbid thee one most heinous crime:
O, carve not with thy hours my love's fair brow,
Nor draw no lines there with thine antique pen;
Him in thy course untainted do allow
For beauty's pattern to succeeding men.
Yet do thy worst, old Time, despite thy wrong,
My love shall in my verse ever live young.

WILLIAM SHAKESPEARE
(1564–1616)

Less is known about William Shakespeare's life than about almost any other major English writer. According to Theophilis Cibber's *Lives of the Poets* (1753), the famous bard's first job in the theater was as a holder of horses for wealthy theatergoers. The addressee of Shakespeare's first 126 sonnets is uncertain, but is usually thought to be a handsome young aristocrat and friend of the author, perhaps the Earl of Southampton, Henry Wriothesley; his stepfather, Sir William Harvey; or William Herbert, third Earl of Pembroke. This sonnet, like all others in the sequence except #126, is in the English form that came to be known as "Shakespearean."

February 8

Overnight

All the familiar contours chasten.
The lake is a pool of dark thought.
There, the clouds bear pale change,
gathered in contemplation.

The lake is a cup of gray fear:
your body in the cold dawn
upturned, and my own drowning eye
opened on the floating light.

And I can see the pines unclasp
each from each, and the sky
rising a little, and always the world
under its leaf of gold.

And I can hear the black ice take
around the island's certainty,
and my own voice, and a pair
of loons unmooring in the mind's ear.

JULIE AGOOS
(1956–)

Julie Agoos was born in Boston, Massachusetts. She holds a B.A. from Harvard University and an M.A. from The Johns Hopkins University. She teaches at the City University of New York, Brooklyn College, where she is an Associate Professor of English. James Merrill selected her first book, *Above the Land,* for the Yale Series of Younger Poets in 1987.

Sonnet 4

Unstable dream, according to the place,
Be steadfast once, or else at least be true.
By tasted sweetness make me not to rue
The sudden loss of thy false feignèd grace.
By good respect, in such a dangerous case,
Thou brought'st not her into this tossing mew,
But madest my sprite live my care to renew,
My body in tempest, her succour to embrace.
The body dead, the sprite had his desire,
Painless was the one, the other in delight.
Why then, alas, did it not keep it right,
Returning to leap into the fire,
And where it was at wish it could not remain?
Such mocks of dreams they turn to deadly pain.

THOMAS WYATT
(1503–1542)

Thomas Wyatt helped popularize the sonnet form in England through his transla-
tions of the Italian sonnets of Petrarch. Wyatt chose to end his own sonnets with
couplets, though he otherwise adhered to the Petrarchan model. The closing couplet
endured through the development of the sonnet in England and remains an element
of the standard English, or Shakespearean, sonnet. It is possible that Wyatt and Anne
Boleyn were romantically involved in the years prior to her fatal marriage to Henry
VIII. Wyatt was arrested shortly before Boleyn's execution on grounds of adultery,
but he regained the king's favor after only a month in the Tower. Wyatt's poems were
circulated in manuscript during his time at court, but most were not published until
after his death from a fever in 1542.

February 10

Jamesian

Their relationship consisted
In discussing if it existed.

THOM GUNN
(1929–)

English by birth, Thom Gunn has lived in California since 1954 and calls San Francisco his permanent home. He was educated at Trinity College, Cambridge, and Stanford University, where he studied with Yvor Winters. He recently retired after teaching in the English Department at the University of California at Berkeley for many years. The title of this poem makes reference to the novelist Henry James.

The Weighing of the Heart: A Prayer

o my mother heart I stand and wait my mouth is empty and dry
o my mother the millions of words in the balance I pray none
will lie o my heart my little heart walking in the darkness
alone I wait while the feather drops while the god listens
and weighs

BEVERLY DAHLEN
(1934–)

Beverly Dahlen was born in Portland, Oregon. With Kathleen Fraser and Frances Jaffer, Dahlen cofounded *HOW(ever)*, a journal of experimental writing by women. She has taught Creative Writing at San Francisco State University and Marin College. The poem included here is part of a series entitled *The Egyptian Poems.*

When I Buy Pictures

or what is closer to the truth,
when I look at that of which I may regard myself as the
                                        imaginary possessor,

I fix upon what would give me pleasure in my average moments:
the satire upon curiosity in which no more is discernible
than the intensity of the mood;
or quite the opposite — the old thing, the medieval decorated
                                        hat-box,

in which there are hounds with waists diminishing like the
                                        waist of the hour-glass,
and deer and birds and seated people;
it may be no more than a square of parquetry; the literal
                                        biography perhaps,
in letters standing well apart upon a parchment-like expanse;
an artichoke in six varieties of blue; the snipe-legged
                                        hieroglyphic in three parts;
the silver fence protecting Adam's grave, or Michael taking
                                        Adam by the wrist.
Too stern an intellectual emphasis upon this quality or that
                                        detracts from one's enjoyment.
It must not wish to disarm anything; nor may the approved
                                        triumph easily be honored —

that which is great because something else is small.
It comes to this: of whatever sort it is,
it must be "lit with piercing glances into the life of things";
it must acknowledge the spiritual forces which have made it.

MARIANNE MOORE
(1887–1972)

Marianne Moore was born in Kirkwood, Missouri. She spent most of her early years in Carlisle, Pennsylvania, and moved to New York City in 1918 where she spent the remainder of her life. An avid sports fan, Moore wrote poems about baseball and boxing and dined with the poetical Cassius Clay (Muhammad Ali) whose famous rhymes she admired. She was so well known that she appeared on the covers of *Vogue, Look,* and *Sports Illustrated,* and once she even threw the first pitch at Yankee Stadium. A friend to many poets of her own generation and advisor to the next, Moore exchanged letters with William Carlos Williams, Wallace Stevens, Elizabeth Bishop, James Merrill, and many others. She suffered a mild stroke in 1961 and a more serious one in 1967, which left her unable to write. She died in her sleep in 1972. Thanks to Moore's habit of keeping meticulous notes on the sources of her own poems, we know that the "silver fence protecting Adam's grave" in this poem was erected by Constantine; the quotation in the penultimate line is from A. R. Gordon's *The Poets of the Old Testament.*

February 13, 1975

Tomorrow is St. Valentine's:
tomorrow I'll think about
that. Always nervous, even
after a good sleep I'd like
to climb back into. The sun
shines on yesterday's new-
fallen snow and yestereven
it turned the world to pink
and rose and steel-blue
buildings. Helene is restless:
leaving soon. And what then
will I do with myself? Some-
one is watching morning
TV. I'm not reduced to that
yet. I wish one could press
snowflakes in a book like flowers.

JAMES SCHUYLER
(1923–1991)

James Schuyler won the Pulitzer Prize in 1981 for his book *The Morning of the Poem,* which included "February 13, 1975." Shy and reclusive, he did not publish his first book of poetry until he was forty-six—more than ten years later than O'Hara, Ashbery, and Koch, the other members of the "New York School." Schuyler often titled poems (as he did this one) with only the date, in the manner of journal entries. As David Lehman has noted, for Schuyler even "a cup of coffee was a lyric occasion."

somewhere i have never travelled, gladly beyond

somewhere i have never travelled, gladly beyond
any experience, your eyes have their silence:
in your most frail gesture are things which enclose me,
or which i cannot touch because they are too near

your slightest look easily will unclose me
though i have closed myself as fingers,
you open always petal by petal myself as Spring opens
(touching skilfully, mysteriously) her first rose

or if your wish be to close me, i and
my life will shut very beautifully, suddenly,
as when the heart of this flower imagines
the snow carefully everywhere descending;

nothing which we are to perceive in this world equals
the power of your intense fragility: whose texture
compels me with the colour of its countries,
rendering death and forever with each breathing

(i do not know what it is about you that closes
and opens; only something in me understands
the voice of your eyes is deeper than all roses)
nobody, not even the rain, has such small hands

E. E. CUMMINGS
(1894–1962)

Edward Estlin Cummings was born in Cambridge, Massachusetts, the son of a
Unitarian minister and Harvard professor. Cummings graduated magna cum laude
from Harvard in 1915. Cummings was a committed pacifist and wanted to avoid
American military service and in 1917 he volunteered for the French ambulance
corps; much to his dismay, he was drafted immediately upon his return to the
United States and served a year in the Army. Though he is best known for his poetry,
Cummings also studied art in Paris and made charming paintings and drawings
throughout his life. The lower-case spelling of his name as well as the quirky typog-
raphy and other oddities of his poetry have made him one of America's most pop-
ular literary figures. Poet and critic Randall Jarrell once dubbed him a "magical
bootlegger or moonshiner of language."

How sad that stupidity should be admired!

February 15

Invocation to Dsilyi N'eyani

Reared Within the Mountains!
Lord of the Mountains!
Young Man!
Chieftain!
I have made your sacrifice.
I have prepared a smoke for you.
My feet restore thou for me.
My legs restore thou for me.
My body restore thou for me.
My mind restore thou for me.
My voice thou restore for me.
Restore all for me in beauty.
Make beautiful all that is before me.
Make beautiful all that is behind me.
It is done in beauty.
It is done in beauty.
It is done in beauty.
It is done in beauty.

NAVAJO SONG

The figure invoked in this poem is Dsilyi N'eyani, whose name literally means "Reared within the Mountains." Navajo spiritual tradition features a cycle of stories based on the life of Dsilyi N'eyani, who was captured by the Utes while out hunting. In the stories, Dsilyi N'eyani is assisted in his escape from the Utes by gods disguised as an old woman and an owl. His journey home is filled with supernatural adventures and takes him across all of the Navajo lands. When he finally returns home, he is washed and dried with cornmeal and ceremonially purified by recounting his adventures in a collection of songs known as the *Dislyidje qacal*. Shortly after his purification, Dsilyi N'eyani is taken up by the gods and is from then on thought to be the voice of the thunder in a storm. The lines of the "Invocation to Dsilyi N'eyani" are traditionally given by the shaman and repeated by the patient as part of a Navajo healing ritual.

#258

There's a certain Slant of light,
Winter Afternoons —
That oppresses, like the Heft
Of Cathedral Tunes —

Heavenly Hurt, it gives us —
We can find no scar,
But internal difference,
Whence the Meanings, are —

None may teach it — Any —
'Tis the Seal Despair —
An imperial affliction
Sent us of the Air —

When it comes, the Landscape listens —
Shadows — hold their breath —
When it goes, 'tis like the Distance
On the look of Death —

EMILY DICKINSON
(1830–1886)

Emily Dickinson's irregular capitalization and habitual dashes were "normalized" in early editions of her poems, but they have since become recognized as important features of her style. The ballad meter, popularly used in Protestant Hymnals to set Psalms and other scriptures to music, is the metrical basis of several of Dickinson's poems, including this one. Ballad meter can be divided into several types, including what is known as Common Meter, with a pattern of 4-3-4-3 stresses in each line of the quatrain, as in "#258." This poem has been dated circa 1861 and thus is relatively early among Dickinson's writings. Poet and critic Yvor Winters numbered this poem among Dickinson's finest and judged her "one of the greatest lyric poets of all time."

Disclaimers

The text of Bach's *St. John Passion,* performed tonight unabridged,
is largely derived from the Gospels, portions of which are alleged
(by some) to be antisemitic. Such passages may well disclose
historical attitudes fastened (by Bach himself) to the Jews,
but must not be taken as having (for that very reason) expressed
convictions or even opinions of the Management or of the cast.

—

The Rape of the Sabine Women, which the artist painted in Rome,
articulates Rubens's treatment of a favorite classical theme.
Proud as we are to display this example of Flemish finesse,
the policy of the Museum is not to be taken amiss:
we oppose all forms of harassment, and just because we have shown
this canvas in no way endorses the actions committed therein.

—

Ensconced in the Upper Rotunda alongside a fossil musk-ox,
the giant *Tyrannosaurus* (which the public has nicknamed "Rex"),
though shown in the act of devouring its still-living prey implies
no favor by public officials to zoophagous public displays;
carnivorous Life-Styles are clearly inappropriate to a State
which has already outlawed tobacco and may soon prohibit meat.

RICHARD HOWARD
(1929–)

Born in Cleveland, Ohio, Richard Howard was educated at Columbia University
and the Sorbonne. He is the poetry editor of *The Paris Review* and *Western
Humanities Review.* The recipient of a PEN Translation Medal and an American
Book Award for Translation, he has also been awarded the Ordre National du Mérite
from the French government. He is a former Chancellor of the Academy of
American Poets and was New York State's Poet Laureate from 1994 to 1996. He has
been a Professor of Writing at Columbia University since 1997.

#31 (from *Astrophel and Stella*)

With how sad steps, O Moon! thou climb'st the skies!
How silently, and with how wan a face!
What! may it be, that even in heavenly place
That busy archer his sharp arrows tries?
Sure, if that long-with-love-acquainted eyes
Can judge of love, thou feel'st a lover's case;
I read it in thy looks; thy languish'd grace,
To me that feel the like, thy state descries.
Then, even of fellowship, O Moon, tell me,
Is constant love deem'd there but want of wit?
Are beauties there as proud as here they be?
Do they above love to be loved, and yet
    Those lovers scorn whom that love doth possess?
    Do they call virtue there ungratefulness?

                    SIR PHILIP SIDNEY
                      (1554–1586)

English poet Philip Sidney was not the only bard in his aristocratic family; his brother Robert Sidney, his sister Mary Sidney, and his niece Mary Wroth were also known for their verse. A fervent Protestant, Sidney was banished from court in 1580 for criticizing Queen Elizabeth's prospective marriage to a Roman Catholic. It was fortunate for him that he was related to the Queen on his mother's side; another critic of the proposed marriage who was not of royal lineage had his hands chopped off for the same offense. Royal disfavor did not prevent Sidney from being knighted in 1583, after which he became governor of Flushing in the English Low Countries. In 1586 he was wounded in a battle to advance Protestantism in the Netherlands, and he died of gangrene at the age of thirty-six. "#31" is from Sidney's sonnet sequence *Astrophel and Stella* ("Starlover and Star"), which contains 108 sonnets and eleven songs. Stella is fashioned after Penelope Devereux who, though engaged to Sidney for a brief time, eventually married someone else.

XXXV. "The moonlight behind the tall branches"

The moonlight behind the tall branches
The poets all say is more
Than the moonlight behind the tall branches.

But for me, who do not know what I think —
What the moonlight behind the tall branches
Is, beyond its being
The moonlight behind the tall branches,
Is its not being more
Than the moonlight behind the tall branches.

FERNANDO PESSOA
(1888–1935)
translated by Edwin Honig and Susan M. Brown

Portuguese poet Fernando Pessoa was one man but several writers. Unlike other writers who have employed simple pseudonyms, Pessoa invented complete personalities, biographies, and even physical profiles of his so-called "heteronyms." Among Pessoa's dramatis personae, three stand out as the most important and most prolific: Albert Caeiro, Ricardo Reis, and Álvaro de Campos. Pessoa's heteronyms vied with one another for fame and publicly reviewed each other's work. "XXXV [The moonlight behind the tall branches]" is from a sequence of forty-nine poems by Albert Caeiro, which he claimed to have written between 1911 and 1912. In fact, Pessoa wrote all of the poems in the sequence after 1914, some much later.

I Know a Man

As I sd to my
friend, because I am
always talking, — John, I

sd, which was not his
name, the darkness sur-
rounds us, what

can we do against
it, or else, shall we &
why not, buy a goddamn big car,

drive, he sd, for
christ's sake, look
out where yr going.

ROBERT CREELEY
(1926–)

Robert Creeley was born in Arlington, Massachusetts, and educated at Harvard, Black Mountain College, and the University of New Mexico. He served as New York State Poet from 1989 to 1991, and in 1999 he was elected Chancellor of the Academy of American Poets. Creeley has taught since 1989 at the State University of New York at Buffalo, where he is Samuel P. Capen Professor of Poetry and the Humanities. Robert Hass has called "I Know a Man" "the poem of the decade about a world gone out of control and the crazy assumption of control that the ego makes."

Upon Julia's washing her self in the river

How fierce was I, when I did see
My *Julia* wash her self in thee!
So *Lillies* thorough Christall look:
So purest pebbles in the brook:
As in the River *Julia* did,
Halfe with a Lawne of water hid,
Into thy streames my self I threw,
And strugling there, I kist thee too;
And more had done (it is confest)
Had not thy waves forbad the rest.

ROBERT HERRICK
(1591–1674)

Robert Herrick was born into a family of wealthy goldsmiths in London. A friend and admirer of Ben Jonson, Herrick happily counted himself among the "Sons of Ben" who gathered around the famous poet in the taverns of London. After quitting a jeweler's apprenticeship to his uncle, Herrick abandoned the family trade and pursued his education at Cambridge. He took Holy Orders in 1623 and afterward became the Dean Prior of Devonshire. Life in that rural setting allowed Herrick to become one of the most prolific among the Cavalier poets, and he wrote more than 2500 poems on religious and secular themes. Most of the secular poems in *Hesperides,* his only book, are dedicated to fourteen muses or fictional "mistresses." Julia, mentioned here, was Herrick's favorite and was the subject of more poems than any of his other imaginary ladies.

Song of Amergin

I am a stag: *of seven tines,*
I am a flood: *across a plain,*
I am a wind: *on a deep lake,*
I am a tear: *the Sun lets fall,*
I am a hawk: *above the cliff,*
I am a thorn: *beneath the nail,*
I am a wonder: *among flowers,*
I am a wizard: *who but I*
Sets the cool head aflame with smoke?

I am a spear: *that roars for blood,*
I am a salmon: *in a pool,*
I am a lure: *from paradise,*
I am a hill: *where poets walk,*
I am a boar: *ruthless and red,*
I am a breaker: *threatening doom,*
I am a tide: *that drags to death,*
I am an infant: *who but I*
Peeps from the unhewn dolmen arch?

I am the womb: *of every holt,*
I am the blaze: *on every hill,*
I am the queen: *of every hive,*
I am the shield: *for every head,*
I am the tomb: *of every hope.*

ANCIENT CELTIC POEM
translated by Robert Graves

In Irish mythology, Amergin is one of the druids who led the Milesian tribes from Iberia (now Spain) to Ireland circa 1530 B.C. Often called the "first poet of Ireland," Amergin used Druidic verses as charms to defeat the Tuantha De Danann who already occupied the island. The "Song of Amergin" is supposed to be the verse Amergin chanted with his right foot on the shore when he and his companions landed at Inber Colptha. The "Song of Amergin" is included in the *Lebor Gabala Erren*, known in English as *The Book of Invasions*, which gives an account of early Ireland made up of folklore, mythology, recounted Biblical narratives, and historical fact. Robert Graves, who translated this poem in his book *The White Goddess*, said, "English poetic education should, really, begin not with *The Canterbury Tales*, not even with Genesis, but with the 'Song of Amergin.'"

Grief

I tell you, hopeless grief is passionless;
That only men incredulous of despair,
Half-taught in anguish, through the mid-night air
Beat upward to God's throne in loud access
Of the absolute Heavens. Deep-hearted man, express
Grief for the Dead in silence like to death —
Most like a monumental statue set
In everlasting watch and moveless woe,
Till itself crumble to the dust beneath.
Touch it; the marble eyelids are not wet.
If it could weep, it could arise and go.

ELIZABETH BARRETT BROWNING
(1806–1861)

As a child, Elizabeth Barrett lived in a mock-Ottoman castle in Herefordshire, England, and began writing poems at the age of four. Her health was frail but she was an extremely bright young woman and excelled in her studies of Greek, Latin, and Hebrew. She and her father were very close, and in time Mr. Barrett's overprotective nature complicated the courtship between Elizabeth and Robert Browning, which started after she praised Browning's verses in one of her own poems. Mutually impressed by each other's work, they began a regular exchange of letters. Mr. Barrett finally permitted Browning to visit Elizabeth. After almost a hundred subsequent visits, the couple eloped to Italy in 1846. Mr. Barrett refused to either speak to Elizabeth or answer her letters after her marriage, and father and daughter were never reconciled. "Grief" is from Barrett Browning's first book *Poems,* published in 1844.

Van Gogh's Face

Noon, streams of the melting crowd,
Paris. On a kiosk, a draft
notice for a new graduation class extorted
from the registry of births
next to ads for fox furs and Beaujolais nouveau.
Among them appears your clear-cut face, the face
of a just man, anxiety
dressed in skin.
We disperse, we pass by, we swim
under the blade of that excruciating look.
And you watch us, rich man,
more alive than living ones and more
collected.

ADAM ZAGAJEWSKI
(1945–)
translated by Renata Gorczynski

Adam Zagajewski was born in Lvov, Poland, which is now part of the Ukraine. He immigrated to France in 1982 and now divides his time between Paris and Houston, Texas, where he has served as Associate Professor of English in the Creative Writing Program at the University of Houston since 1988. He has been awarded the Kurt Tucholsky Prize and a Prix de la Liberté. He is currently coeditor of the Polish-language *Zeszyty literackie* (Literary Review), published in Paris.

February 25

Days

Daughters of Time, the hypocritic Days,
Muffled and dumb like barefoot dervishes,
And marching single in an endless file,
Bring diadems and fagots in their hands.
To each they offer gifts after his will,
Bread, kingdoms, stars, and sky that holds them all.
I, in my pleached garden, watched the pomp,
Forgot my morning wishes, hastily
Took a few herbs and apples, and the Day
Turned and departed silent. I, too late,
Under her solemn fillet saw the scorn.

RALPH WALDO EMERSON
(1803–1882)

Though Ralph Waldo Emerson was the son of a Unitarian minister and was ordained as junior pastor in Boston, he left the church in 1832, unable to deny his serious doubts about organized religion. After reading the philosophy of Plato, Swedenborg, the German Idealists, and sacred Hindu texts, Emerson began to develop his ideas of Transcendentalism. Henry David Thoreau, Nathaniel Hawthorne, and other writers gathered around Emerson in the Transcendental Club. Emerson also influenced and encouraged Walt Whitman, who wrote of him, "His usual manner carried with it something penetrating and sweet beyond mere description. There is in some men an indefinable something which flows out and over you like a flood of light — as if they possessed it illimitable — their whole being suffused with it. Being — in fact that is precisely the word. Emerson's whole attitude shed forth such an impression."

I Will Bow and Be Simple

I will bow and be simple
I will bow and be free
I will bow and be humble
Yea bow like the willow-tree
I will bow this is the token
I will wear the easy yoke
I will bow and be broken
Yea I'll fall upon the rock.

SHAKER HYMN

Known officially as the United Society of Believers in Christ's Second Appearing, among other terms, the Shakers, or Shaking Quakers, came to be known by their popular name due to their practice of trembling in religious ecstasy during worship. Music, dancing, and marching are all vital elements of the Shaker religion, and "I Will Bow and Be Simple" is one of the most enduring Shaker hymns.

The Helmsman

O be swift —
we have always known you wanted us.

We fled inland with our flocks,
we pastured them in hollows,
cut off from the wind
and the salt track of the marsh.

We worshipped inland —
we stepped past wood-flowers,
we forgot your tang,
we brushed wood-grass.

We wandered from pine-hills
through oak and scrub-oak tangles,
we broke hyssop and bramble,
we caught flower and new bramble-fruit
in our hair: we laughed
as each branch whipped back,
we tore our feet in half-buried rocks
and knotted roots and acorn-cups.

We forgot — we worshipped,
we parted green from green,
we sought further thickets,
we dipped our ankles
through leaf-mold and earth,
and wood and wood-bank enchanted us —

and the feel of the clefts in the bark,
and the slope between tree and tree —
and a slender path strung field to field
and wood to wood
and hill to hill
and the forest after it.

We forgot for a moment;
tree-resin, tree-bark,
sweat of a torn branch
were sweet to the taste.

We were enchanted with the fields,
the tufts of coarse grass —
in the shorter grass —
we loved all this.

But now, our boat climbs — hesitates —
    drops —
climbs — hesitates — crawls back —
climbs — hesitates —
O, be swift —
we have always known you wanted us.

H. D.
(1886–1961)

Hilda Doolittle abbreviated her name H. D. on advice from Ezra Pound, who thought the ambiguity of initials might intrigue readers. Pound was the first to read and edit her poems and he immediately sent them to Harriet Monroe at *Poetry*. Upon reading H. D.'s work, Pound invented the Imagist movement, though he later pretended that he, she, and Richard Aldington had agreed upon its principles in advance. Though Pound characteristically credited himself for H. D.'s development as a poet, she was her own woman. She was briefly engaged to Pound, but later married Aldington, and lived most of her life with her lover Winifred Ellerman, the writer better known as Bryher. Her best-known poem is the book-length *Helen in Egypt*, which she began in a sudden frenzy of inspiration after having written nothing for five years. "The Helmsman" was first published in *Sea Garden*, H. D.'s first book, in 1916.

A Sick Child

The postman comes when I am still in bed.
"Postman, what do you have for me today?"
I say to him. (But really I'm in bed.)
Then he says — what shall I have him say?

"This letter says that you are president
Of — this word here; it's a republic."
Tell them I can't answer right away.
"It's your duty." No, I'd rather just be sick.

Then he tells me there are letters saying everything
That I can think of that I want for them to say.
I say, "Well, thank you very much. Good-bye."
He is ashamed, and turns and walks away.

If I can think of it, it isn't what I want.
I want . . . I want a ship from some near star
To land in the yard, and beings to come out
And think to me: "So this is where you are!

Come." Except that they won't do,
I thought of them. . . . And yet somewhere there must be
Something that's different from everything.
All that I've never thought of — think of me!

RANDALL JARRELL
(1914–1965)

Jarrell, who came to be known as one of America's most insightful and outspoken literary critics, was once cautioned by his teacher Robert Penn Warren to "stop terrorizing" his classmates with his opinions. He taught at the University of Texas, Kenyon College, Sarah Lawrence, and the University of North Carolina at Greensboro and proved an extremely popular teacher. In 1942 he enlisted in the army, an experience that provided much material for his poems. "Every inch a poet," as he was described by Robert Lowell, Jarrell frequently reworked his poems even after they were published, making extensive revisions in the pages of his own books. He served as Poetry Consultant to the Library of Congress (a position now known as Poet Laureate) from 1956 to 1958, and he received the National Book Award for *The Woman at the Washington Zoo* in 1961. Jarrell was struck and killed by a car at the age of 50.

February 29

The Meaning of Winter

O I see the
Face — Hideous is selfishness.

(What was summer? It was the descent of
leaves? October is the month of breaking
mind, though I assert with complete certainty,
it is ultimately the oak's strength. What
celebrations! —)

Carolyn told me:

"The winter wind on Amsterdam Avenue
Behind St. Luke's Hospital, listens, halts,
It is a maimed crippled beggar, wanting a
Handout. The sailors talk of big
Times. Then the winter wind begins.

"The winter wind blusters like
A base ingrate; has no patience.
Muck tramples the green film of
Girls in remembered frocks."

(And then, you must add to all this the cold
Sky, the color of a quarrel. Premonitions of
disaster; of course, the month's environment.
Why do I keep thinking of you?)

The principle of our time is
Selfishness.

DAVID SCHUBERT
(1913–1946)

David Schubert published only one volume of poetry, *Initial A,* before succumbing
to tuberculosis at the age of thirty-three. William Carlos Williams described the
experience of reading Schubert's work in a letter to Theodore Weiss: "There is, you
know, a physically new poetry which almost no one yet has sensed. Schubert is a
nova in that sky. I hope I am not using hyperbole to excess. You know how it is when
someone opens a window in a stuffy room." A paranoid schizophrenic, Schubert
apparently destroyed much of his work in fits of rage. "The Meaning of Winter" is
an uncollected poem first published in a special edition of *Quarterly Review of
Literature.*

Homage to Claudius Ptolemy

I am a man: little do I last
and the night is enormous.
But I look up:
the stars write.
Unknowing I understand:
I too am written,
and at this very moment
someone spells me out.

OCTAVIO PAZ
(1914–1998)
translated by Eliot Weinberger

Octavio Paz was born in Mexico City and began publishing poetry at the age of seventeen in a magazine called *Barandal* (Balustrade), which he cofounded. By the age of nineteen, he had published his first book, *Luna silvestre* (Savage Moon). He joined the Mexican Foreign Service, traveling to Paris, New York, San Francisco, Geneva, and New Delhi in this capacity, all the while writing poems and essays, and translating the work of William Carlos Williams, Apollinaire, Fernando Pessoa, Bashō, and others into Spanish. In 1962, Paz was appointed Mexican Ambassador to India and began to study the poetry and philosophy of that country. Paz exhibited the same enthusiasm and energy for the visual arts that he showed for literature, curating the first exhibition of Tantric art in the West, collaborating with Robert Rauschenberg and Robert Motherwell, and publishing a three-volume book on Mexican art and culture. Paz received the Nobel Prize for Literature in 1990. "Homage to Claudius Ptolemy" is a late uncollected poem.

March 2

Dream Variations

To fling my arms wide
In some place of the sun,
To whirl and to dance
Till the white day is done.
Then rest at cool evening
Beneath a tall tree
While night comes on gently,
　　Dark like me —
That is my dream!

To fling my arms wide
In the face of the sun,
Dance! Whirl! Whirl!
Till the quick day is done.
Rest at pale evening . . .
A tall, slim tree . . .
Night coming tenderly
　　Black like me.

LANGSTON HUGHES
(1902–1967)

(John) Langston Hughes

Born in Joplin, Mississippi, the young Langston Hughes displayed a gift with language and was elected Class Poet in elementary school. He was educated at Lincoln University and Columbia University. As a journalist, Hughes supported the Republican side during the Spanish Civil War. He was also briefly associated with the American Communists and as a result was called before Senator Joseph McCarthy's subcommittee on subversive activities in 1953. Hughes once wrote, "Words are the paper and string to package experience, to wrap up from the inside out the poet's concentric waves of contact with the living world. Each poet makes of words his own highly individualized wrappings for the segments of life he wishes to present. . . . Skilled or unskilled, wise or foolish, nobody can write a poem without revealing something of himself. Here are people. Here are poems. Here is revelation."

March 3

Sonnet 65

Since brass, nor stone, nor earth, nor boundless sea,
But sad mortality o'er-sways their power,
How with this rage shall beauty hold a plea,
Whose action is no stronger than a flower?
O how shall summer's honey breath hold out,
Against the wrackful siege of battering days,
When rocks impregnable are not so stout,
Nor gates of steel so strong but Time decays?
O fearful meditation, where, alack,
Shall Time's best jewel from Time's chest lie hid?
Or what strong hand can hold his swift foot back,
Or who his spoil of beauty can forbid?
O none, unless this miracle have might,
That in black ink my love may still shine bright.

WILLIAM SHAKESPEARE
(1564–1616)

Shakespeare is thought to have been more interested in his reputation as a poet than as a playwright, writing drama primarily for financial reasons. In his day, publication of one's verses was not considered respectable, and authors usually feigned indignation when their poems were printed. Shakespeare wrote his sonnets in the 1590s and, though not published until 1609, the poems circulated widely in manuscript and garnered him high praise. "Sonnet 65" shares its theme with sonnets 55, 60, 63, and 64.

Susie Asado

Sweet sweet sweet sweet sweet tea.
    Susie Asado.
Sweet sweet sweet sweet sweet tea.
    Susie Asado.
Susie Asado which is a told tray sure.
A lean on the shoe this means slips slips hers.
When the ancient light grey is clean it is yellow, it is a
silver seller.
This is a please this is a please there are the saids to jelly.
These are the wets these say the sets to leave a crown to
Incy.
Incy is short for incubus.
A pot. A pot is a beginning of a rare bit of trees. Trees
tremble, the old vats are in bobbles, bobbles which shade and
shove and render clean, render clean must.
    Drink pups.
Drink pups drink pups lease a sash hold, see it shine and
a bobolink has pins. It shows a nail.
What is a nail. A nail is unison.
Sweet sweet sweet sweet sweet tea.

GERTRUDE STEIN
(1874–1946)

One of the most influential figures of the Modernist period, Gertrude Stein was friend and patron to Pablo Picasso, Ernest Hemingway, William Faulkner, Juan Gris, Sherwood Anderson, Henri Matisse, Paul Cezanne, and dozens of other important artists and writers of her time. Born in California, she traveled through Europe after attending college at Radcliffe and eventually settled in Paris in 1903 in her legendary apartment at 27 Rue de Fleurus. "Susie Asado" opened Stein's book *Geography and Plays* (1922). She explains her intention for the poem in her characteristic manner in *Lectures in America*: "The strict discipline that I had given myself, the absolute refusal of never using a word that was not an exact word all through the *Tender Buttons* and what I may call the early Spanish and *Geography and Play* (sic) period finally resulted in things like 'Susie Asado' and 'Preciosilla' etc. in an extraordinary melody of words and a melody of excitement in knowing that I had done this thing."

My Last Duchess

That's my last Duchess painted on the wall,
Looking as if she were alive. I call
That piece a wonder, now: Frà Pandolf's hands
Worked busily a day, and there she stands.
Will 't please you sit and look at her? I said
'Frà Pandolf' by design, for never read
Strangers like you that pictured countenance,
The depth and passion of its earnest glance,
But to myself they turned (since none puts by
The curtain I have drawn for you, but I)
And seemed as they would ask me, if they durst,
How such a glance came there; so, not the first
Are you to turn and ask thus. Sir, 't was not
Her husband's presence only, called that spot
Of joy into the Duchess' cheek: perhaps
Frà Pandolf chanced to say, 'Her mantle laps
Over my lady's wrist too much,' or 'Paint
Must never hope to reproduce the faint
Half-flush that dies along her throat:' such stuff
Was courtesy, she thought, and cause enough
For calling up that spot of joy. She had
A heart — how shall I say? — too soon made glad,
Too easily impressed; she liked whate'er
She looked on, and her looks went everywhere.
Sir, 't was all one! My favour at her breast,
The dropping of the daylight in the West,
The bough of cherries some officious fool
Broke in the orchard for her, the white mule
She rode with round the terrace — all and each
Would draw from her alike the approving speech,

Or blush, at least. She thanked men, — good! but thanked
Somehow — I know not how — as if she ranked
My gift of a nine-hundred-years-old name
With anybody's gift. Who'd stoop to blame
This sort of trifling? Even had you skill
In speech — (which I have not) — to make your will
Quite clear to such an one, and say, 'Just this
Or that in you disgusts me; here you miss,
Or there exceed the mark' — and if she let
Herself be lessoned so, nor plainly set
Her wits to yours, forsooth, and made excuse,
— E'en then would be some stooping; and I choose
Never to stoop. Oh, sir, she smiled, no doubt,
Whene'er I passed her; but who passed without
Much the same smile? This grew; I gave commands;
Then all smiles stopped together. There she stands
As if alive. Will 't please you rise? We'll meet
The company below then. I repeat,
The Count your master's known munificence
Is ample warrant that no just pretence
Of mine for dowry will be disallowed;
Though his fair daughter's self, as I avowed
At starting, is my object. Nay, we'll go
Together down, sir. Notice Neptune, though,
Taming a sea-horse, thought a rarity,
Which Claus of Innsbruck cast in bronze for me!

ROBERT BROWNING
(1812–1889)

56 lines

English poet Robert Browning is recognized as a master of the dramatic monologue, and "My Last Duchess" is among his best examples of the genre. Browning was born in a suburb of London and attended London University, though much of his reading was done in his father's library which included more than 6,000 books in Greek, Latin, French, Italian, Hebrew, and Spanish. The precocious Browning wrote his first book of poems at the age of twelve, after the manner of Byron, but despite his parents' efforts it was never published. *Dramatic Lyrics,* in which this poem first appeared, drew the admiration of poet Elizabeth Barrett, among others. In 1846 Browning eloped with Barrett against her father's wishes and the two lived in Italy until her death in 1861, after which Browning returned to England with their son, whom the couple had appropriately named Pen.

Silence

Who was it that took away my voice?
The black wound he left in my throat
Can't even cry.

March is at work under the snow
And the birds of my throat are dead,
Their gardens turning into dictionaries.

I beg my lips to sing.
I beg the lips of the snowfall,
Of the cliff and the bush to sing.

Between my lips, the round shape
Of the air in my mouth.
Because I can say nothing.

I'll try anything
For the trees in the snow.
I breathe. I swing my arms. I lie.

From this sudden silence,
Like death, that loved
The names of all words,
You raise me now in song.

BELLA AKHMADULINA
(1937–)
translated by Daniel Halpern

Bella Akhmadulina was born in Moscow. Her first marriage was to the famous Russian poet Yevgeny Yevtushenko; she is now married to the artist Boris Messerer. In 1960 she graduated from the Gorky Literary Institute. She is an honorary member of the American Academy of Arts and Letters.

Remembrance

Cold in the earth — and the deep snow piled above thee,
Far, far removed, cold in the dreary grave!
Have I forgot, my only Love, to love thee,
Severed at last by Time's all-severing wave?

Now, when alone, do my thoughts no longer hover
Over the mountains, on that northern shore,
Resting their wings where heath and fern leaves cover
Thy noble heart forever, ever more?

Cold in the earth — and fifteen wild Decembers,
From those brown hills, have melted into spring;
Faithful, indeed, is the spirit that remembers
After such years of change and suffering!

Sweet Love of youth, forgive, if I forget thee,
While the world's tide is bearing me along;
Other desires and other hopes beset me,
Hopes which obscure, but cannot do thee wrong!

No later light has lightened up my heaven,
No second morn has ever shone for me;
All my life's bliss from thy dear life was given,
All my life's bliss is in the grave with thee.

But, when the days of golden dreams had perished,
And even Despair was powerless to destroy,
Then did I learn how existence could be cherished,
Strengthened, and fed without the aid of joy.

Then did I check the tears of useless passion —
Weaned my young soul from yearning after thine;
Sternly denied its burning wish to hasten
Down to that tomb already more than mine.

And, even yet, I dare not let it languish,
Dare not indulge in memory's rapturous pain;
Once drinking deep of that divinest anguish,
How could I seek the empty world again?

EMILY BRONTË
(1818–1848)

"Remembrance," like all of Brontë's poems, was originally published pseudony-
mously under the name Ellis Bell. Charlotte Brontë wrote of Emily's natural reti-
cence and her reluctance to publish her writings: "My sister was not a person of
demonstrative character, nor one on the recesses of whose mind and feelings even
those nearest and dearest to her could, with impunity, intrude unlicensed; it took
hours to reconcile her to the discovery I had made, and days to persuade her that
such poems merited publication."

Carrowmore

All about Carrowmore the lambs
Were blotched blue, belonging.

They were waiting for carnage or
Snuff. This is why they are born

To begin with, to end.
Ruminants do not frighten

At anything — gorge in the soil, butcher
Noise, the mere graze of predators.

All about Carrowmore
The rain quells for three days.

I remember how cold I was, the botched
Job of travelling. And just so.

Wherever I went I came with me.
She buried her bone barrette

In the ground's woolly shaft.
A fear of her hair, an old gift

To the burnt other who went
First. My thick braid, my ornament —

My belonging I
Remember how cold I will be.

LUCIE BROCK-BROIDO
(1956–)

Lucie Brock-Broido was born in Pittsburg, Pennsylvania. She was educated at Johns Hopkins and Columbia University. She is an Associate Professor and Director of the Poetry Concentration in the Writing Division at Columbia University. Carrowmore is the largest megalithic burial ground in County Sligo, Ireland, where 200 or more monuments dating as far back as 4,000 B.C. once stood. Unfortunately plunderers and farmers clearing space for their flocks and crops destroyed much of the site, but three large dolmen tombs and a stone circle remain intact.

To His Watch, When He Could Not Sleep

Uncessant Minutes, whilst you move you tell
   The time that tells our life, which though it run
   Never so fast or farr, you'r new begun
Short steps shall overtake; for though life well

May scape his own Account, it shall not yours,
   You are Death's Auditors, that both divide
And summ what ere that life inspir'd endures
   Past a beginning, and through you we bide

The doom of Fate, whose unrecall'd Decree
   You date, bring, execute, making what's new
   Ill and good, old, for as we die in you,
You die in Time, Time in Eternity.

LORD HERBERT OF CHERBURY
(1583–1648)

The eldest brother of poet George Herbert, Edward Herbert was also a friend of Ben Jonson and John Donne. Donne wrote "To Sir Herbert, at Julyers" in his honor, and Herbert addressed "Elegy for Doctor Dunn" to him in return, celebrating their friendship and praising Donne's verses. By most accounts a charismatic if opinionated gentleman, Herbert described himself as an irresistible ladies' man in his *Autobiography*, claiming he knew of several women who fell in love with him after just one look at his portrait. He was an expert lute player who composed popular pieces for the instrument. He briefly served in Parliament and became the British ambassador to France in 1619, but his ambassadorship abruptly ended in 1624 when he spoke out against the policies of King James I. Herbert became first Baron Herbert of Cherbury in 1629 and tried to remain neutral in the English Civil War. In September 1644, he surrendered his castle to parliamentary troops and quietly returned to London. Herbert is widely recognized as an influential philosopher and is the author of a tract on deism, *De Veritate* (1624).

Upper Broadway

The leafbud straggles forth
toward the frigid light of the airshaft   this is faith
this pale extension of a day
when looking up   you know   something is changing
winter has turned   though the wind is colder
Three streets away   a roof collapses   onto people
who thought they still had time   Time out of mind

I have written so many words
wanting to live inside you
to be of use to you

Now I must write for myself   for this blind
woman scratching the pavement   with her wand of thought
this slippered crone   inching on icy streets
reaching into wire trashbaskets   pulling out
what was thrown away   and infinitely precious

I look at my hands and see   they are still unfinished
I look at the vine and see the leafbud
inching towards life

I look at my face in the glass   and see
a halfborn woman

1975

ADRIENNE RICH
(1929–)

Adrienne Rich was born in Baltimore, Maryland. The author of numerous books of poetry, as well as prose, she is also known as an influential feminist and political activist. She has been awarded the National Book Award, and in 1999 she received the Lifetime Achievement Award from the Lannan Foundation. As with "Upper Broadway," under each poem she records the year in which it was written. She lives in northern California.

The Sorrow of Sarajevo

The Sarajevo wind
leafs through newspapers
that are glued by blood to the street;
I pass with a loaf of bread under my arm.

The river carries the corpse of a woman.
As I run across the bridge
with my canisters of water,
I notice her wristwatch, still in place.

Someone lobs a child's shoe
into the furnace. Family photographs spill
from the back of a garbage truck;
they carry inscriptions:
Love from . . . love from . . . love

There's no way of describing these things,
not really. Each night I wake
and stand by the window to watch my neighbour
who stands by the window to watch the dark.

GORAN SIMIĆ
(1952–)
translated by David Harsent

A Bosnian Serb, Goran Simić was born in Bosnia-Herzegovina (formerly Vlasenica, Yugoslavia). After surviving a three-year siege on Sarajevo, Simić and his family immigrated to Canada under the auspices of PEN Canada in 1996. He held a residency at Massey College as part of its writer-in-exile program and has received several awards, including the Hellman-Hammet Grant for Free Expression and the PEN USA West Freedom to Write Award. Simić is the author of seventeen books of poetry, as well as numerous plays and essays.

The Self-Unseeing

Here is the ancient floor,
Footworn and hollowed and thin,
Here was the former door
Where the dead feet walked in.

She sat here in her chair,
Smiling into the fire;
He who played stood there,
Bowing it higher and higher.

Childlike, I danced in a dream;
Blessings emblazoned that day;
Everything glowed with a gleam;
Yet we were looking away!

THOMAS HARDY
(1840–1928)

Thomas Hardy studied architecture and practiced the trade in London and Dorset for ten years, until the success of his first published novel allowed him to pursue his writing full time. Hardy's novels *Tess of the D'Urbervilles* and *Jude the Obscure* drew negative reviews, which criticized Hardy for his pessimism and preoccupation with sex. Hardy wrote poems from his early twenties, but his first collection was not published until he was fifty-eight. The fiddle player in "The Self-Unseeing" is modeled after Hardy's father, who was an accomplished violinist. The "ancient floor" and "former door" in the poem are features of the main room of the Hardy cottage in Dorset. The cottage was remodeled at some point in Hardy's childhood, and the front door with its worn flagstone was filled in and replaced by a window.

March 13

from *King Lear*
Act V, Scene iii

No, no, no, no! Come, let's away to prison;
We two alone will sing like birds i' the cage:
When thou dost ask me blessing, I'll kneel down,
And ask of thee forgiveness: so we'll live,
And pray, and sing, and tell old tales, and laugh
At gilded butterflies, and hear poor rogues
Talk of court news; and we'll talk with them too,
Who loses and who wins; who's in, who's out;
And take upon's the mystery of things,
As if we were God's spies: and we'll wear out,
In a wall'd prison, packs and sects of great ones
That ebb and flow by the moon.

WILLIAM SHAKESPEARE
(1564–1616)

King Lear speaks these lines after being captured by Edmund and his soldiers. Lear is answering Cordelia's question as to whether or not he should confront his other daughters, Regan and Goneril, who have betrayed Lear and cooperated in his deposing. Just after this speech, Edmund sends Lear and Cordelia off to prison with an order for their execution.

Dull Mauve

Twenty miles away, in the colder
waters of the Atlantic, you gaze longingly
toward the coast. Didn't you once love someone
there? Yes, but it was only a cat, and I,
a manatee, what could I do? There are no rewards
in this world for pissing your life away, even
if it means you get to see forgotten icebergs
of decades ago peeling off from the mass
to dive under the surface, raising a
mountain of seething glass before they lunge back up
to start the unknown perilous journey
to the desolate horizon.

      That was the way
I thought of each day when I was young, a sloughing-off,
both suicidal and imbued with a certain ritual grace.
Later, there were so many protagonists
one got quite lost, as in a forest of doppelgängers.
Many things were going on. And the moon, poised
on the ridge like an enormous, smooth grapefruit, understood
the importance of each and wasn't going
to make one's task any easier, though we loved her.

JOHN ASHBERY

(1927–)

John Ashbery's first book, *Some Trees*, was selected by W. H. Auden for the Yale Series
of Younger Poets in 1956. Along with Frank O'Hara, James Schuyler, and Kenneth
Koch, Ashbery is known as one of the major figures of the New York School. Since
1990 he has taught at Bard College as the Charles P. Stevenson, Jr., Professor of
Languages and Literature. Ashbery is one of America's most highly decorated poets and
has received the Pulitzer Prize, among many other honors. He has also been recognized
internationally, receiving the title of Chevalier des Arts et des Lettres from the French
government and the Antonio Feltrinelli International Prize for Poetry in Rome. He
lived in France for a number of years and for many years worked as an art critic.

How Blind and Bright

Light, visibility of light,
Sun, visibility of sun.
Light, sun and seeing,
Visibility of men.

How blind is bright!
How blind is bright!

Eyes looking out for eyes
Meet only seeing, in common faith,
Visibility and brightness.

Night, invisibility of light,
No sun, invisibility of sun,
Eyes in eyes sheltered,
Night, night and night.
All light, all fire, all eyes,
Wrapt in one conference of doubt.

Eyes not looking out for eyes
Look inward and meet sight
In common loneliness,
Invisibility and darkness.

How bright is blind!
How bright is blind!

LAURA RIDING JACKSON
(1901–1991)

Born Laura Reichenthal, the poet changed her name after her marriage to Louis Gottschalk in 1922 and published her first poems as Laura Riding Gottschalk, apparently finding Laura Reichenthal Gottschalk too cumbersome. She and Robert Graves were romantically involved after her first marriage ended in 1925, and they lived together in Deyá, Mallorca, until the Spanish Civil War forced them to flee in 1936. After returning to the United States, Riding met Schuyler Jackson and they married in 1941. The Jacksons retreated from the literary world and made their living by growing citrus in northern Florida. In the end, Riding Jackson renounced poetry completely and disowned her earlier work. In the introduction to her *Selected Poems* in 1970, she wrote, "I judge my poems to be things of the first water as poetry, but that does not make them better than poetry, and I think poetry obstructs general attainment of something better in our linguistic way-of-life than we have."

Pedestrian

What generations could have dreamed
This grandchild of the shopping streets, her eyes

In the buyer's light, the store lights
Brighter than the lighthouses, brighter than moonrise

From the salt harbor so rich
So bright her city

In a soil of pavement, a mesh of wires where she walks
In the new winter among enormous buildings.

GEORGE OPPEN
(1908–1984)

With William Carlos Williams, Louis Zukofsky, and others, George Oppen helped to establish the Objectivist school of poetry, which emphasized clear expression and concrete imagery over formal structure. Oppen and his wife Mary published the *Objectivist Anthology* in 1932 and later participated in the Objectivist Press Co-op in New York. Thy joined the Communist Party in 1935 and George abandoned poetry to focus on politics, delaying his second book until almost thirty years after his first collection. In the 1950s, the Oppens came under the scrutiny of the Un-American Activities Committee and, rather than deny their beliefs or incriminate others, they exiled themselves to Mexico, where George worked as a furniture maker for eight years. After the death of Senator Joe McCarthy, the couple returned to the United States in 1958. Shortly thereafter, Oppen returned to writing and publishing poetry, winning the Pulitzer Prize in 1969 for his book *Of Being Numerous.* "Pedestrian" was written in 1962.

She's Florida Missouri but She Was Born in Valhermosa and Lives in Ohio

My mother's named for places, not Sandusky
that has wild hair soliciting the moon like blue-black
clouds touring. Not Lorain with ways too benevolent
for lay life. Ashtabula comes closer, southern,
evangelical and accented, her feet wide as yams.

She's Florida Missouri, a railroad, sturdy boxcars
without life of their own, filled and refilled with
what no one can carry.

You just can't call somebody Ravenna who's going
to have to wash another woman's bras and panties, who's
going to wear elbow-length dishwater to formal gigs,
who's going to have to work with her hands, folding and
shuffling them in prayer.

THYLIAS MOSS
(1954–)

Thylias Moss was born in Cleveland, Ohio. She earned a B.A. from Oberlin College and an M.A. from the University of New Hampshire. In addition to six books of poetry, she has also written a memoir and two plays. She is a professor of English and Creative Writing at the University of Michigan. "She's Florida Missouri but She Was Born in Valhermosa and Lives in Ohio" is inspired by the poet's mother, whose name is Florida Missouri Brasier. Moss reports that her mother was upset by the description of "her feet wide as yams."

The Beautiful American Word, Sure

The beautiful American word, Sure,
As I have come into a room, and touch
The lamp's button, and the light blooms with such
Certainty where the darkness loomed before,

As I care for what I do not know, and care
Knowing for little she might not have been,
And for how little she would be unseen,
The intercourse of lives miraculous and dear.

Where the light is, and each thing clear,
Separate from all others, standing in its place,
I drink the time and touch whatever's near,

And hope for day when the whole world has that face:
For what assures her present every year?
In dark accidents the mind's sufficient grace.

DELMORE SCHWARTZ
(1913–1966)

Delmore Schwartz's father Harry Schwartz earned a million dollars in real estate after immigrating to Brooklyn from Romania. However, the family was left without means when Harry Schwartz left his wife and sons in 1923; he afterward lost most of his fortune in the stock market crash of 1930. Delmore Schwartz's first book, *In Dreams Begin Responsibilities,* appeared the same week he turned twenty-five and drew comparisons to W. H. Auden and Hart Crane. Unfortunately, Schwartz's alcoholism, barbiturate habit, and mental instability soon overshadowed his auspicious debut. Though he continued to write and kept a fragile hold on his career via editorial and teaching positions, both of his marriages ended in divorce and he was frequently a worry to his friends, editors, and employers. He won both the Bollingen Prize — and was the youngest poet ever to do so — and the Shelley Memorial Award in 1960 for *Summer Knowledge: New and Selected Poems.* In the final years of his life his temper and paranoia got the best of him and he alienated, even sued, his best friends and supporters. Despite the best efforts of his closest friends, he never received adequate treatment for his depression and addictions and died in poverty in 1966 at the Hotel Columbia. His body remained in the morgue for two days before it was claimed. "The Beautiful American Word, Sure" is one of the many poems that provide a glimpse of what James Atlas has described as Schwartz's "tenacious hope."

Many Thousand Gone

No more auction block for me,
No more, no more;
No more auction block for me,
Many thousand gone.

No more peck o' corn for me,
No more, no more;
No more peck o' corn for me,
Many thousand gone.

No more driver's lash for me,
No more, no more;
No more driver's lash for me,
Many thousand gone.

No more pint o' salt for me,
No more, no more;
No more pint o' salt for me,
Many thousand gone.

No more hundred lash for me,
No more, no more;
No more hundred lash for me,
Many thousand gone.

No more mistress' call for me,
No more, no more;
No more mistress' call for me,
Many thousand gone.

UNKNOWN
(CA. 1867)

"Many Thousand Gone" (also known as "No More Auction Block for Me") was first sung by slaves and African-American soldiers who fought in the Union Army during the Civil War. The song is derived from an old African spiritual. As with many folk songs passed down through oral tradition and popular memory, "Many Thousand Gone" exists in several variants. Bob Dylan has recorded his own version of the song under the title "No More Auction Block."

My Life by Water

My life
   by water —
      Hear

spring's
   first frog
      or board

out on the cold
   ground
      giving

to wild green
   arts and letters
      Rabbits

raided
   my lettuce
      One boat

two —
   pointed toward
      my shore

thru birdstart
   wingdrip
      weed-drift

of the soft
   and serious —
      Water

LORINE NIEDECKER
(1903–1970)

Born in Fort Atkinson, Wisconsin, Lorine Niedecker lived in rural isolation on Black Hawk Island along the banks of Rock River in Wisconsin. After her parents died, she was left with two houses that were taken from her in foreclosure and very little money. She worked for several years as a cleaning woman at a local hospital. In a letter to Louis Zukofsky she joked: "I should draw a picture of myself covered with dust mops, pails, kitchen cleanser, cloths, brooms, etc. wondering where I am down those long halls past all those doors." Niedecker was an intensely private person. Many who knew her — even her second husband — had no idea that she wrote poetry at all.

Peace

When will you ever, Peace, wild wooddove, shy wings shut,
Your round me roaming end, and under be my boughs?
When, when, Peace, will you, Peace? — I'll not play hypocrite

To own my heart: I yield you do come sometimes; but
That piecemeal peace is poor peace. What pure peace allows
Alarms of wars, the daunting, wars, the death of it?

O surely, reaving Peace, my Lord should leave in lieu
Some good! And so he does leave Patience exquisite,
That plumes to Peace thereafter. And when Peace here does house
He comes with work to do, he does not come to coo,
              He comes to brood and sit.

GERARD MANLEY HOPKINS
(1844–1889)

English poet and clergyman Gerard Manley Hopkins published only three poems during his lifetime. He converted to Catholicism in 1866 and stopped writing two years later, believing that his poetry was interfering with his religious vocation. He was ordained by the Society of Jesuits in 1877 and taught classics at University College in Dublin, Ireland. After 1875, Hopkins took up writing poems again. He wrote some of his greatest poems, including those known as his Dark Sonnets, during the last years of his life.

VI Love and Knowledge (from *Audubon: A Vision*)

Their footless dance
Is of the beautiful liability of their nature.
Their eyes are round, boldly convex, bright as a jewel,
And merciless. They do not know
Compassion, and if they did,
We should not be worthy of it. They fly
In air that glitters like fluent crystal
And is hard as perfectly transparent iron, they cleave it
With no effort. They cry
In a tongue multitudinous, often like music.

He slew them, at surprising distances, with his gun.
Over a body held in his hand, his head was bowed low,
But not in grief.

He put them where they are, and there we see them:
In our imagination.

What is love?

One name for it is knowledge.

ROBERT PENN WARREN
(1905–1989)

Born in Guthrie, Kentucky, Robert Penn Warren was educated at Vanderbilt University, where he met the other members of a group of Southern poets who came to be known as the Fugitives: John Crowe Ransom, Allen Tate, Donald Davidson, and Merrill Moore. Warren's first poems were published in the group's magazine, *The Fugitive*. Warren was better known as a novelist than a poet, especially early in his career, and won the Pulitzer Prize for his novel *All the King's Men* in 1947. His second Pulitzer came with the publication of *Promises: Poems, 1954–1956* and in 1979 he earned yet another Pulitzer, this time for *Now and Then: Poems, 1976–1978*. Warren was named U.S. Poet Laureate (the first to hold the new title, formerly Poetry Consultant to the Library of Congress). "VI Love and Knowledge" is from Warren's book-length poem about John James Audubon. Warren reported that while working on the poem he was "writing at night, going to sleep, and waking up in the morning early—revising by shouting it all out loud in a Land Rover going to Yale."

Symptom Recital

I do not like my state of mind;
I'm bitter, querulous, unkind.
I hate my legs, I hate my hands,
I do not yearn for lovelier lands.
I dread the dawn's recurrent light;
I hate to go to bed at night.
I snoot at simple, earnest folk.
I cannot take the gentlest joke.
I find no peace in paint or type.
My world is but a lot of tripe.
I'm disillusioned, empty-breasted.
For what I think, I'd be arrested.
I am not sick, I am not well.
My quondam dreams are shot to hell.
My soul is crushed, my spirit sore;
I do not like me any more.
I cavil, quarrel, grumble, grouse.
I ponder on the narrow house.
I shudder at the thought of men . . .
I'm due to fall in love again.

DOROTHY PARKER
(1893–1967)

Born Dorothy Rothschild, Parker began her literary career writing captions for fashion photographs and drawings for *Vogue* in 1916 after selling poems to the magazine's editor. This position led to a job at *Vanity Fair* where she replaced P. G. Wodehouse as drama reviewer in 1918. Though she was fired two years later for being too frank and tough in her criticism, her work at the magazine brought her into contact with the infamous group of literary wits that made up the Algonquin Hotel Round Table, of which she became the pivotal figure. She helped one member of the clique, Harold Ross, establish the tone of the magazine he founded in 1925, *The New Yorker*. The book in which "Symptom Recital" was first published, *Enough Rope* (1926), grounded her reputation as "the wittiest woman in America." In addition to the acclaim she earned as a poet and critic, she also was a well-regarded short-story writer and won, as well, an Academy Award for her work on the screenplay of *A Star Is Born*.

The White Horse

The youth walks up to the white horse, to put its halter on
And the horse looks at him in silence.
They are so silent, they are in another world.

D. H. LAWRENCE
(1885–1930)

One of the twentieth century's greatest novelists, English-born David Herbert Lawrence was also the author of more than a thousand poems. His first published piece was a short story in the *Nottingham Guardian* in 1907; the story had been chosen for the prize in the newspaper's contest, but Lawrence had submitted it under a friend's name so was not properly credited. In 1912 Lawrence left England, which he reviled as "a long gray ashy coffin," and traveled through Mexico, Italy, Ceylon, New Zealand, Tahiti, France, Australia, the United States, and other countries. His novels, especially *Lady Chatterly's Lover* and *The Rainbow,* were banned for obscenity and even burned for the four-letter words and frank depictions of sex they contained. Lawrence died of tuberculosis in France at the age of forty-five.

March 25

Like Attracts Like

like   attracts   like

like   attracts   like

like   attracts   like

like   attracts   like

like   attracts   like

like attracts like

like attracts like

likeattractslike

likattractlike

likttractike

liketradike

likteratike

likrdike

EMMETT WILLIAMS
(1925–)

Poet, performer, and painter Emmett Williams was born in Greenville, South Carolina, and grew up in Newport News, Virginia. After graduating from Kenyon College in 1949, he entered the U. S. Army, later traveling to Poland and Greece, and then living for a time in France, Germany, and Switzerland. A prominent practitioner of concrete poetry, Williams not only publishes and performs his work in the usual senses, he also often displays it as "text art" in galleries and museums. He is associated with the Damstadt Circle of concrete poetry and the Fluxus group, which includes Jackson MacLow, George Brecht, Dick Higgins, Robert Filliou, and others. Williams is the co-founder of the International Symposia of the Arts in Warsaw and has served as Director-President of the Artists' Museum in Lodz, Poland. In 1996 he received the Hannah Höch prize for lifetime achievement in the arts.

Adam Lay I-bounden

Adam lay i-bounden, bounden in a bond;
Foure thousand winter thought he not too long.
And all was for an apple, an apple that he took,
As clerkes finden written in theire book.

Ne hadde the apple take been, the apple taken been,
Ne hadde never our Lady aye been Heaven's queen.
Blessed be the time that apple taken was,
Therefore we may singen, "*Deo gracias!*"

ANONYMOUS
(CA. FIFTEENTH CENTURY)

The text of this poem survives in only one manuscript collection of fifteenth-century carols. The anonymous poet celebrates the *felix culpa* (happy fault) of Original Sin, which allowed the Virgin Mary, "our Lady," to be elevated to the status of "Heaven's queen." "Foure thousand winter" refers to the Middle Age belief that the Creation took place circa 4,000 B.C. The poem has been set to music in several versions and is still included in some modern hymnals.

A Prison Evening

Each star a rung,
night comes down the spiral
staircase of the evening.
The breeze passes by so very close
as if someone just happened to speak of love.
In the courtyard,
the trees are absorbed refugees
embroidering maps of return on the sky.
On the roof,
the moon — lovingly, generously —
is turning the stars
into a dust of sheen.
From every corner, dark-green shadows,
in ripples, come towards me.
At any moment they may break over me,
like the waves of pain each time I remember
this separation from my lover.
This thought keeps consoling me:
though tyrants may command that lamps be smashed
in rooms where lovers are destined to meet,
they cannot snuff out the moon, so today,
nor tomorrow, no tyranny will succeed,

no poison of torture make me bitter,
if just one evening in prison
can be so strangely sweet,
if just one moment anywhere on this earth.

FAIZ AHMED FAIZ
(1910–1984)
translated by Agha Shahid Ali

Urdu poet Faiz Ahmed Faiz was born in the Punjab (now Pakistan). He received an English education at mission school in Sialkto, but also learned Urdu, Persian, and Arabic. He earned his M.A. in English and Arabic literatures from Oriental College, Lahore. During World War II, Faiz served in the Indian Army in Delhi, achieving the rank of Lieutenant Colonel. After the formation of the Islamic republic of Pakistan in 1947, Faiz resigned from the army and moved to Pakistan with his family, where he became editor of the leftist English-language daily, the *Pakistan Times*, and worked as managing editor of the Urdu daily *Imroz*. In 1951 Faiz was implicated in the Rawalpindi Conspiracy case and arrested. The government alleged that Faiz and others were planning a coup d'etat. He spent four years in prison under a sentence of death but was released in 1955. In 1962 he won the Lenin Peace Prize. After a period of exile in war-torn Lebanon from 1979 to 1982, Faiz returned to Pakistan. He died in Lahore on November 20, 1984.

20 years to the day before Bob.

The Star's Whole Secret

Did she drink tea? Yes, please. And after,
the halo of a glass gone.
A taxi appeared out of elsewhere.

Five constellations, Louise said,
but only two bright stars among them. Soon, Ham said,
the whale will reach the knot of the fisherman's net;

the moon will have its face in the water.
And we'll all feel the fury of having been used
up in maelstrom and splendor.

Mother did say, Louise said, try to be popular,
pretty, and charming. Try to make others
feel clever. Without fear, what are we?

the other asked. The will, said Louise. The mill moth
and the lavish wick, breathless in the remnant
of a fire.

MARY JO BANG
(1946–)

Mary Jo Bang was born in Waynesville, Missouri, and grew up in St. Louis. She earned B.A. and M.A. degrees in sociology from Northwestern University, a B.A. in photography from Westminster University (London), and an M.F.A. in creative writing from Columbia University. She is a poetry editor at *Boston Review* and currently teaches at Washington University in St. Louis. The title of "The Star's Whole Secret" comes from Emily Dickinson's poem "451": "The Star's whole Secret — in the Lake — / Eyes were not meant to know."

March 29

West London

Crouch'd on the pavement, close by Belgrave Square,
A tramp I saw, ill, moody, and tongue-tied.
A babe was in her arms, and at her side
A girl; their clothes were rags, their feet were bare.

Some labouring men, whose work lay somewhere there,
Pass'd opposite; she touch'd her girl, who hied
Across, and begg'd, and came back satisfied.
The rich she had let pass with frozen stare.

Thought I: 'Above her state this spirit towers;
She will not ask of aliens, but of friends,
Of sharers in a common human fate.

'She turns from that cold succour, which attends
The unknown little from the unknowing great,
And points us to a better time than ours.'

MATTHEW ARNOLD
(1822–1888)

English poet and critic Matthew Arnold was educated at Baliol College, Oxford, and worked as a government school inspector in England for thirty-five years. In 1857 Arnold accepted a teaching position at Oxford and was the first professor in the school's history to lecture in English rather than Latin. Arnold was equally revered for his poetry and prose, writing popular essays on religion, literature, education, and other topics. In 1883 and again in 1886, Arnold gave lecture tours in the United States. He died in Liverpool, England, in 1888. G. K. Chesterton wrote that Arnold was, "even in the age of Carlyle and Ruskin, perhaps the most serious man alive." This sonnet was set to music by composer Charles Edward Ives in 1921.

Recuerdo

We were very tired, we were very merry —
We had gone back and forth all night on the ferry.
It was bare and bright, and smelled like a stable —
But we looked into a fire, we leaned across a table,
We lay on a hill-top underneath the moon;
And the whistles kept blowing, and the dawn came soon.

We were very tired, we were very merry —
We had gone back and forth all night on the ferry;
And you ate an apple, and I ate a pear,
From a dozen of each we had bought somewhere;
And the sky went wan, and the wind came cold,
And the sun rose dripping, a bucketful of gold.

We were very tired, we were very merry,
We had gone back and forth all night on the ferry.
We hailed, "Good morrow, mother!" to a shawl-covered head,
And bought a morning paper, which neither of us read;
And she wept, "God bless you!" for the apples and pears,
And we gave her all our money but our subway fares.

EDNA ST. VINCENT MILLAY
(1892–1950)

Poet and playwright Edna St. Vincent Millay was born in Rockland, Maine. In 1912 she won a scholarship to Vassar after winning a poetry contest, which she entered at her mother's suggestion. "Vincent," as her friends called her, moved to New York's Greenwich Village after graduating from Vassar and there cultivated a notoriously adventuresome lifestyle as a liberated and openly bisexual woman of the 1920s and 1930s. In 1923 Millay became the first woman ever to win the Pulitzer Prize, which she received for *Ballad of the Harp Weaver.* By all accounts Millay was a beautiful and charming woman. Her readings drew large crowds, in part due to her unique voice, which Louis Untermeyer likened to "the sound of the ax on fresh wood." Millay suffered a nervous breakdown in 1944 and succumbed to alcoholism after the death of her husband Eugen Boissevain in 1949. She died alone, falling from the staircase of her house, in 1950. "Recuerdo" is Spanish for "memory" or "regard."

Song of the Sky Loom

Oh our Mother the Earth, oh our Father the Sky,
Your children are we, and with tired backs
We bring you the gifts that you love.
Then weave for us a garment of brightness;
May the warp be the white light of morning,
May the weft be the red light of evening,
May the fringes be the falling rain,
May the border be the standing rainbow.
Thus weave for us a garment of brightness
That we may walk fittingly where birds sing,
That we may walk fittingly where grass is green,
Oh our Mother the Earth, oh our Father the Sky!

TEWA SONG
translated by Herbert Joseph Spinden

The Tewa were pueblo-dwelling Native Americans of Arizona and New Mexico. In many Southwestern Native American traditions, the image of the loom is associated with the physical appearance of a desert rain, which resembles a loom hung from the sky. A white mantle, here "a garment of brightness," is the ceremonial robe worn by the Tewa on certain occasions. "Song of the Sky Loom" is a prayer for protection and well being. (For other Tewa songs, see June 24 and Spetember 25.)

April 1

from *Spring and All*

By the road to the contagious hospital
under the surge of the blue
mottled clouds driven from the
northeast — a cold wind. Beyond, the
waste of broad, muddy fields
brown with dried weeds, standing and fallen

patches of standing water
and scattering of tall trees

All along the road the reddish
purplish, forked, upstanding, twiggy
stuff of bushes and small trees
with dead, brown leaves under them
leafless vines —

Lifeless in appearance, sluggish
dazed spring approaches —

They enter the new world naked,
cold, uncertain of all
save that they enter. All about them
the cold, familiar wind —

Now the grass, tomorrow
the stiff curl of wildcarrot leaf
One by one objects are defined —
It quickens: clarity, outline of leaf

But now the stark dignity of
entrance — Still, the profound change
has come upon them: rooted, they
grip down and begin to awaken

WILLIAM CARLOS WILLIAMS
(1883–1963)

William Carlos Williams wrote of the book-length *Spring and All*, "Nobody ever saw it—it had no circulation at all—but I had a lot of fun with it. It consists of poems interspersed with prose, the same idea as *Improvisations*. It was written when all the world was going crazy about typographical form and is really a travesty on the idea. Chapter headings are printed upside down on purpose, the chapters are numbered all out of order, sometimes with a Roman numeral, sometimes with an Arabic, anything that came in handy. The prose is a mixture of philosophy and nonsense. . . . But the poems were kept pure—no typographical tricks." *Spring and All* was published in 1923, and Williams dedicated the book to his friend Charles Demuth, a contemporary painter. Demuth repaid Williams's tribute by painting "I Saw the Figure 5 in Gold, (1928)," which borrows Williams's image of a fire truck racing down a Manhattan street and has the poet's name worked into the canvas as a dedication.

Childhood
for Abgar Renault

My father would saddle up and ride to the hills.
My mother would sit home and sew.
My little brother would sleep.
I alone — a boy under the wide mango limbs —
would read all about Robinson Crusoe from his book,
a long story with no end to it.

In the white light of noon, a voice which had learned
to lull babies in the slave quarters long ago, and not forgot,
would call me in for coffee:
black coffee, blacker even than she was,
strong coffee,
and good.

My mother would sit there all vague over her threads
one eye on her boys
— Shh! . . . Don't wake him up! —
and stop the swinging cradle when a mosquito lit,
and loose a sigh . . . come up from, where?

While off in the endless back reaches of our ranch
my father worked the herds.

And I didn't know that my own tale
Was more beautiful than any in Robinson Crusoe's book.

CARLOS DRUMMOND DE ANDRADE
(1902–1987)
translated by Virginia de Araújo

Brazilian modernist poet Carlos Drummond de Andrade worked as a journalist
before earning a degree in pharmacology in 1925. In 1928 Andrade became a civil ser-
vant while working as a newspaper editor. With poet Manuel Bandeira and other
friends, Andrade formed "Semana de Arte Moderna," a group responsible for intro-
ducing the principles of modernism into Brazilian poetry. In addition to achieving
a reputation as one of the best-known Portuguese-language poets, Andrade also
wrote essays and short stories and translated several European writers, including
Proust, Garcia Lorca, Balzac, Hamsun, and Molière. He died in Rio de Janeiro of a
heart attack in 1987. "Childhood" is dedicated to Andrade's contemporary Abgar
Renault, a poet and government official in Brazil.

The Bat

Reading in bed, full of sentiment
for the mild evening and the children
asleep in adjacent rooms, hearing them
cry out now and then the brief reports
of sufficient imagination, and listening
at the same time compassionately
to the scrabble of claws, the fast treble
in the chimney —
                        then it was out,
not a trapped bird
beating at the seams of the ceiling,
but a bat lifting toward us, falling away.

Dominion over every living thing,
large brain, a choice of weapons —
Shuddering, in the lit hall
we swung repeatedly against
its rising secular face
until it fell; then
shoveled it into the yard for the cat
who shuttles easily between two worlds.

ELLEN BRYANT VOIGT
(1943–)

Ellen Bryant Voigt was born in Danville, Virginia. In 1976 she developed and directed the first low-residency writing program in the United States at Goddard College in Vermont, and later Voigt relocated the program to Warren Wilson College in North Carolina, where she has taught since 1981. Ellen Bryant Voigt recently completed her four-year term as Vermont State Poet.

April 4

Quickness

False life! a foil and no more, when
     Wilt thou be gone?
Thou foul deception of all men
That would not have the true come on.

Thou art a Moon-like toil; a blinde
     Self-posing state;
A dark contest of waves and winde;
A meer tempestuous debate.

Life is a fix'd, discerning light,
     A knowing Joy;
No chance, or fit: but ever bright,
And calm and full, yet doth not cloy.

'Tis such a blissful thing, that still
     Doth vivifie,
And shine and smile, and hath the skill
To please without Eternity.

Thou art a toylsom Mole, or less
     A moving mist
But life is, what none can express,
A quickness, which my God hath kist.

HENRY VAUGHAN
(1622–1695)

Welsh poet Henry Vaughan attended Jesus College, Oxford, and studied law, while his twin brother Thomas became renowned as a natural physician and alchemist. There is some indication that, after the Civil War interrupted his law studies, Vaughan may have practiced medicine as well. "Quickness" is from Vaughan's third collection *Silex Scintallans,* the book that marks his turn from secular to religious subjects. The title of the book means "fiery flint" and alludes to the "stony" heart of the author, from which God strikes divine sparks.

April 5

Spring

Ah, this world of ours:
just three days I don't look out —
and cherry blossoms!

ŌSHIMA RYŌTA
(1718–1787)
translated by Steven D. Carter

At least, this translation preserves true Haiku form of 17 syllables.

Ryōta was a Haikai (or Haiku) poet who wrote during the mid-Edo period (1603–1868). Very little is known about this urbane poet other than that he had many followers. Cherry blossoms, a traditional element of haiku and other Japanese forms, are associated with spring.

The Mad Scene

Again last night I dreamed the dream called Laundry.
In it, the sheets and towels of a life we were going to share,
The milk-stiff bibs, the shroud, each rag to be ever
Trampled or soiled, bled on or groped for blindly,
Came swooning out of an enormous willow hamper
Onto moon-marbly boards. We had just met. I watched
From outer darkness. I had dressed myself in clothes
Of a new fiber that never stains or wrinkles, never
Wears thin. The opera house sparkled with tiers
And tiers of eyes, like mine enlarged by belladonna,
Trained inward. There I saw the cloud-clot, gust by gust,
Form, and the lightning bite, and the roan mane unloosen.
Fingers were running in panic over the flute's nine gates.
Why did I flinch? I loved you. And in the downpour laughed
To have us wrung white, gnarled together, one
Topmost mordent of wisteria,
As the lean tree burst into grief.

JAMES MERRILL
(1926–1995)

James Merrill was born in New York City, the son of Hellen Ingram and Charles Merrill, founder of Merrill Lynch & Company. Merrill won three National Book Awards (one in fiction, two in poetry), the Pulitzer Prize, the Bollingen Prize, the National Book Critics Circle Award, and the Bobbit National Prize for Poetry from the Library of Congress, among other honors. In 1956 Merrill used some of his inheritance to set up the Ingram-Merrill Foundation, which has sustained hundreds of writers and artists with grants since that time. Edmund White has described Merrill's poetry as "as funny as Byron's, as elusive as Montale's, as magisterial as Wallace Stevens's, as intelligent as Pope's. He knew better than anyone else how to make a word skip across the smooth surface of the mind and sink deep where it landed. . . . Everything he touched he transformed into art."

His Elegy
Written before His Execution

My prime of youth is but a frost of cares;
My feast of joy is but a dish of pain;
My crop of corn is but a field of tares;
And all my good is but vain hope of gain:
The day is past, and yet I saw no sun;
And now I live, and now my life is done.

My tale was heard, and yet it was not told;
My fruit is fall'n, and yet my leaves are
green;
My youth is spent, and yet I am not old;
I saw the world, and yet I was not seen:
My thread is cut, and yet it is not spun;
And now I live, and now my life is done.

I sought my death, and found it in my womb;
I looked for life, and saw it was a shade;
I trod the earth, and knew it was my tomb;
And now I die, and now I was but made:
My glass is full, and now my glass is run;
And now I live, and now my life is done.

CHIDIOCK TICHBORNE
(1558?–1586)

An ardent papist during the reign of Queen Elizabeth, Tichborne conspired with the King of Spain and other foreign enemies of England, even becoming involved in Anthony Babington's plot against the life of the Queen. He was interrogated several times for indulging in "popish practices" such as attending mass, and once for fingering "popish relics." He was eventually seized and tried, found guilty of conspiracy, and sentenced to be hanged and disemboweled. Tichborne is thought to have composed "His Elegy" while a prisoner in the infamous Tower of London, on the eve of his execution. Only three of Tichborne's poems survived.

April 8

The Open Window

I shaved one morning standing
by the open window
on the second story.
Switched on the razor.
It started to hum.
A heavier and heavier whirr.
Grew to a roar.
Grew to a helicopter.
And a voice — the pilot's — pierced
the noise, shouting:
"Keep your eyes open!
You're seeing this for the last time!"
Rose.
Floated low over the summer.
The small things I love, what do they amount to?
So many variations of green.
And especially in the red of housewells.
Beetles glittered in the dung, in the sun.
Cellars pulled up by the roots
sailed through the air.
Industry.
printing presses crawled along.
People at that instant
were the only things motionless.
They held their minute of silence.
And the dead in the churchyard especially
held still

like those who posed in the early days of the camera.
Fly low!
I didn't know which way
to turn my head —
my sight was divided
like a horse's.

TOMAS TRANSTRÖMER
(1931–)
translated by Robert Bly

The Swedish poet Tomas Tranströmer was born in Stockholm. Known as Sweden's most important poet since World War II, Tranströmer has received Germany's Petrach Prize, the Bonnier Award for Poetry, the Neustadt International Prize for Literature, and the Nordic Prize from the Swedish Academy, among other honors. His work has been translated into thirty languages, including Dutch, Hungarian, and English. In addition to being Sweden's most widely translated contemporary poet, Tranströmer is also a respected psychologist. He spent the early 1960s working at a boys' prison and since then has worked extensively with drug addicts, convicts, and the handicapped.

What Would I Do Without This World Faceless Incurious

what would I do without this world faceless incurious
where to be lasts but an instant where every instant
spills in the void the ignorance of having been
without this wave where in the end
body and shadow together are engulfed
what would I do without this silence where the murmurs die
the pantings the frenzies towards succour towards love
without this sky that soars
above its ballast dust

what would I do what I did yesterday and the day before
peering out of my deadlight looking for another
wandering like me eddying far from all the living
   in a convulsive space
   among the voices voiceless
   that throng my hiddenness

SAMUEL BECKETT
(1906–1989)

Irish playwright, novelist, and poet Samuel Beckett was born in Dublin. He moved to France in 1938 and lived there the rest of his life, writing and translating his work in both French and English. In Paris, Beckett was introduced to James Joyce, whom he assisted with his research for *Finnegan's Wake*. Beckett would also read aloud to the senior author whose eyesight was failing. Beckett won the Nobel Prize for Literature in 1969 and the Grand Prix National du Theatre in 1975. Beckett died of complications from emphysema in Paris in 1989. "What Would I Do Without This World Faceless Incurious" was originally written in French as "que ferais-je sans ce monde . . ." between 1946 and 1948.

Seaweeds

I know a little what it is like, once here at high tide
Stranded, for them to be so attached to the bottom's
Sarcophagus lids, up to their brown green gold wine
Bottle necks in the prevailing booze, riding, as far
As we can see, like a picnic on a blanket.

Whatever plucks them from below the red horizon
Like snapped pulleys and ropes for the pyramidal effort
Of the moon, they come in, they come through the breakers,
Heaps of hair, writing across the beach a collapsed
Script, signers of a huge independence.

Melville thought them pure, bitter, seeing the fog-sized
Flies dancing stiff and renaissance above. But I
Have eaten nori and dulse, and to have gone deep
Before being cast out leaves hardly a taste of loneliness.
And I take in their iodine.

SANDRA McPHERSON
(1943–)

Sandra McPherson was born and raised in San Jose, California. She earned her B.A. at San José State University and did her graduate work under Elizabeth Bishop and David Wagoner at the University of Washington. McPherson has taught at the University of Iowa Writers' Workshop, the University of California at Berkeley, and the Oregon Writers Workshop/Pacific Northwest College of Art. In 1999 McPherson founded Swan Scythe Press, a poetry chapbook publishing house. She currently teaches at the University of California, Davis.

from "Song of Myself" (in *Leaves of Grass*)

31

I believe a leaf of grass is no less than the journey-work of the stars,
And the pismire is equally perfect, and a grain of sand, and the egg
    of the wren,
And the tree-toad is a chef-d'oeuvre for the highest,
And the running blackberry would adorn the parlors of heaven,
And the narrowest hinge in my hand puts to scorn all machinery,
And the cow crunching with depress'd head surpasses any statue,
And a mouse is miracle enough to stagger sextillions of infidels.

I find I incorporate gneiss, coal, long-threaded moss, fruits, grains,
    esculent roots,
And am stucco'd with quadrupeds and birds all over,
And have distanced what is behind me for good reasons,
But call any thing back again when I desire it.

In vain the speeding or shyness,
In vain the plutonic rocks send their old heat against my approach,
In vain the mastodon retreats beneath its own powder'd bones,
In vain objects stand leagues off and assume manifold shapes,
In vain the ocean setting in hollows and the great monsters lying low,
In vain the buzzard houses herself with the sky,
In vain the snake slides through the creepers and logs,
In vain the elk takes to the inner passes of the woods,
In vain the razor-bill'd auk sails far north to Labrador,
I follow quickly, I ascend to the nest in the fissure of the cliff.

WALT WHITMAN
(1819–1892)

Whitman sent *Leaves of Grass* to Ralph Waldo Emerson as a sort of response to Emerson's lament that he had looked in vain for the poet of true genius in America. Emerson was impressed by the work and replied "Dear Sir: I am not blind to the worth of the wonderful gift of 'Leaves of Grass. . . . ' I rubbed my eyes a little to see if this sunbeam were no illusion; but the solid sense of the book is a sober certainty." The letter did not remain private for long; Whitman used the quotation without Emerson's permission in advertising copy for the book. Whitman also published several anonymous reviews of his own book, calling himself in one of them "the begetter of a new offspring out of literature."

Disillusionment of Ten O'clock

The houses are haunted
By white night-gowns.
None are green,
Or purple with green rings,
Or green with yellow rings,
Or yellow with blue rings.
None of them are strange,
With socks of lace
And beaded ceintures.
People are not going
To dream of baboons and periwinkles.
Only, here and there, an old sailor,
Drunk and asleep in his boots,
Catches tigers
In red weather.

WALLACE STEVENS
(1879–1955)

"Disillusionment of Ten O'clock" appeared in Wallace Stevens's first book, *Harmonium*, in 1923. In July of 1922 Stevens wrote to Carl Van Vechten that he felt "frightfully uncertain about a book," but indicated he was certainly willing to discuss the possibility. That conversation must have gone well, because Stevens put aside his uncertainties, Vechten passed the manuscript along, and a contract was signed with Alfred A. Knopf in December of that same year. To Harriet Monroe, editor of *Poetry* and a close friend, Stevens confided: "I have omitted many things, exercising the most fastidious choice, so far as that was possible among my witherlings. To pick a crisp salad from the garbage of the past is no snap." The book was published approximately one month prior to Stevens's forty-fourth birthday. The response to the book was discouraging for Stevens, though Marianne Moore came out as an early fan. He wrote little for the next five or six years, and his second book, *Ideas of Order*, was not published until 1936.

Green Willow

The poor soul sat sighing by a sycamore tree;
    Sing willow, willow, willow!
With his hand in his bosom, and his head upon his knee;
    O! willow, willow, willow, willow,
    O! willow, willow, willow, willow,
        Shall be my garland.
 Sing all a green willow, willow, willow, willow!
Ay me, the green willow must be my garland.

sighed

He sight in his singing, and made a great moan,
I am dead to all pleasure, my true love she is gone.

The mute bird sat by him was made tame by his moans;
The true tears fell from him would have melted the stones.

Come all you forsaken, and mourn you with me;
Who speaks of a false love, mine's falser than she.

Let Love no more boast her, in palace nor bower,
It buds, but it blasteth, ere it be a flower.

Thou fair and more false, I die with thy wound;
Thou hast lost the truest lover that goes upon the ground.

Let nobody chide her, her scorns I approve;
She was born to be false, and I to die for love.

Take this for my farewell and latest adieu;
Write this on my tomb, that in love I was true.

ANONYMOUS

The original author of "Green Willow," a popular folk ballad, is unknown. William Shakespeare has Desdemona sing her own rendition of it in act IV, scene iii, of *Othello.* According to E. Cobham Brewer's *Dictionary of Phrase and Fable* (1898) the willow garland and the "weeping" willow are traditional emblems of forsaken love. Willow garlands were also commonly displayed at funerals and other mournful occasions.

April 14

Easter-Wings

Lord, who createdst man in wealth and store,
    Though foolishly he lost the same,
        Decaying more and more,
           Till he became
             Most poore:
             With thee
           O let me rise
        As larks, harmoniously,
    And sing this day thy victories:
Then shall the fall further the flight in me.

My tender age in sorrow did beginne:
    And still with sicknesses and shame
        Thou didst so punish sinne,
           That I became
            Most thinne.
            With   thee
         Let me combine
      And feel this day thy victorie:
    For, if I imp my wing on thine,
Affliction shall advance the flight in me.

GEORGE HERBERT
(1593–1633)

Like "The Windows" (see February 4), "Easter-Wings" appeared in *The Temple: Sacred Poems and Private Ejaculations* in 1633. One of George Herbert's pattern poems, "Easter-Wings" is one of the best-known examples of shaped verse. In the original edition, the stanzas were printed sideways, one to a page, to represent two birds flying upward with outspread wings. The word "imp," from the penultimate line, refers to the falconer's practice of grafting new feathers onto a hawk's wing to improve its flight.

The Owl

Downhill I came, hungry, and yet not starved;
Cold, yet had heat within me that was proof
Against the North wind; tired, yet so that rest
Had seemed the sweetest thing under a roof.

Then at the inn I had food, fire, and rest,
Knowing how hungry, cold, and tired was I.
All of the night was quite barred out except
An owl's cry, a most melancholy cry

Shaken out long and clear upon the hill,
No merry note, nor cause of merriment,
But one telling me plain what I escaped
And others could not, that night, as in I went.

And salted was my food, and my repose,
Salted and sobered, too, by the bird's voice
Speaking for all who lay under the stars,
Soldiers and poor, unable to rejoice.

EDWARD THOMAS
(1878–1917)

English poet Edward Thomas was born of Welsh parents in the London suburb of Lambeth. A precocious child interested in nature, he began writing and publishing his natural observations at the age of seventeen, and his first book, *The Woodland Life*, was published before he was twenty. Thomas worked very hard as a prolific author of essays, biographies, and criticism to support his wife and two children. He published some verse under the pseudonym Edward Eastaway but became serious about his poetry after being encouraged by Robert Frost, whom he greatly admired. Thomas joined the British Army in 1915 and was killed at the battle of Arras in France two years later. He wrote almost all of his poems in his diary between December 1914 and January 1917.

Midnight Flowers

I go down step by step.
The house is quiet, full of trapped heat and sleep.
In the kitchen everything is still.
Nothing is distinct; there is no moon to speak of.

I could be undone every single day by
paradox or what they call in the countryside
blackthorn winter,
when hailstones come with the first apple blossom.

I turn a switch and the garden grows.
A whole summer's work in one instant!
I press my face to the glass. I can see
shadows of lilac, of fuchsia; a dark likeness of blackcurrant:

little clients of suddenness, how sullen they are at
the margins of the light.
They need no rain, they have no roots.
I reach out a hand; they are gone.

When I was a child a snapdragon was
held an inch from my face. Look, a voice said, this
is the color of your hair. And there it was, my head,
a pliant jewel in the hands of someone else.

EAVAN BOLAND
(1944–)

Irish poet Eavan Boland was born in Dublin and educated in Dublin, London, and New York. She has taught at Trinity College, University College, and Bowdoin College, and she was a member of the International Writing Program at the University of Iowa. From 1995 to 2000 Boland served as the Director of the Creative Writing Program at Stanford University, where she is currently a professor of English. In her book *Object Lessons,* Boland notes that she "began writing in a country where the word woman and the word poet were almost magnetically opposed."

Editor Whedon

To be able to see every side of every question;
To be on every side, to be everything, to be nothing long;
To pervert truth, to ride it for a purpose,
To use great feelings and passions of the human family
For base designs, for cunning ends;
To wear a mask like the Greek actors —
Your eight-page paper — behind which you huddle,
Bawling through the megaphone of big type;
"This is I, the giant."
Thereby also living the life of a sneak-thief,
Poisoned with the anonymous words
Of your clandestine soul.
To scratch dirt over scandal for money,
And exhume it to the winds for revenge,
Or to sell papers,
Crushing reputations, or bodies, if need be;
To win at any cost, save your own life.
To glory in demoniac power, ditching civilization,
As a paranoiac boy puts a log on the track
And derails the express train.
To be an editor, as I was.
Then to lie here close by the river over the place
Where the sewage flows from the village,
And the empty cans and garbage are dumped,
And abortions are hidden.

EDGAR LEE MASTERS
(1868–1950)

Edgar Lee Masters was born in Garnett, Kansas, and grew up in Lewiston, Illinois. His most popular work, *Spoon River Anthology*, contains "Editor Whedon" and hundreds of similar portraits of the real and imagined citizens of Spoon River, Illinois. Masters began writing the book while maintaining a career as a prominent lawyer in Chicago. After a visit to his mother sparked his memories of his small-town youth, he wrote with such intensity of vision that the 214 poems in the book were completed within ten months. *Spoon River* was Masters' twelfth book, and it immediately drew both notoriety and fame for the heretofore little known author. It also earned more money for Masters and his publisher than any previously published book of American poetry.

from "The Prairies"

These are the gardens of the Desert, these
The unshorn fields, boundless and beautiful,
For which the speech of England has no name —
The Prairies. I behold them for the first,
And my heart swells, while the dilated sight
Takes in the encircling vastness. Lo! they stretch,
In airy undulations, far away,
As if the ocean, in his gentlest swell,
Stood still, with all his rounded billows fixed,
And motionless forever. — Motionless? —
No — they are all unchained again. The clouds
Sweep over with their shadows, and, beneath,
The surface rolls and fluctuates to the eye;
Dark hollows seem to glide along and chase
The sunny ridges. Breezes of the South!
Who toss the golden and the flame-like flowers,
And pass the prairie-hawk that, poised on high,
Flaps his broad wings, yet moves not — ye have played
Among the palms of Mexico and vines
Of Texas, and have crisped the limpid brooks
That from the fountains of Sonora glide
Into the calm Pacific — have ye fanned
A nobler or a lovelier scene than this?

WILLIAM CULLEN BRYANT
(1794–1878)

William Cullen Bryant was born in Cummington, Massachusetts, and published his first poem at the age of ten in the *Northampton Hampshire Gazette*. Because of his family's financial situation, he was unable to attend Yale as he planned, but he passed the bar exam and worked as a lawyer in Plainfield, Massachusetts, until 1825, when he moved to New York as the editor of the *New York Review*. In 1827, Bryant became editor-in-chief and part owner of the New York *Evening Post*, from which platform he spoke out against slavery and on behalf of other causes. After publishing four books of poems, he became the country's most prominent poet and the best-known American poet abroad. Despite his long career as an outspoken journalist, he wrote in a letter to his friend Richard Henry Dana, "I do not like politics any better than you do; but they get only my mornings and politics and a bellyful are better than poetry and starvation."

Tunnel Music

Times Square, the shuttle's quick chrome
flies open and the whole car floods with
— what is it? Infernal industry, the tunnels
under Manhattan broken into hell at last?

Guttural churr and whistle and grind
of the engines that spin the poles?
Enormous racket, ungodly. What it is
is percussion: nine black guys

with nine lovely and previously unimagined
constructions of metal ripped and mauled,
welded and oiled: scoured chemical drums,
torched rims, unnameable disks of chrome.

Artifacts of wreck? The end of industry?
A century's failures reworked, bent,
hammered out, struck till their shimmying
tumbles and ricochets from tile walls:

anything dinged, busted or dumped
can be beaten till it sings.
A kind of ghostly joy in it, though
this music's almost unrecognizable,

so utterly of the coming world it is.

Mark Doty
(1953–)

Mark Doty divides his time between Provincetown, Massachusetts, and Houston, Texas, where he teaches in the Creative Writing Program at the University of Houston. He has taught at the University of Utah, the University of Iowa, Columbia University, Sarah Lawrence College, and other universities. Doty has received the T. S. Eliot Prize from the United Kingdom. He has also written several autobiographical prose works.

miss rosie

when i watch you
wrapped up like garbage
sitting, surrounded by the smell
of too old potato peels
or
when i watch you
in your old man's shoes
with the little toe cut out
sitting, waiting for your mind
like next week's grocery
i say
when i watch you
you wet brown bag of a woman
who used to be the best looking gal in georgia
used to be called the Georgia Rose
i stand up
through your destruction
i stand up

LUCILLE CLIFTON
(1936–)

Lucille Clifton was born in Depew, New York. She won the National Book Award for her new and selected poems in 2000. She has also been honored with an Emmy from the American Academy of Television Arts and Sciences, and in 1999 she was elected a Chancellor of the Academy of American Poets. She has been the Poet Laureate for the State of Maryland and is Distinguished Professor of Humanities at St. Mary's College, Maryland. As a young poet, Clifton was inspired by the success of Robert Hayden and sent him some of her poems. "He was very kind about them," she says. "What you want to understand is that 50 years ago, one never saw a person who looked like me as a published poet. I certainly didn't in the schools in Buffalo, New York, where I grew up."

April 21

She Dwelt among the Untrodden Ways

She dwelt among the untrodden ways
    Beside the springs of Dove,
A maid whom there were none to praise
    And very few to love:

A violet by a mossy stone
    Half hidden from the eye!
— Fair as a star, when only one
    Is shining in the sky.

She lived unknown, and few could know
    When Lucy ceased to be;
But she is in her grave, and, oh,
    The difference to me!

WILLIAM WORDSWORTH
(1770–1850)

William Wordsworth was born in Cockermouth, Cumbria, England. "She Dwelt among the Untrodden Ways" has been dated to 1798, when Wordsworth was traveling in Germany. Lucy, named in line ten, is also the subject of five other poems by Wordsworth. It is unknown whether Lucy was a real person or a creation of the poet, but some feel that she is a stand-in for Wordsworth's much-loved sister Dorothy who went with him everywhere. While in Germany, Wordsworth wrote to his close friend and sometime collaborator Samuel Taylor Coleridge, "As I had not books I have been obliged to write in self-defense." Inserted in the letter were the original versions of this poem and another Lucy piece, "Strange Fits of Passion."

For My Mother

It was better when we were
together in one body.
Thirty years. Screened
through the green glass
of your eye, moonlight
filtered into my bones
as we lay
in the big bed, in the dark,
waiting for my father.
Thirty years. He closed
your eyelids with
two kisses. And then spring
came and withdrew from me
the absolute
knowledge of the unborn,
leaving the brick stoop
where you stand, shading
your eyes, but it is
night, the moon
is stationed in the beech tree,
round and white among
the small tin markers of the stars:
Thirty years. A marsh
grows up around the house.
Schools of spores circulate
behind the shades, drift through
gauze flutterings of vegetation.

LOUISE GLÜCK
(1943–)

Louise Glück was born in New York, New York, and raised on Long Island. She won the Pulitzer Prize for her book *The Wild Iris*. Glück teaches at Williams College and lives in Cambridge, Massachusetts. In 1999 she was elected a Chancellor of the Academy of American Poets.

April 23

from CXV (in *The Cantos*)

The scientists are in terror
        and the European mind stops
Wyndham Lewis chose blindness
        rather than have his mind stop.
Night under wind mid garofani,
        the petals are almost still
Mozart, Linnaeus, Sulmona,
When one's friends hate each other
        how can there be peace in the world?
Their asperities diverted me in my green time.
A blown husk that is finished
        but the light sings eternal
a pale flare over marshes
        where the salt hay whispers to tide's change
Time, space,
        neither life nor death is the answer.
And of man seeking good,
        doing evil.
In meiner Heimat
        where the dead walked
          and the living were made of cardboard.

EZRA POUND
(1885–1972)

Ezra Pound was born in Hailey, Idaho. Considered the founder of Imagism and a major proponent of modernist American poetry, Pound spent much of his adult life abroad. He was a tireless promoter and supporter of his contemporaries. T. S. Eliot, in particular, benefited from Pound's advice when he allowed him a free hand in the editing of "The Waste Land." Pound served as a secretary to William Butler Yeats and was a champion of the work of James Joyce (once even buying the impoverished writer a new pair of shoes). Pound began his master work, *The Cantos,* in about 1915 and continued to work on the "endless poem" (as he called it) for the rest of his life, revising and adding sections for more than fifty years. "Canto CXV" was contained in the final New Directions volume *Drafts & Fragments of Cantos CX–CXVII,* published in 1969. Pound was jailed at an internment camp in Pisa, Italy, in 1945 as a traitor to his country after giving radio broadcasts in support of Mussolini, and he was eventually sentenced to confinement in Saint Elizabeth's Federal Hospital for the Insane in Washington, D.C.. Many poets worked for his release and, after a number of years, he was discharged, returning to Italy where he lived out the rest of years.

Loveliest of Trees

Loveliest of trees, the cherry now
Is hung with bloom along the bough,
And stands about the woodland ride
Wearing white for Eastertide.

Now, of my threescore years and ten,
Twenty will not come again,
And take from seventy springs a score,
It only leaves me fifty more.

And since to look at things in bloom
Fifty springs are little room,
About the woodlands I will go
To see the cherry hung with snow.

A. E. HOUSMAN
(1859–1936)

Alfred Edward Housman was born in Frockbury, Worcestershire, England, and grew up in nearby Bromsgrove. After the death of his friend and companion Adalbert Jackson from typhoid fever, Housman lived as a recluse, shunning honors and avoiding most of the trappings of fame, though he continued to work as a well-regarded classicist scholar and lecturer. He published only two volumes of poetry in his lifetime, though his brother published a third volume of his work after Housman's death. "Loveliest of Trees" is from Housman's first and best-known book, *A Shropshire Lad,* printed at the author's own expense in 1896. Though slow to catch on, *A Shropshire Lad* contained several poems on military subjects and became a bestseller after the Boer War broke out in 1899, and it was made popular again during World War I.

April 25

Song of the Galley-Slaves

We pulled for you when the wind was against us and the sails
    were low.
        Will you never let us go?
We ate bread and onions when you took towns, or ran aboard
    quickly when you were beaten back by the foe.
The Captains walked up and down the deck in fair weather
    singing songs, but we were below.
We fainted with our chins on the oars and you did not see that
    we were idle, for we still swung to and fro.
        Will you never let us go?
The salt made the oar-handles like shark-skin; our knees were
    cut to the bone with salt-cracks; our hair was stuck to
    our foreheads; and our lips were cut to the gums, and you
    whipped us because we could not row.
        Will you never let us go?
But, in a little time, we shall run out of the port-holes as the
    water runs along the oar-blade, and though you tell the
    others to row after us you will never catch us till you catch
    the oar-thresh and tie up the winds in the belly of the
    sail. Aho!
        Will you never let us go?

RUDYARD KIPLING
(1865–1936)

Rudyard Kipling was born in Bombay, India, to British parents. In 1871 he was sent to
live with a relative in England where he would receive his education. Best known for his
novels *The Jungle Book, The Second Jungle Book,* and *Kim,* Kipling was a renowned
journalist who also wrote several books of poetry. He received the Nobel Prize for
Literature in 1907. Poet and critic Randall Jarrell once wrote of Kipling, "If I had to pick
one writer to invent a conversation between an animal, a god, and a machine, it would
be Kipling. To discover what, if they ever said, the dumb would say — this takes real
imagination; and this imagination of what isn't is the extension of a real knowledge of
what is, the knowledge of a consummate observer who took no notes."

Soloing

My mother tells me she dreamed
of John Coltrane, a young Trane
playing his music with such joy
and contained energy and rage
she could not hold back her tears.
She sits awake now, her hands
crossed in her lap as the tears start
in her blind eyes. The TV set
behind her is gray, expressionless.
It is late, the neighbors quiet,
even the city — Los Angeles — quiet.
I have driven for hours down 99,
over the Grapevine into heaven
to be here. I place my left hand
on her shoulder, and she smiles.
What a world, a mother and son
finding solace in California
just where we were told it would
be, among the palm trees and all-
night supermarkets pushing orange
backlighted oranges at two A.M.
"He was alone," she says, and does
not say, just as I am, "soloing."
What a world, a great man half
her age comes to my mother
in sleep to give her the gift
of song, which — shaking the tears
away — she passes on to me, for now
I can hear the music of the world
in the silence and that word:
soloing. What a world — when I
arrived the great bowl of mountains

was hidden in a cloud of exhaust,
the sea spread out like a carpet
of oil, the roses I had brought
from Fresno browned on the seat
beside me, and I could have
turned back and lost the music.

Philip Levine
(1928–)

Philip Levine was born in Detroit, Michigan. Well known for his portrayals of working-class Americans, Levine has won most of this country's highest literary honors, including the Pulitzer Prize. He has served as the chair of the Literature Panel of the National Endowment for the arts, and has taught at New York University and California State University, Fresno. Levine was elected a Chancellor of The Academy of American Poets in 2000.

Bonie Doon

Ye flowery banks o' bonie Doon,
　　How can ye blume sae fair?
How can ye chant, ye little birds,
　　And I sae fu' o' care?

Thou'll break my heart, thou bonie bird,
　　That sings upon the bough;
Thou minds me o' the happy days,
　　When my fause luve was true.

Thou'll break my heart, thou bonie bird,
　　That sings beside thy mate;
For sae I sat, and sae I sang,
　　And wist na o' my fate.

Aft hae I roved by bonie Doon
　　To see the wood-bine twine,
And ilka bird sang o' its luve,
　　And sae did I o' mine.

Wi' lightsome heart I pu'd a rose
　　Frae aff its thorny tree;
And my fause luver staw my rose
　　But left the thorn wi' me.

　　　　　　　Robert Burns
　　　　　　　(1759–1796)

Robert Burns was born the son of a tenant farmer and wrote his first poem at the age of fifteen, after falling in love with a local girl. After leaving the farm behind him, Burns became a tax inspector, father to fourteen children, a renowned Scots-dialect poet, and eventually a national emblem for individual mobility and Scottish independence. So great was his status in Scotland that after his death people developed the habit of telling one another stories about their experiences with the man known for his generous and patriotic character and adventures with drink and women. This grew into a "calendar custom" called the Burns Supper in which his fans repeat these legendary stories, recite his poems, and celebrate at an annual gathering in his honor on January 25, Burns's birthday. The Doon is a river in Ayrshire near Alloway, where he was born.

April 28

Moesta et Errabunda

Tell me, Perdita, does not your heart sometimes
From this black ocean of the shameless town
Will to fly far, into another sea
Whose sparkling blue is of a virgin's gown?
Tell me, Perdita, does not your heart sometimes?

O sea, O great sea, after our labouring
Rest us! what spirit gifted you, who high
Howl to the growling organ of the winds,
The holy function of a lullaby,
O sea, O great sea, after our labouring?

Carry me, train! and ferry me, packet-boat,
Far far from here whose mud is of our tears!
Is it not true, your sad heart, Perdita,
Murmurs at times: From evil, guilt and fears,
Carry me, train, and ferry me, packet-boat?

How far you are O heaven of delicate scent
Where love and pleasure gaze without a frown,
And what one loves is worthy to be loved,
And in its pure desire the heart goes down!
How far you are O heaven of delicate scent!

But the grass-greenest heaven of childish loves,
The races, songs, the kisses and the flowers,
The violins that called behind the hills,
The crocks of cider in the evening bowers —
But the grass-greenest heaven of childish loves,

The simple heaven full of stolen joys,
Is it so farther than the China seas
And not to be recalled with bitter cries
Or woken at a treble's silver voice,
The simple heaven full of stolen joys?

CHARLES BAUDELAIRE
(1821–1867)
translated by Hilary Corke

Charles Baudelaire was born in Paris. As a young man he contracted syphilis after being expelled from military school. His bohemian lifestyle concerned his mother and stepfather, who sent him on a voyage to India in 1841. This reformative measure was unsuccessful, and Baudelaire jumped shipped and returned to Paris, where his inheritance allowed him to write and lay-about with some of the finest artists of his generation. With the publication of *Les Fleurs du Mal* in 1857, Baudelaire became the target of censors who found his treatment of lesbian sex and vampirism obscene. On the other hand, he drew praise from figures such as Gustave Flaubert and Victor Hugo. Hugo was particularly impressed and wrote to Baudelaire, remarking, "You have created a new shudder." Baudelaire's influence, especially his development of the prose poem, has been widely felt, and he is recognized as an important precursor for writers such as Stephane Mallarmé, Paul Verlaine, and Arthur Rimbaud. Suffering from self-induced poverty and the effects of strokes and syphilis, Baudelaire eventually became weak, nervous, and aphasic, reduced to speaking only in monosyllables. He died at the age of forty-six.

Incident

for Eric Walrond

Once riding in old Baltimore,
    Heart-filled, head-filled with glee,
I saw a Baltimorean
    Keep looking straight at me.

Now I was eight and very small,
    And he was no whit bigger,
And so I smiled, but he poked out
    His tongue, and called me, "Nigger."

I saw the whole of Baltimore
    From May until December;
Of all the things that happened there
    That's all that I remember.

COUNTEE CULLEN
(1903–1946)

Born Countee LeRoy Porter, Cullen took the surname of Reverend Frederic A. Cullen, the Harlem pastor who adopted him after his grandmother died. Cullen began writing poetry at the age of fourteen, and by the time he attended New York University and Harvard his work had been published in W. E. B. Dubois's *The Crisis, Harper's, Poetry,* and *Century Magazine.* His first collection *Color,* as the title suggests, dealt with racial issues and drew substantial attention, but black readers responded negatively to *Copper Sun,* his second volume, charging that he had stepped back from the platform he had built with his earlier work. Cullen was also a successful novelist and translator. Eric Walrond, named in the dedication, was another writer of the Harlem Renaissance and a friend and contemporary of Cullen.

#341

After great pain, a formal feeling comes —
The Nerves sit ceremonious, like Tombs —
The stiff Heart questions was it He, that bore,
And Yesterday, or Centuries before?

The Feet, mechanical, go round —
Of Ground, or Air, or Ought —
A Wooden way
Regardless grown,
A Quartz contentment, like a stone —

This is the Hour of Lead —
Remembered, if outlived,
As Freezing persons, recollect the Snow —
First — Chill — then Stupor — then the letting go —

EMILY DICKINSON
(1830–1886)

Poet and critic Louise Bogan called Dickinson a "mystical poet" who could "describe with clinical precision the actual emotional event, the supreme moment of anguish, and even her own death itself. And she finds symbols which fit the event — terrible symbols." This poem has been dated to 1862.

May I

307

You took away my seas and running jumps and sky
And propped my foot against the violent earth.
Where could this brilliant calculation get you?
You couldn't take away my muttering lips.

May 1935

OSIP MANDELSTAM
(1891–1938)
translated by James Greene

Osip Mandelstam was born in Warsaw, Poland, and grew up in St. Petersburg, Russia. Though he initially supported the Russian Revolution, Mandelstam came to strongly oppose the Bolshevik regime and was forced to spend his later years in work camps and prisons. After living in abject poverty and under persecution for many years, he died in the Gulag Archipelago a few days after Christmas in 1938. "307" is a late poem in Mandelstam's oeuvre and its survival, along with the almost four hundred other poems by the poet, is somewhat miraculous. Mandelstam and his wife would often either hide his work in shoes or pots and pans or commit poems to memory to prevent them from being lost.

May 2

Someday I'd like to go
to Atlantic City with you
not to gamble (just being
there with you is enough
of a gamble) but to ride
the high white breakers
have a Manhattan and listen
to a baritone saxophone
play a tune called "Salsa
Eyes" with you beside me
on a banquette but why
stop there let's go to
Paris in November when
it's raining and we read
the *Tribune* at La Rotonde
our hotel room has a big
bathtub I knew you'd like
that and we can be a couple
of unknown Americans what
are we waiting for let's go

DAVID LEHMAN
(1948–)

Poet and critic David Lehman was born in New York City and educated at
Columbia University and Cambridge University. Lehman is the series editor of the
popular *Best American Poetry Series* and he also co-directs the KGB Bar poetry
reading series with Star Black. He is on the core faculty of the writing programs at
New School University and Bennington College. Inspired by Frank O'Hara's "I do
this I do that" poems and Robert Bly's *Morning Poems*, Lehman began writing a
poem a day as an experiment in 1996. Like "May 2," each poem takes as its title the
date of its composition.

May 3

Saint Francis and the Sow

The bud
stands for all things,
even for those things that don't flower,
for everything flowers, from within, of self-blessing;
though sometimes it is necessary
to reteach a thing its loveliness,
to put a hand on its brow
of the flower
and retell it in words and in touch
it is lovely
until it flowers again from within, of self-blessing;
as Saint Francis
put his hand on the creased forehead
of the sow, and told her in words and in touch
blessings of earth on the sow, and the sow
began remembering all down her thick length,
from the earthen snout all the way
through the fodder and slops to the spiritual curl of the tail,
from the hard spininess spiked out from the spine
down through the great broken heart
to the blue milken dreaminess spurting and shuddering
from the fourteen teats into the fourteen mouths sucking and
        blowing beneath them:
the long, perfect loveliness of sow.

GALWAY KINNELL
(1927–)

Galway Kinnell was born in Providence, Rhode Island. He received a B.A. from Princeton University and an M.A. from the University of Rochester. Kinnell has served in the United States Navy, been a Fulbright Fellow in Paris, and worked on the Congress on Racial Equality. He was awarded the Pulitzer Prize in 1983, the National Book Award for Poetry in 1984, and the National Book Critics Circle Award in 1986. He was Vermont State Poet from 1989 until 1993. He has been teaching at New York University since 1985 and is currently the Erich Maria Remarche Professor of Creative Writing in the M.F.A. program there.

May 4

Village Mystery

The woman in the pointed hood
And cloak blue-gray like a pigeon's wing,
Whose orchard climbs to the balsam-wood,
Has done a cruel thing.

To her back door-step came a ghost,
A girl who had been ten years dead,
She stood by the granite hitching-post
And begged for a piece of bread.

Now why should I, who walk alone,
Who am ironical and proud,
Turn, when a woman casts a stone
At a beggar in a shroud?

I saw the dead girl cringe and whine,
And cower in the weeping air —
But, oh, she was no kin of mine,
And so I did not care!

ELINOR WYLIE
(1885–1928)

Beautiful, talented, and notorious for her amorous affairs, Wylie died of a stroke at the age of forty-three. Seen as "hatchet minded" and "cadaverous" by Virginia Woolf, she was described as a "master of the divine language" and "the Edith Wharton of our poets" by Edmund Wilson. Such ambivalence has been characteristic in assessments of her work since her death, as well as of the attention she received during her lifetime. Wylie served as the Poetry Editor at *Vanity Fair, New Republic,* and *Literary Guild.* She made the gossip columns for running off to England with Horace Wylie in 1910, leaving her first husband, her son, and Wylie's wife behind. She later divorced Wylie to marry (in 1923) William Rose Benét, who collected the final editions of her work.

May 5

Proud Error

Once upon a time there was an error
So ridiculous so minute
No one could have paid attention to it

It couldn't stand
To see or hear itself

It made up all sorts of nonsense
Just to prove
That it really didn't exist

It imagined a space
To fit all its proofs in
And time to guard its proofs
And the world to witness them

All that it imagined
Was not so ridiculous
Or so minute
But was of course in error

Was anything else possible

VASKO POPA
(1922–1991)
translated by Charles Simic

Yugoslav poet Vasko Popa fought in World War II and afterward spent time in a Nazi concentration camp. Written in Serbian, his eight collections of poetry have been widely translated and concern the themes of Serbian culture, traditions, folklore, and history. A major figure in the postwar literature of Eastern Europe, Popa has been memorialized by a prize awarded in his name for the best book of Serbian poetry published in a given year. Popa died of cancer in 1991. Octavio Paz remarked after Popa's death that "poets have the gift to speak for others, . . . [but] Vasko Popa had the very rare quality to hear the others."

Moon, Flowers, Man

I raise my cup and invite
The moon to come down from the
Sky. I hope she will accept
Me. I raise my cup and ask
The branches, heavy with flowers,
To drink with me. I wish them
Long life and promise never
To pick them. In company
With the moon and the flowers,
I get drunk, and none of us
Ever worries about good
Or bad. How many people
Can comprehend our joy? I
Have wine and moon and flowers.
Who else do I want for drinking companions?

Su Tung P'o
(1037–1101)
translated by Kenneth Rexroth

Born Su Shih, Su Tung P'o came from a family of intellectuals. His work includes poetry, essays, calligraphy, and painting. He compared poetry to painting, pointing out that both should run spontaneously, like streaming water. An outspoken critic of the emperor Wang An-Shih, he was often demoted and sent to posts in remote provinces. In later years, he grew to cherish his life as a farmer in the isolated setting of Huang-Chou and he changed his name to that of his farm, Tung P'o.

Ode on a Grecian Urn

1

Thou still unravished bride of quietness,
　Thou foster child of silence and slow time,
Sylvan historian, who canst thus express
　A flowery tale more sweetly than our rhyme:
What leaf-fringed legend haunts about thy shape
　Of deities or mortals, or of both,
　　In Tempe or the dales of Arcady?
　What men or gods are these? What maidens loath?
What mad pursuit? What struggle to escape?
　　What pipes and timbrels? What wild ecstasy?

2

Heard melodies are sweet, but those unheard
　Are sweeter; therefore, ye soft pipes, play on;
Not to the sensual ear, but, more endeared,
　Pipe to the spirit ditties of no tone:
Fair youth, beneath the trees, thou canst not leave
　Thy song, nor ever can those trees be bare;
　　Bold Lover, never, never canst thou kiss,
Though winning near the goal — yet, do not grieve;
　　She cannot fade, though thou hast not thy bliss,
Forever wilt thou love, and she be fair!

3

Ah, happy, happy boughs! that cannot shed
　Your leaves, nor ever bid the Spring adieu;
And, happy melodist, unweariéd,
　Forever piping songs forever new;
More happy love! more happy, happy love!
　Forever warm and still to be enjoyed,
　　Forever panting, and forever young;
All breathing human passion far above,
　That leaves a heart high-sorrowful and cloyed,
　　A burning forehead, and a parching tongue.

4

Who are these coming to the sacrifice?
　To what green altar, O mysterious priest,
Lead'st thou that heifer lowing at the skies,
　And all her silken flanks with garlands dressed?
What little town by river or sea shore,
　Or mountain-built with peaceful citadel,
　　Is emptied of this folk, this pious morn?
And, little town, thy streets forevermore
　Will silent be; and not a soul to tell
　　Why thou art desolate, can e'er return.

5

O Attic shape! Fair attitude! with brede
　Of marble men and maidens overwrought,
With forest branches and the trodden weed;
　Thou, silent form, dost tease us out of thought
As doth eternity: Cold Pastoral!
　When old age shall this generation waste,
　　Thou shalt remain, in midst of other woe
Than ours, a friend to man, to whom thou say'st,
"Beauty is truth, truth beauty," — that is all
　Ye know on earth, and all ye need to know.

JOHN KEATS
(1795–1821)

As a boy, John Keats did not show outward signs of becoming a great poet, or even a poet at all. He preferred to fight and roughhouse with his friends and brothers, and he cared little for reading. By the age of fourteen, however, Keats had discovered verse and become a voracious reader. When the death of his mother left him an orphan at the age of fifteen, he found himself reluctantly apprenticed to an apothecary. He went on to train as a surgeon, but his mind was not in it; he wrote poems instead of taking notes during anatomy lectures, eventually abandoning medicine altogether in favor of his writing. "Ode on a Grecian Urn" was written in 1819, the same year Keats wrote "Ode to a Nightingale," "The Eve of St. Agnes," and "To Autumn," which are among his best-known poems. In fact, Keats wrote most of his major poems in that year, between January and September. A few months later, he began to suffer the first symptoms of tuberculosis, which he contracted while caring for a younger brother, who died of the disease in the previous year. His illness worsened quickly and interfered with his poetry. In a letter to his love Fanny Brawne written a year before his death, he wrote, "Take care of yourself my dear that we may both be well in the Summer. I do not at all fatigue myself with writing, having merely to put a line or two here and there, a Task which would worry a stout state of the body and mind, but which just suits me as I can do no more." He died at the age of twenty-five.

Styrofoam Cup

thou still unravished   thou
thou,   thou bride

thou unstill,
thou unravished   unbride

unthou   unbride

BRENDA HILLMAN
(1951–)

Brenda Hillman was born in Tucson, Arizona. She received her B.A. from Pomona College and M.F.A. from the University of Iowa. Hillman teaches at St. Mary's College in Moraga, California. She lives in the San Francisco Bay Area with her husband, former U.S. Poet Laureate Robert Hass. Barbara Fischer in the *Boston Review* called "Styrofoam Cup" a witty "anti-ode to an anti-urn."

May 9

The Maldive Shark

About the Shark, phlegmatical one,
Pale sot of the Maldive sea,
The sleek little pilot-fish, azure and slim,
How alert in attendance be.
From his saw-pit of mouth, from his charnel of maw
They have nothing of harm to dread,
But liquidly glide on his ghastly flank
Or before his Gorgonian head;
Or lurk in the port of serrated teeth
In white triple tiers of glittering gates,
And there find a haven when peril's abroad,
An asylum in jaws of the Fates!
They are friends; and friendly they guide him to prey,
Yet never partake of the treat —
Eyes and brains to the dotard lethargic and dull,
Pale ravener of horrible meat.

HERMAN MELVILLE
(1819–1891)

Born Herman Melvill in New York City in 1819, the author's mother added an *e* to his name in the 1830s, after his father's death. At the age of fifteen, Melville quit school in order to help support his struggling family. In 1839 he took his first voyage as a cabin boy on a trip to Liverpool, at which time he first recognized his love for the sea. In 1841 Melville jumped ship from a whaling vessel and was captured by cannibalistic natives in the Marquesas Islands. He managed to escape to Tahiti where he worked in the fields as a laborer. He eventually made his way to Honolulu, where he again enlisted as a seaman. Returning to New York after these high-sea adventures, he began writing romantic novels in 1843. After *Moby Dick* and his other works failed to bring him commercial or literary success, Melville turned to poetry in the 1870s, but his verse was also largely ignored. Today revered as a major figure in American Literature, Melville died poor and in relative obscurity in 1891. "The Maldive Shark" appeared in the volume *John Marr and Other Sailors with Some Sea-Pieces* (1888).

May 10

XLII

I WALKED IN A DESERT.
AND I CRIED,
"AH, GOD, TAKE ME FROM THIS PLACE!"
A VOICE SAID, "IT IS NO DESERT."
I CRIED, "WELL, BUT —
THE SAND, THE HEAT, THE VACANT HORIZON."
A VOICE SAID, "IT IS NO DESERT."

STEPHEN CRANE
(1871–1900)

Stephen Crane was born in Newark, New Jersey, the youngest of fourteen children. His father was a Methodist minister and author of religious articles, and his mother also wrote on religious themes. In 1891 Crane abandoned his courses at Syracuse University when he decided "humanity was more interesting study" and went to work for the *New York Tribune* as a reporter. After being rejected by several publishers, Crane self-published his novella *Maggie: A Girl of the Streets* under a pseudonym in 1893. "XLII" is from *The Black Riders and Other Lines,* published in 1895. Comparing this book with his best-selling novel, Crane said, "Personally, I like my little book of poems, *The Black Riders,* better than I do *The Red Badge of Courage.* The reason is, I suppose, that the former is the more ambitious effort. In it I aim to give my ideas of life as a whole, so far as I know it, and the latter is a mere episode, or rather an amplification." Crane died in Germany at the age of twenty-eight, while traveling through Europe in search of an effective cure for his tuberculosis.

After This Deluge

After this deluge
I would like to see the dove,
and nothing but the dove,
saved once more.

For I'd perish in this sea!
if she didn't fly away,
if she didn't bring back,
in the last hour,
the leaf.

INGEBORG BACHMANN
(1926–1973)
translated by Mark Anderson

Ingeborg Bachmann was born in Klagenfurt, Austria, and was a composer, fiction writer, translator, and playwright in addition to being one of the most well-known German-language poets of the postwar period. She grew up under the National Socialist regime and remembered the day Nazi troops marched through Klagenfurt as the final day of her childhood. Bachmann spent most of her adult life in Rome, Italy, where she died at the age of forty-seven from burns she suffered after her apartment caught on fire. There is a museum dedicated to her life and work in Klagenfurt, and in 1977 the Ingeborg Bachmann Literary Prize for young writers was established in her honor. Her papers, which include more than six thousand pages of handwritten documents and typescript pages, are held in the Austrian National Library in Vienna.

Nulla Fides

For God's sake mark that fly:
See what a poor, weak, little thing it is.
When thou hast marked, and scorned it, know that this,
This little, poor, weak fly
Has killed a pope; can make an emp'ror die.

Behold yon spark of fire:
How little hot! how near to nothing 'tis!
When thou hast done despising, know that this,
This contemned spark of fire,
Hast burnt whole towns; can burn a world entire.

That crawling worm there see:
Ponder how ugly, filthy, vile it is.
When thou hast seen and loathed it, know that this,
This base worm thou dost see,
Has quite devoured thy parents; shall eat thee.

Honor, the world, and man,
What trifles are they; since most true it is
That this poor fly, this little spark, this
So much abhorred worm, can
Honor destroy; burn worlds; devour up man.

PATRICK CAREY
(1623–1657)

Born Patrick Cary, Patrick Carey was the tenth of eleven children whose father was a Royalist courtier named Henry Cary, a man who served both as First Viscount of Falkland and Lord Deputy of Ireland. Several members of the Cary family were writers, including Patrick's parents, some of his siblings, and several descendents. Carey's Catholic mother arranged for him and his younger brother to "escape" Ireland, and he was eventually sent to Rome to live under the protection of a group of English Benedictine monks. During these years, Carey is known to have dined with visiting poets John Milton and Richard Crashaw at English College, and he himself became a Benedictine novice in 1650. He lasted only three and a half months in monastic life, however, and eventually reconverted to Protestantism in hopes of inheriting his family's former Falkland estates. Carey's extant writing consists of a single volume of poems never published during his lifetime, though it is thought to have been circulated among his friends. More than one hundred years after the poet's death, nine of Carey's poems were printed by Reverend Pierrepont Cromp as *Poems from a Manuscript Written in the Time of Oliver Cromwell.*

There Is No Forgetfulness
(*Sonata*)

If you ask where I have been
I have to say, "It so happens . . ."
I have to talk about the earth turned dark with stones,
and the river which ruins itself by keeping alive;
I only know about objects that birds lose,
the sea far behind us, or my sister crying.
Why so many different places, why does one day
merge with another day? Why does a black night
gather in the mouth? Why all these people dead?

If you ask where I come from I have to start talking with
        broken objects,
with kitchenware that has too much bitterness,
with animals quite often rotten,
and with my heavy soul.

What have met and crossed are not memories,
nor the yellow pigeon that sleeps in forgetfulness;
but they are faces with tears,
fingers at the throat,
anything that drops out of the leaves:
the shadowiness of a day already passed by,
of a day fed with our own mournful blood.

Look and see violets, swallows,
all those things we love so much and can see
on the tender greeting-cards with long tails
where time and sweetness are sauntering.

But let's not go deeper than those teeth,
nor bite into the rinds growing over the silence,
because I don't know what to say:
there are so many people dead
and so many sea-walls that the red sun used to split,
and so many heads that the boats hit,
and so many hands that have closed around kisses,
and so many things I would like to forget.

PABLO NERUDA
(1904–1973)
translated by Robert Bly

Chilean poet Neftalí Ricardo Reyes Basoalto took the name Pablo Neruda to avoid upsetting his disapproving family when he published his first book at the age of nineteen in 1923. His second book, *Twenty Love Poems and a Song of Despair*, launched the twenty-year-old poet to instant fame. The Chilean government selected Neruda for a series of diplomatic posts, including consulates in Burma, Buenos Aires, and Madrid. When the Spanish Civil War broke out, Neruda spoke out against the execution of poet and friend Federico Garcia Lorca and revealed himself as a strong supporter of the loyalists, a move which caused him to be recalled from his post. He was later named consul to Mexico and served in the Chilean senate, but after his government declared Communism illegal, Neruda — who had joined the party in 1943 — was expelled and went into exile until the order to arrest communist artists was lifted. Neruda received the International Peace Prize in 1950, the Lenin and Stalin Peace Prizes in 1953, and the Nobel Prize in literature in 1971. He died of leukemia in Santiago, Chile, in 1973.

The Day Dreamers

All day all over the city every person
Wanders a different city, sealed intact
And haunted as the abandoned subway stations
Under the city. Where is my alley doorway?

Stone gable, brick escarpment, cliffs of crystal.
Where is my terraced street above the harbor,
Café and hidden workshop, house of love?
Webbed vault, tiled blackness. Where is my park, the path

Through conifers, my iron bench, a shiver
Of ivy and margin birch above the traffic?
A voice. *There is a mountain and a wood
between us* — one wrote, lovesick — *Where the late*

Hunter and the bird have seen us. Aimless at dusk,
Heart muttering like any derelict,
Or working all morning, violent with will,
Where is my garland of lights? My silver rail?

ROBERT PINSKY
(1940–)

Robert Pinsky was born in Long Branch, New Jersey. After being named Poet Laureate
of the United States in 1997, Pinsky founded the Favorite Poem Project of the Library
of Congress, which collects recordings and videos of Americans reading their best-
loved poems. Pinsky served a total of three terms as Poet Laureate. He is the poetry
editor of *Slate* and teaches in the graduate writing program at Boston University.

Humming-Bird

I can imagine, in some otherworld
Primeval-dumb, far back
In that most awful stillness, that only gasped and hummed,
Humming-birds raced down the avenues.

Before anything had a soul,
While life was a heave of Matter, half inanimate,
This little bit chipped off in brilliance
And went whizzing through the slow, vast, succulent stems.

I believe there were no flowers, then,
In the world where the humming-bird flashed ahead of creation.
I believe he pierced the slow vegetable veins with his long beak.

Probably he was big
As mosses, and little lizards, they say were once big.
Probably he was a jabbing, terrifying monster.
We look at him through the wrong end of the long telescope of
    Time,
Luckily for us.

D. H. LAWRENCE
(1885–1930)

"Humming-Bird" was published in a book of unrhymed poems titled *Birds, Beasts and Flowers* in 1923. Lawrence began composing poems as a teenager and described the occasion in an unpublished preface to his *Collected Poems:* "[On a] slightly self-conscious Sunday afternoon, when I was nineteen, . . . I 'composed' my first two 'poems.' One was 'Guelder-roses,' and one was to 'Campions,' and most young ladies would have done better."

Birth Stone

The older women wise and tell Anna
first time baby mother,
"hold a stone upon your head and follow
a straight line go home."

For like how Anna was working in the
field, grassweeder
right up till the appointed hour
that the baby was to come.

Right up till the appointed hour
when her clear heraldic water
broke free and washed her down.

Dry birth for you young mother;
the distance between the field and home
come in like the Gobi desert now.
But your first baby must born abed.

Put the woman stone on your head
and walk through no man's land
go home. When you walk, the stone
and not you yet, will bear down.

LORNA GOODISON
(1947–)

Born in Kingston, Jamaica, Lorna Goodison has been a visiting professor of English at the University of Michigan, Ann Arbor, and a visiting fellow at the Bunting Institute of Radcliffe College and the University of Toronto. Goodison is also a short-story writer and an accomplished artist whose book covers feature her paintings. She has been awarded the Commonwealth Poetry Prize, Americas Region, among other honors. She is currently an Associate Professor at the University of Michigan, where she teaches Afro-Caribbean poetry. "Birth Stone" is from Goodison's sixth book of poetry, *To Us, All Flowers Are Roses*.

May 17

from "Song of Myself" (in *Leaves of Grass*)
    8

The little one sleeps in its cradle,
I lift the gauze and look along time, and silently brush away flies
    with my hand.
The youngster and the red-faced girl turn aside up the bushy hill,
I peeringly view them from the top.

The suicide sprawls on the bloody floor of the bedroom,
I witness the corpse with its dabbled hair, I note where the pistol
    has fallen.

The blab of the pave, tires of carts, sluff of boot-soles, talk of the
    promenaders,
The heavy omnibus, the driver with his interrogating thumb, the
    clank of the shod horses on the granite floor,
The snow-sleighs, clinking, shouted jokes, pelts of snowballs,
The hurrahs for popular favorites, the fury of rous'd mobs,
The flap of the curtain'd litter, a sick man inside borne to the
    hospital,
The meeting of enemies, the sudden oath, the blows and fall,
The excited crowd, the policeman with his star quickly working his
    passage to the centre of the crowd,
The impassive stones that receive and return so many echoes,
What groans of over-fed or half-starv'd who fall sunstruck or in fits,
what exclamations of women taken suddenly who hurry home and
    give birth to babes,

What living and buried speech is always vibrating here, what howls
    restrain'd by decorum,
Arrests of criminals, slights, adulterous offers made, acceptances,
    rejections with convex lips,
I mind them or the show or resonance of them — I come and I depart.

WALT WHITMAN
(1819–1892)

Walt Whitman's work has exerted a profound influence on American poetry, map-
ping out an entirely new direction when it first began to be read in the 1850s. Writers
from D. H. Lawrence and Oscar Wilde to Allen Ginsberg and Federico García Lorca
paid homage to his unique genius. Randall Jarrell wrote of Whitman, "They might
have put on his tombstone WALT WHITMAN: HE HAD NERVE. He is the rashest, the
most inexplicable and unlikely — the most impossible, one wants to say — of poets.
He somehow is in a class by himself. . . . [O]ne Whitman is miracle enough, and
when he comes again it will be the end of the world."

Carmel Point

The extraordinary patience of things!
This beautiful place defaced with a crop of suburban houses —
How beautiful when we first beheld it,
Unbroken field of poppy and lupin walled with clean cliffs;
No intrusion but two or three horses pasturing,
Or a few milch cows rubbing their flanks on the outcrop rockheads —
Now the spoiler has come: does it care?
Not faintly. It has all time. It knows the people are a tide
That swells and in time will ebb, and all
Their works dissolve. Meanwhile the image of the pristine beauty
Lives in the very grain of the granite.
Safe as the endless ocean that climbs our cliff. — As for us:
We must uncenter our minds from ourselves;
We must unhumanize our views a little, and become confident
As the rock and ocean that we were made from.

ROBINSON JEFFERS
(1887–1962)

Robinson Jeffers was the son of a learned Presbyterian minister, and as a precocious fifteen-year-old he completed college in two years. After studying both philosophy and forestry in graduate school, Jeffers gave up both. He began an affair with former classmate Una Call, and the couple married (after Una divorced her first husband) and moved to Carmel-by-the-Sea, California, which was still a small village at the time. Jeffers was born in Pittsburgh, Philadelphia, but is considered a Californian poet because so much of his work evokes the rough landscape of his seaside home. Tor House, as it was called, is a museum today, as is Hawk Tower, the structure Jeffers built with his own hands and used as a writing studio. Though he appeared on the cover of *Time* magazine in 1932, his reclusive nature and controversial politics led to a decline in his reputation after the beginning of World War II, and his collection of anti-war poetry, *The Double-Ax*, carried with it a disclaimer from his publisher. Louise Bogan wrote in 1970 that "Jeffers' nightmare world, in which reality is squeezed and beaten into the shape of a brutal adolescent's dream, is, however, more relevant to our present situation than it was when it burst in upon us, twenty years or so ago. If Jeffers now pitches his tone so high that it becomes a shriek of hysteria, he is only screwing up to their utmost the tensions of our scene."

from *The Tempest*
Act V, Scene i

Ye elves of hills, brooks, standing lakes, and groves;
And ye, that on the sands with printless foot
Do chase the ebbing Neptune and do fly him
When he comes back; you demi-puppets, that
By moonshine do the green sour ringlets make
Whereof the ewe not bites; and you, whose pastime
Is to make midnight mushrooms; that rejoice
To hear the solemn curfew; by whose aid, —
Weak masters though ye be — I have bedimm'd
The noontide sun, call'd forth the mutinous winds,
And 'twixt the green fire and rifted Jove's stout oak
With his own bolt; the strong-bas'd promontory
Have I made shake; and by the spurs pluck'd up
The pine and cedar; graves at my command
Have wak'd their sleepers, op'd, and let them forth
By my so potent art. But this rough magic
I here abjure; and, when I have requir'd
Some heavenly music, — which even now I do, —
To work mine end upon their senses that
This airy charm is for, I'll break my staff,
Bury it certain fathoms in the earth,
And, deeper than did ever plummet sound,
I'll drown my book.

WILLIAM SHAKESPEARE
(1564–1616)

In *The Tempest* these lines are spoken by Prospero, the magician and former Duke of Milan who has been exiled to a remote island. Prospero's enchanted books and an "airy spirit" named Ariel allow him to stir up storms, conjure visions, toss the seas, and thereby control the island and its inhabitants. Some critics have proposed the character of Prospero as a stand-in for Shakespeare himself. Shakespeare also seems to have been partially inspired by accounts of the shipwreck of the *Sea Venture* in the Bermudas in 1609, after which several survivors lived on an island for nine months. This speech in particular is thought to echo that of the sorceress Medea in Ovid's *Metamophoses,* which begins in one translation, "Ye Ayres and windes: ye Elves of Hilles, of Brookes, of Woods alone, Of standing Lakes. . . ."

Riddle #47 (from the *Exeter Book*)

I heard of a wonder, of words moth-eaten;
that is a strange thing, I thought, weird
that a man's song be swallowed by a worm,
his binded sentences, his bedside stand-by
rustled in the night — and the robber-guest
not one whit the wiser for the words he had mumbled.

ANONYMOUS
translated by Michael Alexander

Like "Riddle #68" this poem is one of a series of ninety-five riddles preserved in the *Exeter Book*, one of the largest and most important collections of Anglo-Saxon writing. (See also: January 9 and July 8.) The riddles are thought to have been composed by various authors, though a single scribe copied them into the *Exeter Book*. They are written in the West Saxon literary dialect of Old English and some contain runic characters which provide clues to the riddles' answers. The opening line of this translation is similar to that of many of the other riddles, which often begin with the statement "I saw a marvelous creature" or "I saw a strange thing." As with the bookworm that becomes a moth in this poem, many of the riddles portray their subjects in various stages of transformation to heighten the mystery of the puzzle. The answer to "Riddle #47" is: *bookworm*.

Canary

for Michael S. Harper

Billie Holiday's burned voice
had as many shadows as lights,
a mournful candelabra against a sleek piano,
the gardenia her signature under that ruined face.

(Now you're cooking, drummer to bass,
magic spoon, magic needle.
Take all day if you have to
with your mirror and your bracelet of song.)

Fact is, the invention of women under siege
has been to sharpen love in the service of myth.

If you can't be free, be a mystery.

RITA DOVE
(1952–)

Rita Dove was born in Akron, Ohio. A recipient of the Pulitzer Prize, she served as
Poet Laureate of the United States from 1993 to 1995; she was the youngest poet to
be appointed to the post. Dove is currently the Commonwealth Professor of English
at the University of Virginia. Legendary jazz singer Billie Holiday, or "Lady Day,"
died in 1959 at the age of forty-four, after years of heroin addiction and alcoholism.

The Dancing

In all these rotten shops, in all this broken furniture
and wrinkled ties and baseball trophies and coffee pots
I have never seen a post-war Philco
with the automatic eye
nor heard Ravel's "Bolero" the way I did
in 1945 in that tiny living room
on Beechwood Boulevard, nor danced as I did
then, my knives all flashing, my hair all streaming,
my mother red with laughter, my father cupping
his left hand under his armpit, doing the dance
of old Ukraine, the sound of his skin half drum,
half fart, the world at last a meadow,
the three of us whirling and singing, the three of us
screaming and falling, as if we were dying,
as if we could never stop — in 1945 —
in Pittsburgh, beautiful filthy Pittsburgh, home
of the evil Mellons, 5,000 miles away
from the other dancing — in Poland and Germany —
oh God of mercy, oh wild God.

GERALD STERN
(1925–)

Gerald Stern was born in "beautiful, filthy" Pittsburgh, Pennsylvania. He received his B.A. from the University of Pittsburgh and graduate degrees from Columbia and the University of Paris. He served in the U.S. Army Air Corps from 1946 to 1947, and he was the principal of Lake Grove School in Lake Grove, New York, from 1951 until 1953. He has received numerous awards for his poetry, including the National Book Award. He taught for many years at the University of Iowa Writers' Workshop, until his retirement in 1995.

A Description of the Morning

Now hardly here and there a hackney-coach
Appearing, showed the ruddy morn's approach.
Now Betty from her master's bed had flown,
And softly stole to discompose her own;
The slip-shod 'prentice from his master's door
Had pared the dirt and sprinkled round the floor.
Now Moll had whirled her mop with dext'rous airs,
Prepared to scrub the entry and the stairs.
The youth with broomy stumps began to trace
The kennel-edge, where wheels had worn the place.
The small-coal man was heard with cadence deep,
Till drowned in shriller notes of chimney-sweep:
Duns at his lordship's gate began to meet;
And brickdust Moll had screamed through half the street.
The turnkey now his flock returning sees,
Duly let out a-nights to steal for fees:
The watchful bailiffs take their silent stands,
And schoolboys lag with satchels in their hands.

JONATHAN SWIFT
(1667–1745)

Best known for his novel *Gulliver's Travels* and his satirical treatise *A Modest Proposal,*
Jonathan Swift began his career as a writer of Pindaric odes. Swift was born in
Dublin, Ireland, educated at Trinity College, and took Anglican orders in the
Church of Ireland in 1695. Though he sought an English bishopric, he never
attained one, but was instead appointed Dean of St. Patrick's Cathedral in Dublin
in 1713. Swift published *Gulliver's Travels* under a pseudonym and maintained the
fiction that he was not the book's author, though he took pains to make sure his
identity was known in literary circles. "Description of the Morning" was published
in Richard Steele's magazine, *The Tatler,* in 1709 along with another poem depicting
urban scenes of London, "Description of a City Shower."

Passage over Water

We have gone out in boats upon the sea at night,
lost, and the vast waters close traps of fear about us.
The boats are driven apart, and we are alone at last
under the incalculable sky, listless, diseased with stars.

Let the oars be idle, my love, and forget at this time
our love like a knife between us
defining the boundaries that we can never cross
nor destroy as we drift into the heart of our dream,
cutting the silence, slyly, the bitter rain in our mouths
and the dark wound closed in behind us.

Forget depth-bombs, death and promises we made,
gardens laid waste, and, over the wastelands westward,
the rooms where we had come together bombed.

But even as we leave, your love turns back. I feel
your absence like the ringing of bells silenced. And salt
over your eyes and the scales of salt between us. Now,
you pass with ease into the destructive world.
There is a dry crash of cement. The light fails,
falls into the ruins of cities upon the distant shore
and within the indestructible night I am alone.

ROBERT DUNCAN
(1919–1988)

Born in Oakland, California, Robert Duncan is associated with the poets of the San Francisco Renaissance as well as the Black Mountain School. He founded and edited the magazine *Experimental Review* with Sanders Russell and published the work of Henry Miller, Anais Nin, Kenneth Patchen, Lawrence Durrell, and others. Duncan is credited with exploring the idea of the poem as a "compositional field" to which the poet may bring whatever material he likes. This concept is one of the many subjects of his most famous book, *The Opening of the Field.* In an essay titled "Equilibrations" Duncan wrote, "Working in words I am an escapist; as if I could step out of my clothes and move naked as the wind in a world of words. But I want every part of the actual world involved in my escape. I bring the laws that bound me into an aerial structure in which they are unbound as outlines of a prison unfolding."

Planting Song

I have made a footprint, a sacred one.
I have made a footprint, through it the blades push upward.
I have made a footprint, through it the blades radiate.
I have made a footprint, over it the blades float in the wind.
I have made a footprint, over it the ears lean toward one another.
I have made a footprint, over it I bend the stalk to pluck the ears.
I have made a footprint, over it the blossoms lie gray.
I have made a footprint, smoke arises from my house.
I have made a footprint, there is cheer in my house.
I have made a footprint, I live in the light of day.

Osage song
translated by Dr. Francis La Flesche

An important crop for the Osage people, corn played a significant role in their ceremonies. The speaker of this song is female, as women of the Osage were responsible for fields and crops. It was sung as part of a ritualistic ceremony for which a woman painted part of her hair red before sunrise and kept it that way until sunset. During the Planting Song a messenger would give each woman a planting pole and sack. The women would then use these objects as they acted out the stages of clearing and planting.

When You Leave

This sadness could only be a color
if we call it *momoiro,* Japanese

for *peach-color,* as in the first story
Mother told us: It is the color of the hero's skin

when the barren woman discovered him
inside a peach floating down the river.

And of the banner and gloves she sewed
when he left her to battle the horsemen, then found himself

torn, like fruit off a tree. Even when he met a monkey
dog and bird he could not release

the color he saw when he closed his eyes.
    In his boat
the lap of the waves against the hold

was too intimate as he leaned back to sleep.
    He wanted
to leave all thoughts of peach behind him —

the fruit that brought him to her
and she, the one who opened the color forever.

KIMIKO HAHN
(1955–)

Kimiko Hahn was born in Mt. Kisco, New York, and received her B.A. from the University of Iowa and M.A. from Columbia University, where she studied Japanese. She is an Associate Professor of English at Queens College, City University of New York.

Written in Prison

I envy e'en the fly its gleam of joy
In the green woods; from being but a boy
Among the vulgar and the lowly bred,
I envied e'en the hare her grassy bed.
Inured to strife and hardship from a child,
I traced with lonely step the desert wild,
Sighed o'er bird pleasures, but no nest destroyed,
With pleasure felt the singing they enjoyed,
Saw nature smile on all and shed no tears,
A slave through ages, though a child in years —
The mockery and scorn of those more old,
An Æsop in the world's extended fold.
The fly I envy settling in the sun
On the green leaf, and wish my goal was won.

JOHN CLARE
(1793–1864)

Mental illness and the memory of his first love and ideal woman Mary Joyce plagued Romantic poet John Clare. During his first breakdown in 1836, he was confined to High Beech Asylum in Essex, where he remained for several years. In 1841 he wandered off the grounds and headed for his home in Northamptonshire, walking for four days without food. He had hoped to find Mary upon his return, but found out that she had died three years earlier. His wife, Martha "Patty" Turner, found Clare's insanity and obsession with Mary Joyce too difficult to handle and Clare was again committed. As the title suggests, "Written in Prison" was composed during his subsequent stay in the Northampton Lunatic Asylum where he remained until his death from a paralytic seizure in 1864. In *Other Traditions,* John Ashbery cites Clare as one of his favorite poets and explains that "[a]nother side of Clare's modernity is a kind of nakedness of vision that we are accustomed to, at least in America, from the time of Walt Whitman and Emily Dickinson, down to Robert Lowell and Allen Ginsberg. Like these poets, Clare grabs hold of you—no he doesn't grab hold of you, he is already there, talking to you before you've arrived on the scene, telling you about himself, about the things that are closest and dearest to him, and it would no more occur to him to do otherwise than it would occur to Whitman to stop singing you his song of himself."

May 28

What Issa Heard

Two hundred years ago
Issa heard
the morning birds
singing sutras
to this suffering world.

I heard them too,
this morning,
which must mean

since we will always have
a suffering world
we must also always
have a song.

DAVID BUDBILL
(1940–)

David Budbill was born in Cleveland, Ohio. He attended Muskingum College and Columbia University and earned a Masters of Divinity from Union Theological Seminary. He lives in Wolcott, Vermont, and has also written novels, short stories, librettos, and children's fiction. He has been a commentator on National Public Radio's *All Things Considered.*

#528

Mine — by the Right of the White Election!
Mine — by the Royal Seal!
Mine — by the Sign in the Scarlet prison —
Bars — cannot conceal!

Mine — here — in Vision — and in Veto!
Mine — by the Grave's Repeal —
Titled — Confirmed —
Delirious Charter!
Mine — long as Ages steal!

EMILY DICKINSON
(1830–1886)

This poem has been dated to 1862, the same year Dickinson sought out the advice of the well-known editor Thomas Wentworth Higginson. She wrote in her first letter to him: "Are you too deeply occupied to say if my Verse is alive? The Mind is so near itself — it cannot see, distinctly — and I have none to ask — Should you think it breathed — and had you the leisure to tell me, I should feel quick gratitude . . . I enclose my name — asking you, if you please — Sir — to tell me what is true?" Although at the time Higginson felt Dickinson's work was not publishable, and wrote her so, he later recalled his experience of reading Dickinson's work for the first time, writing that "[t]he impression of a wholly new and original poetic genius was distinct on my mind at the first reading of these four poems as it is now, after thirty years of further knowledge."

May 30

from "Thorow"

The origin of property
that leads here Depth

Indian names lead here

Bars of a social system
Starting for Lost Pond

psychology of the lost
First precarious Eden

a scandal of materialism

My ancestors tore off
the first leaves

picked out the best stars
Cries accompany laughter

Winter of the great Snow
Life surrounded by snows

The usual loggers camp
the usual bark shelter

Fir floor and log benches

Pines seem giant phenomena

Child of the Adirondacks
taking notes like a spy

SUSAN HOWE
(1937–)

Susan Howe was born in Boston, Massachusetts. She is a Chancellor of the Academy of American Poets. Since 1989 she has been a professor of English at the State University of New York, Buffalo, where she was recently named a SUNY Distinguished Professor. In a piece titled "There Are Not Leaves Enough to Crown to Cover to Crown to Cover," Howe has written "Poetry brings similitude and representations to configurations waiting from forever to be spoken. . . . I write to break out into perfect primeval Consent. I wish I could tenderly lift from the dark side of history, voices that are so anonymous, slighted — inarticulate." She is also a prose writer, known especially for her study of Dickinson, *My Emily Dickinson*.

The City Limits

When you consider the radiance, that it does not withhold
itself but pours its abundance without selection into every
nook and cranny not overhung or hidden; when you consider

that birds' bones make no awful noise against the light but
lie low in the light as in a high testimony; when you consider
the radiance, that it will look into the guiltiest

swervings of the weaving heart and bear itself upon them,
not flinching into disguise or darkening; when you consider
the abundance of such resource as illuminates the glow-blue

bodies and gold-skeined wings of flies swarming the dumped
guts of a natural slaughter or the coil of shit and in no
way winces from its storms of generosity; when you consider

that air or vacuum, snow or shale, squid or wolf, rose or lichen,
each is accepted into as much light as it will take, then
the heart moves roomier, the man stands and looks about, the

leaf does not increase itself above the grass, and the dark
work of the deepest cells is of a tune with May bushes
and fear lit by the breadth of such calmly turns to praise.

A. R. AMMONS
(1926–2001)

Archie Randolph Ammons was born near Whiteville, North Carolina. Before
devoting himself entirely to poetry, he worked as the principal of an elementary
school and as the executive vice-president of his father's glassware factory in Atlantic
City, New Jersey. Archie, as he was known to his friends and fans, taught English and
Creative Writing as the Golden Smith Professor of Poetry at Cornell University from
1964 until his retirement in 1998. One of this country's major literary figures,
Ammons garnered many of American poetry's highest honors including the National
Book Award. He wrote more than thirty books before his death in February 2001.
Ammons once told an interviewer, "I never dreamed of being a Poet poet. I think I
always wanted to be an amateur poet." In a tribute to Ammons written in 1998,
David Lehman remembered that "despite all the recognitions, he remains what he has
always been: independent, unaligned, a bit ornery, and as removed as one can be from
any of poetry's supposed centers of power. He is an American original not only in his
poetry but in the way he has conducted his literary life."

June I

from "Jubilate Agno"
  (*iii*)

For the doubling of flowers is the improvement of the gardners talent.
For the flowers are great blessings.
For the Lord made a Nosegay in the meadow with his disciples and
    preached upon the lily.
For the angels of God took it out of his hand and carried it to the Height.
For a man cannot have publick spirit, who is void of private benevolence.
For there is no Height in which there are not flowers.
For flowers have great virtues for all the senses.
For the flower glorifies God and the root parries the adversary.
For the flowers have their angels even the words of God's Creation.
For the warp and woof of flowers are worked by perpetual moving spirits.
For flowers are good both for the living and the dead.
For there is a language of flowers.
For there is a sound reasoning upon all flowers.
For elegant phrases are nothing but flowers.
For flowers are peculiarly the poetry of Christ.
For flowers are medicinal.
For flowers are musical in ocular harmony.
For the right names of flowers are yet in heaven. God make gard'ners
    better nomenclators.
For the Poorman's nosegay is an introduction to a Prince.

CHRISTOPHER SMART
(1722–1771)

Christopher Smart lived in London, was incarcerated for insanity in 1757, and lived out much of the rest of his life in an asylum. One of his symptoms was said to be a compulsion to fall upon his knees and pray in the street. In Boswell's *Life of Johnson,* Samuel Johnson is recorded as saying, "I did not think he ought to be shut up. His infirmities were not noxious to society. He insisted on people praying with him; and I'd as lief pray with Kit Smart as anyone else." Smart's "Jubilate Agno" ("Rejoice in the Lamb") is an unfinished work in numerous sections, composed mostly while he was in the asylum. In 1770 he was arrested for debt and went to prison, where he died.

A Giant Has Swallowed the Earth

What will it do for him, to have internalized
The many slender stems of riverlets and funnels,
The blunt toes of the pine cone fallen, to have ingested
Lakes in gold slabs at dawn and the peaked branches
Of the fir under snow? He has taken into himself
The mist of the hazel nut, the white hairs of the moth,
And the mole's velvet snout. He remembers, by inner
Voice alone, fogs over frozen grey marshes, fine
Salt on the blunt of the cliff.

What will it mean to him to perceive things
First from within — the mushroom's fold, the martin's
Tongue, the spotted orange of the wallaby's ear,
To become the object himself before he comprehends it,
Putting into perfect concept without experience
The din of the green gully in spring mosses?

And when he stretches on his bed and closes his eyes,
What patterns will appear to him naturally — the schematic
Tracings of the Vanessa butterfly in migration, tacks
And red strings marking the path of each mouse
In the field, nucleic chromosomes aligning their cylinders
In purple before their separation? The wind must settle
All that it carries behind his face and rise again
In his vision like morning.

A giant has swallowed the earth,
And when he sleeps now, o when he sleeps,
How his eyelids murmur, how we envy his dream.

PATTIANN ROGERS
(1940–)

Pattiann Rogers was born in Joplin, Missouri. She earned her B.A. at the University of Missouri and her M.A. at the University of Houston. Though her degrees were taken in English and Creative Writing, Rogers minored in zoology. Known for her meditative, poetic treatments of natural and scientific subjects, she once remarked that her goal is "to express the kind of wonder and exhilaration that I felt was contained in much of what science has been discovering and also to reflect in my poetry how some of these discoveries affect our ways of seeing ourselves. I felt that somehow poetry was going to have to deal with the process of science and what science is saying."

The Month of June: 13½

As my daughter approaches graduation and
puberty at the same time, at her
own calm deliberate serious rate,
she begins to kick up her heels, jazz out her
hands, thrust out her hip-bones, chant
I'm great! I'm great! She feels 8th grade coming
open around her, a chrysalis cracking and
letting her out, it falls behind her and
joins the other husks on the ground,
7th grade, 6th grade, the
purple rind of 5th grade, the
hard jacket of 4th when she had so much pain,
3rd grade, 2nd, the dim cocoon of
1st grade back there somewhere on the path, and
kindergarten like a strip of thumb-suck blanket
taken from the actual blanket they wrapped her in at birth.
The whole school is coming off her shoulders like a
cloak unclasped, and she dances forth in her
jerky sexy child's joke dance of
self, self, her throat tight and a
hard new song coming out of it, while her
two dark eyes shine
above her body like a good mother and a
good father who look down and
love everything their baby does, the way she
lives their love.

SHARON OLDS
(1942–)

Sharon Olds was born in San Francisco, California, and educated at Stanford
University and Columbia University. She is the former Director of the Creative
Writing Program at New York University where she is currently a professor and
permanent faculty member and is the founding chairperson of the Writing
Program at Goldwater Hospital on Roosevelt Island. In 1998 Olds was appointed
New York State Poet.

Stanzas for Music

O Lachrymarum fons, tenero sacros
Ducentium ortus ex animo: quater
Felix! in imo qui scatentem
Pectore te, pia Nympha, sensit.

GRAY'S *Poemata*

1

There's not a joy the world can give like that it takes away,
When the glow of early thought declines in feeling's dull decay;
'Tis not on youth's smooth cheek the blush alone, which fades so fast,
But the tender bloom of heart is gone, ere youth itself be past.

2

Then the few whose spirits float above the wreck of happiness,
Are driven o'er the shoals of guilt or ocean of excess:
The magnet of their course is gone, or only points in vain
The shore to which their shiver'd sail shall never stretch again.

3

Then the mortal coldness of the soul like death itself comes down;
It cannot feel for others' woes, it dare not dream its own;
That heavy chill has frozen o'er the fountain of our tears,
And tho' the eye may sparkle still, 'tis where the ice appears.

4

Tho' wit may flash from fluent lips, and mirth distract the breast,
Through midnight hours that yield no more their former hope of rest;
'Tis but as ivy-leaves around the ruin'd turret wreath,
All green and wildly fresh without but worn and grey beneath.

Oh could I feel as I have felt, — or be what I have been,
Or weep as I could once have wept, o'er many a vanished scene:
As springs in deserts found seem sweet, all brackish though they be,
So midst the wither'd waste of life, those tears would flow to me.

GEORGE GORDON, LORD BYRON
(1788–1824)

George Gordon Byron was born near Aberdeen, Scotland, in 1788. Infamous, exceedingly handsome, and always at the center of a scandal, Byron achieved instant celebrity with his first collection of poems. By 1816 he had become weary of the hypocrisies and pieties of English society and left the country, never to return. He died at the age of thirty-six while fighting with the Greeks against the Turks. Though the exact cause of his death was never determined, it is known that Byron suffered a series of fevers and convulsions, perhaps due to the combined effects of alcohol, opium, and malaria or other disease. Byron wrote "Stanzas for Music" in 1815 for a close childhood friend, the Duke of Dorset, who was killed while hunting in Ireland. The epigraph from Thomas Gray's *Poemata* translates: "O fount of tears, that have their sacred sources in the tender spirit; four times blessed is he who has felt you, Holy Nymph, gushing forth from the depths of his heart."

June 5

History

History has to live with what was here,
clutching and close to fumbling all we had —
it is so dull and gruesome how we die,
unlike writing, life never finishes.
Abel was finished; death is not remote,
a flash-in-the-pan electrifies the skeptic,
his cows crowding like skulls against high-voltage wire,
his baby crying all night like a new machine.
As in our Bibles, white-faced, predatory,
the beautiful, mist-drunken hunter's moon ascends —
a child could give it a face: two holes, two holes,
my eyes, my mouth, between them a skull's no-nose —
O there's a terrifying innocence in my face
drenched with the silver salvage of the mornfrost.

ROBERT LOWELL
(1917–1977)

Robert Trail Spence Lowell IV was born in Boston, Massachusetts, and was distantly related to poets James Russell Lowell and Amy Lowell. By the age of thirty, Lowell had already published two collections and been awarded the Pulitzer Prize and by all accounts was well on his way to becoming one of America's most prominent literary figures. He married the novelist and essayist Elizabeth Hardwick in 1949, shortly after his divorce from novelist Jean Stafford. Lowell married his third wife, Lady Caroline Blackwood, in 1972. "History" shares its form with the pieces in Lowell's *Notebook, 1967-1968,* a book that includes poems on Caligula, Robert Kennedy, Napoleon, and Norman Mailer, as well as "confessional" material about the poet and his family. Lowell revised and republished this book twice: as *Notebook* in 1970 and again as *History* (the version that contained this poem as its title piece) in 1973. In a note to the original edition, Lowell wrote, "My meter, fourteen line unrhymed blank verse sections, is fairly strict at first and elsewhere, but often corrupts in single lines to the freedom of prose. Even with this license, I fear I have failed to avoid the themes and gigantism of the sonnet. A poet can be intelligent and on to what he does; yet he walks, half-balmy, and over-accounted — caught by his gentle amnesia, his rude ignorance, his too meticulous education. I had good guides when I began. They have gone on with me by now the echoes are so innumerable that I almost lack the fineness of ear to distinguish them." Lowell died of a heart attack in the back-seat of a New York City taxicab in 1977.

The Nature of Musical Form

It is hard to believe of the world that there should be
music in it: these certainties against
the all-uncertain, this ordered fairness beneath
the tonelessness, the confusion of random noise.

It is tempting to say of the incomprehensible,
the formlessness, there is only order as we
so order and ordering, make it so; or this,
there is natural order which music apprehends

which apprehension justifies the world;
or even this, these forms are false, not true,
and music irrelevant at least, the world
is stated somewhere else, not there. But no.

How is it? There is a fairness of person too,
which is not a truth of persons or even, we learn,
a truth of that person, particularly.
It is only fairness stating only itself:

as though we could say of music only, it is.

WILLIAM BRONK
(1918–1999)

William Bronk was born in Fort Edward, New York, and educated at Dartmouth and Harvard. He served in the United States Army during World War II, after which he taught at Union College in Schenectady, New York, and also ran his family's lumber business. Though he did not travel much or give many readings (he never drove a car), Bronk was a gourmet chef who entertained writers and artists in his large Victorian house in Hudson Falls, New York. Bronk felt that poems "happened" to him and should also "happen" to the reader, who should invest as much in a poem as the author. He once remarked, "Such acceptance as I've had is very small, and I don't care whether the most respected critics are reading it at all."

June 7

Haiku

The short night:
A scarlet flower has bloomed
At the tip of the vine.

ISSA
(1762–1827)
translated by R. H. Blyth

Eighteenth-century Japanese poet Kobayashi Issa's original name was Kobayashi Nobuyki. He was also sometimes called Kobayashi Yataro. Issa, as he is most often called, became popular in the late Edo period partly for the sense of humor often evident in his haiku. In an essay called "Issa's Comic Vision," David G. Lanoue has written that, though the poet had "reason enough to succumb to depression and bitterness, he chose to greet the improbable universe of day-to-day, most often, with a smile. In the many thousands of haiku that he left behind for us, that warm, mischievous smile of his lives on."

June 8

The Smaller Orchid

Love is a climate
small things find safe
to grow in — not
(though I once supposed so)
the demanding cattleya
du côté de chez Swann,
glamor among the faubourgs,
hothouse overpowerings, blisses
and cruelties at teatime, but this
next-to-unidentifiable wildling,
hardly more than a
sprout, I've found
flourishing in the hollows
of a granite seashore —
a cheerful tousle, little,
white, down-to-earth orchid
declaring its authenticity,
if you hug the ground
close enough, in a powerful
outdoorsy-domestic
whiff of vanilla.

AMY CLAMPITT
(1920–1994)

Born in New Providence, Iowa, Amy Clampitt earned a B.A. from Grinnell College and attended graduate school at Columbia University, but left without completing her degree. Though Clampitt began writing poetry in high school, she focused on fiction for many years and did not publish her first poem until 1978, in the *New Yorker.* Her first collection, *The Kingfisher,* appeared in 1983 when Clampitt was sixty-three years old. *The Collected Poems of Amy Clampitt* was published in 1997, three years after her death from ovarian cancer at the age of seventy-four. Poet Mary Jo Salter recalls her first encounter with Clampitt: "Tall, seemingly weighing nothing at all in her ballet slippers, she had a lightness of foot and manner that put one in mind, immediately, of a child. Her dark brown hair, graying only a little then, was put up behind with a hippie's leather barrette, though she had also trained two wide chin-length locks to fall over her rather comically large ears. She was less able (though she tried, with long, elegant fingers that were always flying upward) to hide a beautiful gap-toothed smile. She listened intently, but when she spoke she became a rapid, revved-up, high-pitched machine that rarely paused except for an attack of the giggles."

Cupid, I Hate Thee

Cupid, I hate thee, which I'd have thee know,
A naked starveling ever may'st thou be,
Poor rogue, go pawn thy fascia and thy bow,
For some few rags wherewith to cover thee;
Or if thou'lt not, thy archery forbear,
To some base rustic do thyself prefer,
And when corn's sown, or grown into the ear,
Practice thy quiver and turn crow-keeper;
Or being blind (as fittest for the trade),
Go hire thyself some bungling harper's boy;
They that are blind are minstrels often made,
So may'st thou live, to thy fair mother's joy:
That whilst with Mars she holdeth her old way,
Thou, her blind son, may'st sit by them, and play.

MICHAEL DRAYTON
(1563–1631)

A contemporary of William Shakespeare and Ben Jonson, Michael Drayton was born in Warwickshire, England, and brought up as a page in the house of Sir Henry Goodyere. At the age of ten, Drayton declared himself a poet and, despite his lack of formal education, became a master of Renaissance poetic forms. He published his first book in 1591—a collection of verse paraphrases of the Bible entitled *The Harmony of the Church*. Authorities suppressed the volume, perhaps due to Drayton's reliance on the Geneva Bible as his source rather than the more acceptable Anglican Bible. "Cupid, I Hate Thee" is from his 1593 collection of sonnets, *Idea: The Shepherd's Garland*. The poem is sometimes referred to as "Sonnet XLVIII."

Written on the Wall at Chang's Hermitage

It is Spring in the mountains.
I come alone seeking you.
The sound of chopping wood echos
Between the silent peaks.
The streams are still icy.
There is snow on the trail.
At sunset I reach your grove
In the stony mountain pass.
You want nothing, although at night
You can see the aura of gold
And silver ore all around you.
You have learned to be gentle
As the mountain deer you have tamed.
The way back forgotten, hidden
Away, I become like you,
An empty boat, floating, adrift.

TU FU
(712–770)
translated by Kenneth Rexroth

Chinese poet Tu Fu was born in Kung-hsien, Honan, China, and was also known as Tu Kung-pu. He held a variety of minor positions in the imperial court, including Office of the Right Commander of the Heir Apparent's Palace Guard, though he was eventually banished from the capital for his outspoken advice to the Emperor. Tu Fu met and became friends with poet Li Po in 744 and their travels together are the subject of many of Tu Fu's poems. Tu Fu composed more than fifteen hundred poems and his place in Chinese literature may be compared to Shakespeare's canonical position in the West, though there is evidence that he was not highly esteemed in his own lifetime. As Tu Fu himself remarked in a poem titled "Chance Topic," "Literature is a matter of a thousand ages; / Its success is known in one's heart. / Writers all stand in different ranks, / But fame is surely no random favor."

June II

Work without Hope

All Nature seems at work. Slugs leave their lair —
The bees are stirring — birds are on the wing —
And Winter, slumbering in the open air,
Wears on his smiling face a dream of Spring!
And I the while, the sole unbusy thing,
Nor honey make, nor pair, nor build, nor sing.

Yet well I ken the banks where amaranths blow,
Have traced the fount whence streams of nectar flow.
Bloom, O ye amaranths! bloom for whom ye may,
For me ye bloom not! Glide, rich streams, away!
With lips unbrightened, wreathless brow, I stroll:
And would you learn the spells that drowse my soul?
Work without Hope draws nectar in a sieve,
And Hope without an object cannot live.

SAMUEL TAYLOR COLERIDGE
(1772–1834)

Samuel Taylor Coleridge was born in Otter, St. Mary, in Devon, England, and raised
in London, the youngest child of a vicar. He abandoned his studies at Jesus College,
Cambridge, to flee from his debtors and enlisted as a soldier. In 1794 he met Robert
Southey, who was soon to become England's Poet Laureate. The two planned a
"Pantisocrasy" — a utopian community on the banks of the Susquehanna River —
but never achieved their idealist dream. In 1795 Coleridge met William Wordsworth,
with whom he collaborated on the anonymous and revolutionary *Lyrical Ballads*,
published in 1798. Coleridge is best known for "Kubla Kahn," a hallucinatory vision
he claimed came to him in an opium dream. "Work without Hope" has been dated
to 1825, and was composed in Highgate, where Coleridge had retired while recuper-
ating from his severe opium addiction.

June 12

Lambs

Under branches of white lilac
They crop the wet grass just before dawn.
They move smokily through the half-light, smudge pots
Pulsing against a thick morning frost.
My watch glows like a small, improbable moon. Six o'clock.
I have been driving into the dark too long.

I pull to the side of the road.
I am a branch, a stone. The lambs are not aware of me.
They have been fading into the hillside
Like shadows that have peopled someone's fever
In the shut room of a dilapidated farmhouse
Where the walls reiterate a spray of honeysuckle.

They ignore one another. They are blanketed with thistles,
A little out of sorts in this shabby light.
Five or six of them are wandering through a peach orchard,
Not even aware of my personal squalor.
What stumbles from their tongues is never music;
It is the echo of a badly damaged shell.

Now they are moving by a ditch of rainwater,
Inspected for flaws in the foggy mirror.
I walk into the field, I am not afraid of them —
They scatter like the last edges of a sickness.
The sun has begun to enlarge its tawny fleeces
At the expense of no one in particular.

THOMAS JAMES
(1946–1974)

Thomas James published one book of poems, *Letters to a Stranger*, before his death by suicide, not long after the deaths of both his parents. He took as the epigraph for his book these sentences from James Baldwin's novel *Giovanni's Room*: "Perhaps everybody has a garden of Eden. I don't know; but they have scarcely seen their garden before they see the flaming sword. Then, perhaps, life only offers the choice of remembering the garden or forgetting it. Either, or: it takes strength to remember, it takes another kind of strength to forget, it takes a hero to do both."

June 13

The Soote Season

The soote season, that bud and bloom forth brings,
With green hath clad the hill and eke the vale;
The nightingale with feathers new she sings;
The turtle to her make hath told her tale.
Summer is come, for every spray now springs;
The hart hath hung his old head on the pale;
The buck in brake his winter coat he flings,
The fishes float with new repairéd scale;
the adder all her slough away she slings,
The swift swallow pursueth the flies small;
The busy bee her honey now she mings.
Winter is worn, that was the flowers' bale.
And thus I see among these pleasant things,
Each care decays, and yet my sorrow springs.

HENRY HOWARD, EARL OF SURREY
(1517–1547)

Henry Howard, Earl of Surrey was born to an illustrious family and was heir to the dukedom of Norfolk. In his early years, he seemed to live comfortably as a courtier, but by 1537, when he was twenty, he'd become rebellious and aggressive. He was imprisoned in Windsor Castle for several months for violent behavior in the presence of the court, though King Henry VIII could have ordered him put to death. He drew further displeasure from the court for similar outbursts and bad behavior, including eating meat during Lent. He was eventually charged with treason for attacking George Blage and was finally beheaded in 1547. With the exception of a few poems on the death of Sir Thomas Wyatt, none of Surrey's poems were published during his lifetime, and his verse was not widely published until ten years after his execution. "The Soote Season," a sonnet adaptation of Petrarch's "Rime 310," was first published along with poems by Wyatt and others in an anthology known as *Tottel's Songs and Sonnets* in 1557.

June 14

Progress and Retrogression

They invented a kind of glass which let flies through. The fly would come, push a little with his head and pop, he was on the other side. Enormous happiness on the part of the fly.

All this was ruined by a Hungarian scientist when he discovered that the fly could enter but not get out, or vice versa, because he didn't know what gimmick was involved in the glass or the flexibility of its fibers, for it was very fibroid. They immediately invented a fly trap with a sugar cube inside, and many flies perished miserably. So ended any possible brotherhood with these animals, who are deserving of better luck.

JULIO CORTÁZAR
(1914–1984)
translated by Paul Blackburn

Julio Cortázar was born in Brussels to Argentinean parents. He spent his childhood and young adulthood in Argentina, moving to Paris in 1951. Cortázar earned his living as a translator and professor and became internationally known for his novel *Hopscotch*. He is also considered a modern master of the short story for collections such as *Blow Up and Other Stories*. He died from the effects of leukemia and heart disease in Paris in 1984. "Progress and Retrogression" is from his book *Cronopios and Famas*.

I Find No Peace
Description of the Contrarious Passions in a Lover

I find no peace, and all my war is done;
I fear and hope, I burn, and freeze like ice;
I fly aloft, yet can I not arise;
And nought I have, and all the world I seize on,
That locks nor loseth, holdeth me in prison,
And holds me not, yet can I scape no wise:
Nor letteth me live, nor die, at my devise,
And yet of death it giveth me occasion.
Without eye I see; without tongue I plain:
I wish to perish, yet I ask for health;
I love another, and I hate myself;
I feed me in sorrow, and laugh in all my pain.
Lo, thus displeaseth me both death and life,
And my delight is causer of this strife.

THOMAS WYATT
(1503–1542)

Though it is clear from the state of his manuscripts that Wyatt intended to publish a collection of his poems, no such book made it into print during his lifetime. Several of his sonnets were collected and published with work by Henry Howard, Earl of Surrey, and others in a volume called *Tottel's Songs and Sonnets* or simply *Tottel's Miscellany* in 1557. Tottel was not a responsible editor, however, and he "improved" many of the poems, obscuring the subtlety of Wyatt's poetic effects. The subtitle "Description of the Contrarious Passions in a Lover" seems to have been added by Tottel to this poem as well. "I Find No Peace" is Wyatt's version of Petrarch's "Sonnet 134."

June 16

Ebbtide at Sundown

How larger is remembrance than desire!
How deeper than all longing is regret!
The tide is gone, the sands are rippled yet;
The sun is gone; the hills are lifted higher,
Crested with rose. Ah, why should we require
Sight of the sea, the sun? The sands are wet,
And in their glassy flaws huge record set
Of the ebbed stream, the little ball of fire.
Gone, they are gone! But, oh, so freshly gone,
So rich in vanishing we ask not where —
So close upon us is the bliss that shone,
And, oh, so thickly it impregns the air!
Closer in beating heart we could not be
To the sunk sun, the far, surrendered sea.

MICHAEL FIELD

"Michael Field" is the pseudonym of Katherine Harris Bradley (1846–1914) and Edith Emma Cooper (1862–1913). These prolific collaborators were close relatives (aunt and niece, respectively) and together they authored twenty-eight plays and eight collections of poetry. They also used the pseudonyms Arran and Isla Leigh, as well as the epithet "the author of *Borgia*" after the publication of their anonymous play of that title. After 1884 they used "Michael Field" exclusively and their works received high praise until their true identities were discovered. In 1878 Cooper and Bradley moved from Birmingham to Bristol to attend University College, where they became known on campus for their theatrical clothes, interest in paganism, and use of elaborate nicknames among their circle of friends. Their plays explored themes that shocked many Victorians, including atheism, feminine sexuality, homosexuality, and women's rights. After receiving a letter from Robert Browning — who addressed his correspondence to Michael Field — Cooper confessed the truth about their authorship. The women became close friends with Robert and Elizabeth Barrett Browning, who faithfully kept their secret, agreeing with Bradley that the two had "many things to say that the world will not tolerate from a woman's lips."

Thorns and Roses

Radiant and white
Saint Ignatius
passed near a rose
and threw himself onto the bush
injuring his body

with the bell of his black habit
he wanted to extinguish
the world's beauty
that sprang from the earth as if from a wound

and when he lay at the bottom
of the cradle of thorns
he saw
that the blood trickling down his forehead
congealed on his eyelashes
in the shape of a rose

and the blind hand
groping for the thorns
was pierced
by the sweet touch of petals

the cheated saint wept
in the mockery of flowers

thorns and roses
roses and thorns
we search happiness

ZBIGNIEW HERBERT

(1924–1998)

translated by John and Bogdana Carpenter

Zbigniew Herbert was born in Lvov, Poland. During the German occupation, Herbert studied at the underground King John Casimir University, where he majored in Polish Literature. He went on to study economics and law, eventually studying philosophy at the University of Warsaw. Despite his broad and excellent education, Herbert worked at many low-paying jobs during the 1950s. He published his first collection, *The Chord of Light,* in 1956 after the Soviet "thaw." A playwright and essayist as well as a poet, Herbert went on to become one of Poland's most well-respected authors. He died in Warsaw in 1998 at the age of seventy-four.

Together, We All Go Out under the Cypress Trees in the Chou Family Burial-Grounds

Today's skies are perfect for a clear
flute and singing *koto*. And touched

this deeply by those laid under these
cypress trees, how could we neglect joy?

Clear songs drift away anew. Emerald wine
starts pious faces smiling. Not knowing

what tomorrow brings, it's exquisite
exhausting whatever I feel here and now.

T'AO CH'IEN
(365–427)
translated by David Hinton

T'ao Ch'ien, also known as T'ao Yüan-ming, is considered the first modern Chinese poet. He was born into a once illustrious family who had fallen on hard times and he held a series of minor government positions, a career he did not enjoy. He turned to farming and a simple lifestyle that enabled him to write the best of his poems, which like his chosen life bucked the ornate style in fashion at the time. Huang T'ing-chien, the Sung Dynasty poet, once wrote of T'ao Ch'ien, "when you've just come of age, reading these poems will seem like gnawing on withered wood. But reading them after long experience in the world, it seems the decisions of your life were all made in ignorance."

Moonrise June 19, 1876

I awoke in the midsummer not-to-call night, | in the white and the walk
    of the morning:
The móon, dwíndled and thínned to the fringe | of a fíngernail héld to
    the cándle,
Or páring of páradisáïcal frúit, | lóvely in wáning but lústreless,°
Stepped from the stool, drew back from the barrow, | of dark Maenefa
    the mountain;°
A cusp still clasped him, a fluke yet fanged him, | entangled him, not quit
    utterly.°
This was the prized, the desirable sight, | unsought, presented so easily,°
Parted me leaf and leaf, divided me, | eyelid and eyelid of slumber.

GERARD MANLEY HOPKINS
(1844–1889)

Almost thirty years after his death, Gerard Manley Hopkins's mature poems were
finally published. His literary executor, English Poet Laureate Robert Bridges,
painstakingly gathered and compared the extant manuscripts and the resulting col-
lection was released in 1918. In "A Note (on Gerard Manley Hopkins)" Robert
Lowell wrote, "Hopkins's epitaph, I think, should run something like this: He wrote
religious lyrics that are thoroughly of the nineteenth century and yet are unsurpassed
by anything written in the great ages of religion. He is probably the finest of English
poets of nature; i.e., of inanimate creation."

June 20

The Dreamt-of Place

I saw two towering birds cleaving the air
And thought they were Paolo and Francesca
Leading the lost, whose wings like silver billows
Rippled the azure sky from shore to shore,
They were so many. The nightmare god was gone
Who roofed their pain, the ghastly glen lay open,
The hissing lake was still, the fiends were fled,
And only some few headless, footless mists
Crawled out and in the iron-hearted caves.
Like light's unearthly eyes the lost looked down,
And heaven was filled and moving. Every height
On earth was thronged and all that lived stared upward.
I thought, This is the reconciliation,
This is the day after the Last Day,
The lost world lies dreaming within its coils,
Grass grows upon the surly sides of Hell,
Time has caught time and holds it fast for ever.
And then I thought, Where is the knife, the butcher,
The victim? Are they all here in their places?
Hid in this harmony? But there was no answer.

EDWIN MUIR
(1887–1959)

Scottish poet Edwin Muir was born in the Orkney Islands. When he was fourteen years old his family relocated to Glasgow, hoping to find work, but they lived in poverty and within five years both of his parents and two of his brothers had died. Though he left school at the age of eleven to work in a beer-bottling factory, Muir was an enthusiastic autodidact. He began writing in earnest after he moved to London in 1919 and he began teaching, translating, and working as a journalist. He is credited with introducing English-speaking audiences to the work of Franz Kafka with his translations of *The Castle, The Trial, In the Penal Colony, America,* and other works. His autobiography, *The Story and the Fable,* was published in 1940. Paolo and Francesca in line two of "The Dreamt-of Place" are the same star-crossed lovers who appear in Dante's *Inferno.*

My Papa's Waltz

The whiskey on your breath
Could make a small boy dizzy;
But I hung on like death:
Such waltzing was not easy.

We romped until the pans
Slid from the kitchen shelf;
My mother's countenance
Could not unfrown itself.

The hand that held my wrist
Was battered on one knuckle;
At every step you missed
My right ear scraped a buckle.

You beat time on my head
With a palm caked hard by dirt,
Then waltzed me off to bed
Still clinging to your shirt.

THEODORE ROETHKE
(1908–1963)

Born in Saginaw, Michigan, Theodore Roethke grew up near the greenhouses of his German grandfather, uncle, and father, and the imagery of these surroundings permeates his poetry. Roethke was fourteen at the time of his father's death from cancer. He was plagued by alcoholism and poor mental health and suffered a series of debilitating breakdowns that often left him hospitalized. From 1947 until his death in 1963, he taught poetry at the University of Washington, where his students included James Wright, Richard Hugo, Carolyn Kizer, and David Wagoner. Roethke published sparingly, but he increased his reputation with each book and was awarded the Pulitzer Prize. He died at the age of fifty-five of a coronary occlusion while swimming in a friend's pool.

June 22

Insects

Thou tiney loiterer on the barleys beard
And happy unit of a numerous herd
Of playfellows the laughing summer brings
Mocking the suns face in their glittering wings
How merrily they creep and run and flye
No kin they bear to labours drudgery
Smoothing the velvet of the pale hedge rose
And where they flye for dinner no one knows
The dewdrops feed them not — they love the shine
Of noon whose sun may bring them golden wine
All day theyre playing in their sunday dress
Till night goes sleep and they can do no less
Then in the heath bells silken hood they flie
And like to princes in their slumber lie
From coming night and dropping dews and all
In silken beds and roomy painted hall
So happily they spend their summer day
Now in the corn fields now the new mown hay
One almost fancys that such happy things
In coloured moods and richly burnished wings
Are fairey folk in splendid masquerade
Disguised through fear of mortal folk affraid
Keeping their merry pranks a mystery still
Lest glaring day should do their secrets ill

JOHN CLARE
(1793–1864)

With the publication of his first book of poetry, *Poems Descriptive of Rural Life and Scenery* (1820), John Clare became a celebrity who found himself the target of curious visitors who frequently traveled to his home. While some critics claimed that Clare's poetry was compelling because of the author's lowly educational and economic background, others praised the book generously, concurring with the observation in *New Monthly Magazine* (March 1820) that the poetry was distinguished for its "minute delineations of external nature."

June 23

Strange Fruit

Here is the girl's head like an exhumed gourd.
Oval-faced, prune-skinned, prune-stones for teeth.
They unswaddled the wet fern of her hair
And made an exhibition of its coil,
Let the air at her leathery beauty.
Pash of tallow, perishable treasure:
Her broken nose is dark as a turf clod,
Her eyeholes blank as pools in the old workings.
Diodorus Siculus confessed
His gradual ease among the likes of this:
Murdered, forgotten, nameless, terrible
Beheaded girl, outstaring axe
And beatification, outstaring
What had begun to feel like reverence.

SEAMUS HEANEY
(1939–)

Seamus Heaney was born in Castledawson, County Derry, in Northern Ireland. A prolific poet, essayist, and translator, Heaney received the Nobel Prize for literature in 1995. He lives in Dublin, Ireland. He won the Whitbread Book of the Year Award for his acclaimed translation of *Beowulf* in 2000. Diodorus Siculus in line eight was a Sicilian historian (90–21 B.C.) who wrote the *Bibliotheca Historica* and was a contemporary of Julius Caesar.

June 24

The Willows by the Water Side

My little breath, under the willows by the water side we used to sit
And there the yellow cottonwood bird came and sang.
That I remember and therefore I weep.
Under the growing corn we used to sit,
And there the little leaf bird came and sang.
That I remember and therefore I weep.
There on the meadow of yellow flowers we used to walk
Oh, my little breath! Oh, my little heart!
There on the meadow of blue flowers we used to walk.
Alas! how long ago that we two walked in that pleasant way.
Then everything was happy, but, alas! how long ago.
There on the meadow of crimson flowers we used to walk.
Oh, my little breath, now I go there alone in sorrow.

TEWA SONG
translated by Herbert Joseph Spinden

The willow tree played an important part in Tewa culture, supplying materials for weaving baskets and bark for medicinal use. The Tewa migrated from their original settlements in New Mexico to Arizona, where they joined with the Hopi and other pueblo groups. The New Mexican Tewa settlements were near Taos and Santa Fe, and the "Taos" is an approximation of the Tewa (or Tenoan) word for "red willow place." (For other Tewa songs, see March 31 and September 25.)

June 25

Psyche's Dream

If dreams could dream, beyond the canon of landscapes
Already saved from decorum, including mute
Illicit girls cowering under eaves
Where the books are stacked and which they
Pillage, hoping to find not events but response

If dreams could dream, free from the damp crypt
And from the bridge where she went
To watch the spill and the tree
Standing on its head, huge and rootless
(Of which the wasp is a cruel illustration

Although its sting is not), the decay
Now spread into the gardens, their beds
Tethered to weeds and to all other intrusions;
Then the perishing house, lost from view
So she must, and you, look out to see
Not it but an image of it, would be

Nowhere and would not resemble, but would languish
On the other side of place where the winged boy
Touches her ear far from anywhere
But gathered like evening around her waist
So that within each dream is another, remote
And mocking and a version of his mouth on her mouth.

ANN LAUTERBACH
(1942–)

Ann Lauterbach was born in Manhattan, New York, and educated at the University of Wisconsin and Columbia University. She teaches at Bard College, where she is the David and Ruth Schwab III Professor of Language and Literature and co-director of the M.F.A. program in the Writing Division.

And Suddenly It Is Evening

Everyone stands alone at the heart of this earth
Stunned by a ray of sunlight
and suddenly it is evening.

SALVATORE QUASIMODO

(1901–1968)

translated by J. Ruth Gendler

Italian poet, translator, and critic Salvatore Quasimodo was born in Modica, Sicily. The central figure of Hermeticism — an Italian movement that took its initial inspiration from the work of the French symbolists — Quasimodo is closely associated with poets Giuseppe Ungaretti and Eugenio Montale. Quasimodo was briefly imprisoned during World War II for his anti-fascist activities and afterward turned his poetry toward topics of social conditions and contemporary history. He was awarded the Nobel Prize for literature in 1959. In his acceptance speech, he spoke about the importance of poetry in contemporary society, saying, "The world today seems allied with the side opposed to poetry. And for the world, the poet's very presence is an obstacle to be overcome. He must be annihilated. The force of poetry, on the other hand, fans out in every direction in organized societies; and if literary games escape the sensibilities of men everywhere, a poetic activity that is inspired by humanism does not."

A Pause

That little brown bird visiting
one corner of the meadow, then another,
for a wrapper, a twig, some fuzz-color,
is unerring, it seems, though maybe,
the world so various, so much of it dangling,
there's not much possibility of error,
and any looping out and returning
tightens, by nature, into a nest.
What is it about wonder,
strong weakness, will to be surprised,
that where there is no home, lets us live,
and just when we forget how, flies?

                              JAMES RICHARDSON
                              (1950–)

James Richardson was born in Bradenton, Florida. He received an A.B. from Princeton University and a Ph.D. from University of Virginia. Richardson is the author of four collections of poems, as well as a book of aphorisms, and critical studies of Thomas Hardy and others. He teaches English and creative writing at Princeton University.

June 28

Pastoral

When I was younger
it was plain to me
I must make something of myself.
Older now
I walk back streets
admiring the houses
of the very poor:
roof out of line with sides
the yards cluttered
with old chicken wire, ashes,
furniture gone wrong;
the fences and outhouses
built of barrel-staves
and parts of boxes, all,
if I am fortunate,
smeared a bluish green
that properly weathered
pleases me best
of all colors.
      No one
will believe this
of vast import to the nation.

WILLIAM CARLOS WILLIAMS
(1881–1963)

"Pastoral" shares its ironic title with several other poems by William Carlos Williams. This particular "Pastoral" was written in 1917 and included in Williams's book *Al Que Quiere,* which he translated as "To him who wants it." Technically, *Al Que Quiere* was Williams's second book, after the privately printed *Poems* by "William C. Williams," published in 1909. Williams later discounted *Poems* when listing his books. "The poems were bad Keats, nothing more," he wrote in his *Autobiography.* "[O]h well, bad Whitman too. But I sure loved them. Where does a young man get the courage for such abortions? I can tell you my need must have been great. There is not one thing of the slightest value in the whole thin booklet — except the intent."

Sparkles from the Wheel

Where the city's ceaseless crowd moves on the livelong day,
Withdrawn I join a group of children watching, I pause aside with them.

By the curb toward the edge of the flagging,
A knife-grinder works at his wheel sharpening a great knife,
Bending over he carefully holds it to the stone, by foot and knee,
With measur'd tread he turns rapidly, as he presses with light but
    firm hand,
Forth issue then in copious golden jets,
Sparkles from the wheel.

The scene and all its belongings, how they seize and affect me,
The sad sharp-chinn'd old man with worn clothes and broad
    shoulder-band of leather,
Myself effusing and fluid, a phantom curiously floating, now here
    absorb'd and arrested,
The group, (an unminded point set in a vast surrounding,)
The attentive, quiet children, the loud, proud, restive base of the streets,
The low hoarse purr of the whirling stone, the light-pressd'd blade,
Diffusing, dropping, sideways-daring, in tiny showers of gold,
Sparkles from the wheel.

WALT WHITMAN
(1819–1892)

Walt Whitman had not yet written "Sparkles from the Wheel" when he published
the first edition of *Leaves of Grass* in 1855. The poem has been dated to 1870 in
Whitman's "Good Gray Poet" years and was included in a section of the book called
"Autumn Rivulets" in all subsequent editions.

The Frog

When little matchsticks of rain bounce off drenched fields, an amphibian dwarf, a maimed Ophelia, barely the size of a fist, sometimes hops under the poet's feet and flings herself into the next pond.

Let the nervous little thing run away. She has lovely legs. Her whole body is sheathed in waterproof skin. Hardly meat, her long muscles have an elegance neither fish nor fowl. But to escape one's fingers, the virtue of fluidity joins forces with her struggle for life. Goitrous, she starts panting . . . And that pounding heart, those wrinkled eyelids, that drooping mouth, move me to let her go.

FRANCIS PONGE
(1899–1988)
translated by Beth Archer

Francis Jean Gaston Alfred Ponge was born in Montpellier, France, and educated at the Sorbonne and Ecole de Droit in Paris. He served in the French military from 1918 to 1919, and afterward he began his career as a secretary and insurance salesman, but was soon turning out journalism, essays, poems, and other writings and gaining a formidable reputation as a major French writer. Like Pablo Neruda, Ponge was often attracted to simple objects as his subjects. One remarkable example of his preoccupation with quotidian things is his book *Le Savon (The Soap)*, a series of prose poems in the voice of a bar of soap as it "lives" through its various experiences of being wetted, lathered, and left to dry. Ponge spent the last thirty years of his life as a recluse in his country home *Mas du Vergers* and frequently suffered from nervous exhaustion and psychosomatic illnesses, though he continued to write up until his death in 1988.

Fragment 1

Loveliest of what I leave behind is the sunlight,
and loveliest after that the shining stars, and the moon's face,
but also cucumbers that are ripe, and pears, and apples.

PRAXÍLLA OF SÍCYON
(CA. 450 B.C.)
translated by Richmond Lattimore

According to the Greek rhetorician Athenaeus, Praxílla of Sícyon was the composer of *scolia* (short lyric poems for after-dinner entertainment, or drinking songs), and as great a poet as Alcaeus and Anacreon. Of her dithyrambs, hymns, and scolia on mystic and mythological topics only eight fragments survive. She was distinguished enough to be called one of the lyric Muses and was the subject of a sculpture by Lysippos which stood in Sicyon and is known from several later Roman copies.

The Mower to the Glowworms

1

Ye living lamps, by whose dear light
The nightingale does sit so late,
And studying all the summer-night,
Her matchless songs does meditate;

2

Ye country comets, that portend
No war, nor prince's funeral,
Shining unto no higher end
Than to presage the grass's fall;

3

Ye glowworms, whose officious flame
To wand'ring mowers shows the way,
That in the night have lost their aim,
And after foolish fires do stray;

4

Your courteous lights in vain you waste,
Since *Juliana* here is come,
For she my mind hath so displaced
That I shall never find my home.

ANDREW MARVELL
(1621–1678)

Andrew Marvell was born in Hull, Yorkshire, England, the son of a reverend at Trinity Church. A precocious child, he began his studies at Trinity College at the age of twelve, and by the age of sixteen he had published two poems (one in Latin, the other in Greek) in an anthology of Cambridge poets. He completed his B.A. in 1639 but abandoned his M.A. studies after his father drowned in the Hull estuary in 1641. He later served as John Milton's Latin secretary and was elected to the British Parliament in 1660 and used his political power to free the elder poet from prison. Marvell died suddenly from a fever in 1678, prompting some to suggest he was poisoned by Jesuit opponents. "The Mower to the Glowworms" was first published in *Miscellaneous Poems* in 1681, with a preface by "Mary Marvell." It was later discovered that "Mary Marvell" was actually Mary Palmer, Marvell's housekeeper, who was posing as his wife to protect his small estate from creditors and business partners.

Naima

for John Coltrane

Propped against the crowded bar
he pours into the curved and silver horn
his old unhappy longing for a home

the dancers twist and turn
he leans and wishes he could burn
his memories to ashes like some old notorious emperor

of rome. but no stars blazed across the sky when he was born
no wise men found his hovel. this crowded bar
where dancers twist and turn

holds all the fame and recognition he will ever earn
on earth or heaven. he leans against the bar
and pours his old unhappy longing in the saxophone

KAMAU BRAITHWAITE
(1930–)

Kamau Brathwaite was born Lawson Edward Brathwaite in Bridgetown, Barbados. He attended Harrison College in Barbados and received a B.A. with honors in history from Pembroke College, Cambridge, on a Barbados Island scholarship. He is a professor of comparative literature at New York University and divides his time between Barbados and New York. John Coltrane in the dedication is the legendary jazz saxophonist, also mentioned in "Soloing " by Philip Levine (see April 26). "Naima" is the name of John Coltrane's wife and also the name of a song he wrote and recorded for his album *Giant Steps* in December 1959.

from "Song of Myself" (in *Leaves of Grass*)

52

The spotted hawk swoops by and accuses me, he complains of my
    gab and my loitering.

I too am not a bit tamed, I too am untranslatable,
I sound my barbaric yawp over the roofs of the world.

The last scud of day holds back for me,
It flings my likeness after the rest and true as any on the shadow'd wilds,
It coaxes me to the vapor and the dusk.

I depart as air, I shake my white locks at the runaway sun,
I effuse my flesh in eddies, and drift it in lacy jags.

I bequeath myself to the dirt to grow from the grass I love,
If you want me again look for me under your boot-soles.

You will hardly know who I am or what I mean,
But I shall be good health to you nevertheless,
And filter and fiber your blood.

Failing to fetch me at first keep encouraged,
Missing me one place search another,
I stop somewhere waiting for you.

WALT WHITMAN
(1819–1892)

This is the final section in Walt Whitman's wide-ranging "Song of Myself," which
was included in the premier edition of *Leaves of Grass* in 1855. Whitman once wrote,
"In my poems all revolves around, concentrates in, radiates from myself. I have but
one central figure, the general human personality typified in myself. But my book
[*Leaves of Grass*] compels, absolutely necessitates, every reader to transpose himself
or herself into the central position, and become the living fountain, actor, experi-
encer himself or herself, of every page, every aspiration, every line."

Out of Sight in the Direction of My Body

All the trees all their boughs all their leaves
The grass at the base the rocks the massed houses
Afar the sea that thine eye washes
Those images of one day and the next
The vices the virtues that are so imperfect
The transparence of men that pass in the streets of hazard
And women that pass in a fume from thy dour questing
The fixed ideas virgin-lipped leaden-hearted
The vices the virtues that are so imperfect
The eyes consenting resembling the eyes though didst
                                                        vanquish
The confusion of the bodies the lassitudes the ardours
The imitation of the words the attitudes the ideas
The vices the virtues that are so imperfect

Love is man unfinished.

PAUL ÉLUARD
(1895–1952)
translated by Samuel Beckett

Paul Éluard was the pen name for Eugène Grindel, who was born in Saint Denis, a working-class suburb of Paris. He was a founding member of the surrealist movement with Tristan Tzara, Louis Aragon, and André Breton. A prolific poet, he also published several prose collections and collaborative works done with Breton, Aragon, and others. Éluard broke with the Surrealist movement in 1938 and joined the Communist Party. He remained in Paris as a member of the French Resistance during the German Occupation. He died from heart failure in Paris in 1952. Though thousands of admirers came to see his body lying in state, he was denied burial with national honors by the French government because of his membership in the Communist Party.

July 6

A Slumber Did My Spirit Seal

A slumber did my spirit seal;
    I had no human fears:
She seemed a thing that could not feel
    The touch of earthly years.

No motion has she now, no force;
    She neither hears nor sees;
Rolled round in earth's diurnal course,
    With rocks, and stones, and trees.

WILLIAM WORDSWORTH
(1770–1850)

"A Slumber Did My Spirit Seal" has been dated to 1799 and was composed while Wordsworth was traveling in Germany. Wordsworth sent it to his friend and collaborator Samuel Coleridge, who in turn forwarded it on to Tomas Poole, with this comment on the poem: "Some months ago Wordsworth transmitted to me a most sublime Epitaph . . . whether it had any reality, I cannot say. — Most probably, in some gloomier moment he had fancied the moment in which his Sister might die."

Question

Body my house
my horse my hound
what will I do
when you are fallen

Where will I sleep
How will I ride
What will I hunt

Where can I go
without my mount
all eager and quick
How will I know
in thicket ahead
is danger or treasure
when Body my good
bright dog is dead

How will it be
to lie in the sky
without roof or door
and wind for an eye
With cloud for shift
how will I hide?

MAY SWENSON
(1919–1989)

May Swenson was born in Logan, Utah, and educated at Utah State Agricultural College where she earned her B.S. She met Elizabeth Bishop, who would serve as a sort of mentor, at Yaddo in 1950, and the two became close correspondents and friends over the next twenty-odd years. At the time, Bishop wrote in a letter to Marianne Moore: "There's another girl [here at Yaddo] who writes poetry, May Swenson — not bad either." Swenson died of complications from chronic asthma at the age of seventy in Oceanview, Delaware. "Question" comes from a volume of poetry for children, *The Complete Poems to Solve.*

Riddle #60 (from the *Exeter Book*)

I was by the sand at the sea-wall once:
where the tide comes I kept my dwelling,
fast in my first seat. There were few indeed
of human kind who cared to behold
my homeland in that lonely place,
but in every dawning the dark wave
lapped about me. Little did I think
that early or late I ever should
speak across the meadbench, mouthless as I am,
compose a message. It is a mysterious thing,
dark to the mind that does not know,
how a knife's point and a clever hand,
a man's purpose and a point also,
have pressed upon me to the purpose that
I might fearlessly announce, for none but us two,
a message to you, so that no man beside
might spread abroad what is spoken between us.

ANONYMOUS
translated by Michael Alexander

Another of the ninety-five Anglo-Saxon riddles preserved in the *Exeter Book*, "Riddle #60" may be answered with *reed*. (See also: January 9 and May 20.)

Untitled

There's nothing now
We can't expect to happen!
Anything at all, you can bet,
Is ready to jump out at us.
No need to wonder over it.
Father Zeus has turned
Noon to night, blotting out
The sunshine utterly,
Putting cold terror
At the back of the throat.
Let's believe all we hear.
Even that dolphins and cows
Change places, porpoises and goats,
Rams booming along in the offing,
Mackerel nibbling in the hill pastures.
I wouldn't be surprised,
I wouldn't be surprised.

ARCHILOCHUS
(CA. SEVENTH CENTURY B.C.)
translated by Guy Davenport

One of the earliest notable poets after Homer, Archilochus of Páros lived in the middle of the seventh century B.C. His work survives only in fragments, of which this piece is one. Though little biographical information about Archilochus can be verified, some scholars credit him with the invention of the elegiac couplet. Ancient tradition holds that Archilochus was forbidden to marry Neobule by her father Lycambes, and in retaliation the poet wrote such venomous verses about the girl and her father that they hanged themselves in shame.

All Night by the Rose

All night by the rose, rose —
    All night by the rose I lay;
Dared I not the rose steal,
    And yet I bore the flower away.

ANONYMOUS

(CA. 1300)

This poem was written in Middle English. The original reads as follows:
    Al nist by þe rose, rose —
    al nist bi the rose i lay;
    darf ich noust þe rose stele,
    ant ʒet ich bar þe flour away.

Air

Naturally it is night.
Under the overturned lute with its
One string I am going my way
Which has a strange sound.

This way the dust, that way the dust.
I listen to both sides
But I keep right on.
I remember the leaves sitting in judgment
And then winter.

I remember the rain with its bundle of roads.
The rain taking all its roads.
Nowhere.

Young as I am, old as I am,

I forget tomorrow, the blind man.
I forget the life among the buried windows.
The eyes in the curtains.
The wall
Growing through the immortelles.
I forget silence
The owner of the smile.

This must be what I wanted to be doing,
Walking at night between the two deserts,
Singing.

W. S. Merwin
(1927–)

William Stanley Merwin was born in New York City and educated at Princeton University. Merwin has been awarded an impressive collection of honors, including a Pulitzer Prize. W. H. Auden selected Merwin's first book, *A Mask for Janus,* for the Yale Series of Younger Poets in 1952. Merwin later served as the judge for this same award. An active environmentalist, Merwin has lived in Hawaii, cultivating endangered plants, since 1970.

July 12

The River-Merchant's Wife: a Letter

While my hair was still cut straight across my forehead
I played about the front gate, pulling flowers.
You came by on bamboo stilts, playing horse,
You walked about my seat, playing with blue plums.
And we went on living in the village of Chokan:
Two small people, without dislike or suspicion.

At fourteen I married My Lord you.
I never laughed, being bashful.
Lowering my head, I looked at the wall.
Called to, a thousand times, I never looked back.

At fifteen I stopped scowling,
I desired my dust to be mingled with yours
Forever and forever and forever.
Why should I climb the look out?

At sixteen you departed,
You went into far Ku-to-yen, by the river of swirling eddies,
And you have been gone five months.
The monkeys make sorrowful noise overhead.

You dragged your feet when you went out.
By the gate now, the moss is grown, the different mosses,
Too deep to clear them away!
The leaves fall early this autumn, in wind.
The paired butterflies are already yellow with August
Over the grass in the West garden;

They hurt me. I grow older.
If you are coming down through the narrows of the river Kiang,
Please let me know before hand,
And I will come out to meet you
    As far as Cho-fu-Sa.

RIHAKU (LI PO)
(701–762)
translated by Ezra Pound

Rihaku is another name of the Chinese poet Li Po. Li Po lived in T'ang Dynasty China and his work shows influences of both Taoism and Ch'an (Zen) Buddhism. Chokan, in line five, is a suburb of Nanking. Cho-fu-Sa in the last line is several hundred miles upriver from Nanking. Cho-fu-Sa is also known as Chang-feng Sha and can be literally translated "the Long Wind Beach." This version of the poem is one made famous by Ezra Pound. David Hinton has also translated the poem, though he titles it "Ch'ang-Kan Village Song" and argues that there is no evidence in the original to suggest that the speaker's husband is a river merchant and supposes Li Po may have been thinking of his own wife when composing the poem.

Autistic Child, No Longer Child

Flywheel, whirligig, hummingbird, singing the same
cruel tune, a drone, a dirge, a nursery tune, which year
have we now, which birthday? — kitchen-bright the eyes,
rubber-smooth the skin,
your gaze slyly hooded,
your grin fierce in place.

So quick! — so cute! — monkey-nimble in your mock dance,
which season is this now, which anniversary, inside
the rocking waste motion, left to right to left,
the silence you wetly chew like your lips, the lullaby,
the hum, left to right, which year? — inside your empty stare,
what voltage?

        I cannot look into you
as into a mirror, though you mirror me, sister,
and were born on my birthday eighteen years after me
and late, very late.

Now you crackle with spirit, on Sundays most dead,
now you navigate the room, left to right, the relentless tune,
the moon-blank stare, what year have we now, what weather? —
how far it carries, your cheerful baby-dirge!

You hear us but will not, O never!
You see us but cannot, O no one dares force you,
what an insult to your soul!

To touch you, sister, is to feel that voltage.

To touch you, sister, is not our privilege.

JOYCE CAROL OATES
(1938–)

Joyce Carol Oates was born in Lockport, New York. She received a B.A. from
Syracuse University and an M.A. from the University of Wisconsin. She is a prolific
writer of novels and criticism in addition to poetry, and she is a playwright as well.
Oates won a National Book Award in 1970 for her fourth novel, *Them*. She is the
Roger S. Berlind '52 Professor in the Humanities at Princeton University.

from *Romeo and Juliet*
Act II, Scene ii

But, soft! what light from yonder window breaks?
It is the east, and Juliet is the sun!
Arise, fair sun, and kill the envious moon,
Who is already sick and pale with grief,
That thou her maid art far more fair than she:
Be not her maid, since she is envious;
Her vestal livery is but sick and green,
And none but fools do wear it; cast it off.
It is my lady; O! it is my love:
O! that she knew she were.
She speaks, yet she says nothing: what of that?
Her eye discourses; I will answer it.
I am too bold, 'tis not to me she speaks:
Two of the fairest stars in all the heaven,
Having some business, do entreat her eyes
to twinkle in their spheres till they return.
What if her eyes were there, they in her head?
The brightness of her cheek would shame those stars
As daylight doth a lamp; her eyes in heaven
Would through the airy region stream so bright
That birds would sing and think it were not night.
See! how she leans her cheek upon her hand:
O! that I were a glove upon that hand,
That I might touch that cheek.

WILLIAM SHAKESPEARE
(1564–1616)

A love-struck Romeo speaks this poem from the garden below Juliet's window after meeting her at the masquerade ball. His professed deep feelings for Rosalind so in evidence only hours before have been obliterated by the sunlight that is Juliet's beauty. Just after this speech, Juliet answers with one of her own, beginning with the famous lines "Romeo, O Romeo. Wherefore art thou, Romeo. / Deny thy father and refuse thy name!"

July 15

1079. Written after thieves had broken into his hut

At least the robbers
    left this one thing behind —
moon in my window.

MONK RYŌKAN

(1758–1831)

translated by Steven D. Carter

Ryōkan was born in Echigo, Niigata Prefecture, the eldest son of a Shinto priest. He entered the Soto sect of Zen Buddhism at the age of seventeen and later became a Buddhist monk and Zen master. Ryōkan lived an austere existence in a mountain he called "Gogo An" and supported himself by the traditional practice of begging. He wrote *waka,* a specialized form of the *tanka,* in Japanese, as well as *kanshi* in Chinese.

England in 1819

An old, mad, blind, despised, and dying king —
Princes, the dregs of their dull race, who flow
Through public scorn — mud from a muddy spring;
Rulers who neither see, nor feel, nor know,
But leechlike to their fainting country cling,
Till they drop, blind in blood, without a blow;
A people starved and stabbed in the untilled field —
An army, which liberticide and prey
Makes as a two-edged sword to all who wield;
Golden and sanguine laws which tempt and slay;
Religion Christless, Godless — a book sealed;
A Senate — Time's worst statute unrepealed —
Are graves, from which a glorious phantom may
Burst, to illumine our tempestuous day.

PERCY BYSSHE SHELLEY
(1792–1822)

English Romantic poet Percy Bysshe Shelley was born in Field Place, near Horsham, Sussex. In 1816, after his first wife committed suicide, Shelley married Mary Wollstonecraft Godwin, the future author of *Frankenstein*. The couple left England in 1818 and traveled in Italy with the infamous George Gordon, Lord Byron, Leigh Hunt, and other members of the so-called Pisan Circle. Shelley drowned at the age of twenty-nine, attempting to sail from Leghorn to La Spezia, Italy, during a violent storm. As the title suggests, this sonnet was composed in 1819, and Shelley sent it off in a letter to Hunt, then editor of *The Examiner*. "I don't expect you to publish it," he wrote, "but you may show it to whomever you wish." "England in 1819" was not in fact published until the posthumous collection edited by Mary Shelley appeared in 1839.

The Day Lady Died

It is 12:20 in New York a Friday
three days after Bastille day, yes
it is 1959 and I go get a shoeshine
because I will get off the 4:19 in Easthampton
at 7:15 and then go straight to dinner
and I don't know the people who will feed me

I walk up the muggy street beginning to sun
and have a hamburger and a malted and buy
an ugly NEW WORLD WRITING to see what the poets
in Ghana are doing these days
                                                    I go on to the bank
and Miss Stillwagon (first name Linda I once heard)
doesn't even look up my balance for once in her life
and in the GOLDEN GRIFFIN I get a little Verlaine
for Patsy with drawings by Bonnard although I do
think of Hesiod, trans. Richmond Lattimore or
Brendan Behan's new play or *Le Balcon* or *Les Nègres*
of Genet, but I don't, I stick with Verlaine
after practically going to sleep with quandariness

and for Mike I just stroll into the PARK LANE
Liquor Store and ask for a bottle of Strega and
then I go back where I came from to 6th Avenue
and the tobacconist in the Ziegfeld Theatre and
casually ask for a carton of Gauloises and a carton
of Picayunes, and a NEW YORK POST with her face on it

and I am sweating a lot by now and thinking of
leaning on the john door in the 5 SPOT
while she whispered a song along the keyboard
to Mal Waldron and everyone and I stopped breathing

FRANK O'HARA
(1926–1966)

Francis Russell O'Hara was born in Baltimore, Maryland, and educated at Harvard, where he majored in music and met fellow poets John Ashbery and Kenneth Koch. These three, along with James Schuyler, would later come together in New York and eventually become known as the founders of the so-called New York School of poetry. Gregarious and energetic, O'Hara often composed poems on the fly, while running from his job as curator at the Museum of Modern Art to meet a friend in Greenwich village and back again. His *Lunch Poems* is arguably the best-known example of his "I do this I do that" style of poetry, and it was a popular success when it was published in 1964. O'Hara was killed at the age of forty in a tragic accident on Fire Island: He was hit by a dune buggy traversing the beach at night. "The Day Lady Died" is O'Hara's casual, yet moving elegy for Billie Holiday, who died of a heroin overdose on July 17, 1959. The Five Spot, mentioned three lines from the end, was a popular jazz club where O'Hara and his circle also frequently gave poetry readings.

The Sound of Trees

I wonder about the trees.
Why do we wish to bear
Forever the noise of these
More than another noise
So close to our dwelling place?
We suffer them by the day
Till we lose all measure of place,
And fixity in our joys,
And acquire a listening air.
They are that that talks of going
But never gets away;
And that talks no less for knowing,
As it grows wiser and older,
That now it means to stay.
My feet tug at the floor
And my head sways to my shoulder
Sometimes when I watch trees sway,
From the window or the door.
I shall set forth for somewhere,
I shall make the reckless choice
Some day when they are in voice
And tossing so as to scare
The white clouds over them on.
I shall have less to say,
But I shall be gone.

ROBERT FROST
(1874–1963)

Though known best for his poems set in snowy New England, Robert Frost was born in San Francisco, California. He dropped out of Dartmouth after less than one semester, but later attended Harvard for eighteen months. Though he wrote steadily, by the time he was forty Frost had managed to publish only in small literary journals and remained obscure. In 1912, Frost moved his family to England, where he finally published his first book. He also met Ezra Pound, who became an important facilitator in Frost's career. Frost returned to the United States in 1915 and discovered that he had become a star poet. He became a national figure when he read a poem at the inauguration of President John F. Kennedy. Frost won most of the major awards for poetry, including four Pulitzer Prizes.

The Infinite

This lonely hill was always dear to me,
And this hedgerow, that hides so large a part
Of the far sky-line from my view. Sitting and gazing
I fashion in my mind what lie beyond —
Unearthly silences, and endless space,
And very deepest quiet; until almost
My heart becomes afraid. And when I hear
The wind come blustering among the trees
I set that voice against this infinite silence:
And then I call to mind Eternity,
The ages that are dead, and the living present
And all the noise of it. And thus it is
In that immensity my thought is drowned:
And sweet to me the foundering in that sea.

GIACOMO LEOPARDI
(1798–1837)
translated by John Heath-Stubbs

Giacomo Leopardi was born to an aristocratic family in Recanati, Italy. An extremely bright child whose parents hoped he would be a scholar and cleric, Leopardi was tutored in Latin, Spanish, French, theology, history, rhetoric, science, and mathematics. He soon outpaced his teachers and in his teens continued his studies on his own in his father's library, learning Greek, Hebrew, English, and German. Leopardi later came to blame these years of intense study for his various physical ailments, including a severely malformed spine, near blindness, and weakness of the heart, bones, and lungs. He died at the age of thirty-eight, after contracting cholera in an outbreak at Naples. Leopardi wrote "The Infinite" sometime between 1818 and 1822.

From Outer Space

Moving & delicate
                    we saw you
that time, fragile as a raindrop
                                    you seemed then
shining & vulnerable,   in colors
we had not known to be yours,
                                    rare, jewel-like,
but more alive than a jewel,
                              grained & printed,
scratched by the finger-nails of living,
                                    a thousand
ways of life, millions, even,
                                    with that first
lifting of man's foot,   heavy on
the surface of the stony moon-rock   we saw you
for the first time, earth, our earth, young,
fresh, bestowed on us as new,   newest of
all possible new stars,   even knowing you
stained, soiled & trampled
                              by our filth,
all of it transmuted somehow into living sapphire.
emerald breathing,   topaz, carnelian   alight with
fire
          O small bell,   lit with living,
swinging into danger —
                              where is our tenderness
enough to care for you?

HILDA MORLEY
(1919–1998)

Hilda Morley was born Hilda Auerbach in New York, New York. Though she wrote poetry from the age of nine and published widely in literary journals, her first book, *A Blessing Outside Us,* did not appear until 1976 when she was already fifty-five years old. She once remarked to *Contemporary Authors,* "The capacity to look and to imagine freed me from confusion. They were my windows, connecting me to the world and the poems were a way of giving back what had been given me — the gifts and offerings the visible, tangible, audible world gave me." Morley died of liver failure at the age of seventy-nine.

July 21

Let Evening Come

Let the light of late afternoon
shine through chinks in the barn, moving
up the bales as the sun moves down.

Let the cricket take up chafing
as a woman takes up her needles
and her yarn. Let evening come.

Let dew collect on the hoe abandoned
in long grass. Let the stars appear
and the moon disclose her silver horn.

Let the fox go back to its sandy den.
Let the wind die down. Let the shed
go black inside. Let evening come.

To the bottle in the ditch, to the scoop
in the oats, to air in the lung
let evening come.

Let it come, as it will, and don't
be afraid. God does not leave us
comfortless, so let evening come.

JANE KENYON
(1947–1995)

Jane Kenyon was born in Ann Arbor, Michigan, and educated at the University of Michigan. In 1972 she married the poet Donald Hall and the couple settled at Eagle Pond Farm in Wilmot, New Hampshire. She wrote four books of poetry and acclaimed translations of the work of Anna Akhmatova. Kenyon was poet laureate of New Hampshire at the time of her death from leukemia in 1995.

July 22

Weeds as Partial Survivors

The chorus of the weeds, unnameably
profuse, sings Courage, Courage, like
an India of unemployables who have
no other word to say and say it.
Too bendable to break, bowing away
together from the wind although
the hail or hurricane can knock them flat,
they rise up wet by morning. This
morning erection of the weeds
is not so funny: It
is perseverance dancing: some of them,
the worst, are barely rooted and
a lady gardener can pull them out
ungloved. Nevertheless, they do do
what they do or die, surviving all
catastrophes except the human: they
extend their glosses, like the words I said,
on sun-cracked margins of the sown
lines of our harrowed grains.

ALAN DUGAN
(1923–)

Alan Dugan was born in Brooklyn, New York. He received his B.A. from Mexico City College and was drafted into the Army Air Forces during World War II. He won the Pulitzer Prize for poetry in 1962. He is a member of the faculty at the Fine Arts Work Center in Provincetown, Massachusetts. In a 2001 interview with Linda Wertheimer on NPR's *All Things Considered,* Dugan remarked, "You can't say poetry should be about something or shouldn't be about something. Poems are, the poem is, and that is all there is to it."

July 23

A Silent Love

The lowest trees have tops, the ant her gall,
The fly her spleen, the little spark his heat;
The slender hairs cast shadows, though but small,
And bees have stings, although they be not great;
 Seas have their source, and so have shallow springs;
 And love is love, in beggars and in kings.

Where waters smoothest run, there deepest are the fords,
The dial stirs, yet none perceives it move;
The firmest faith is found in fewest words,
The turtles do not sing, and yet they love;
 True hearts have ears and eyes, no tongues to speak;
 They hear and see, and sigh, and then they break.

SIR EDWARD DYER
(1543–1607)

Edward Dyer was born in Sharpham Park, Somersetshire, England, and knighted by
Queen Elizabeth I in 1596. A mostly successful courtier, Dyer was sent on a number
of official missions by the queen and served in the British Parliament in 1589 and
again in 1593. He is thought to be among the earliest of Elizabeth's courtiers to write
vernacular love poetry, and he is closely associated with Sir Philip Sidney, who
exerted a powerful influence on his later work. Dyer contracted tuberculosis in 1573,
though he managed to survive to the age of sixty-four.

July 24

Poem

I'm inside the advancing light,
my hands are hungry, the world beautiful.

My eyes can't get enough of the trees —
they're so hopeful, so green.

A sunny road runs through the mulberries,
I'm at the window of the prison infirmary.

I can't smell the medicines —
carnations must be blooming somewhere.

It's like this:
being captured is beside the point,
the point is not to surrender.

NAZIM HIKMET
(1902–1963)
translated by Randy Blasing and Mutlu Konuk

Turkish poet Nazim Hikmet was born in Salonika, Greece, when it was under
Turkish rule. He went to Russia in 1921 to study at the University of the Workers of
the East and returned to Turkey in 1924. A staunch communist in a country that
forbade communism, Hikmet found his poems, plays, and prose banned in Turkey
during most of his lifetime. Because he refused to remain silent about his political
beliefs he was imprisoned a number of times, his longest term in jail lasting about
twelve years. In 1950, after an international protest of prominent intellectuals helped
secure his release from yet another prison sentence, Hikmet shared the International
Peace Prize with Pablo Neruda.

The Woodspurge

The wind flapped loose, the wind was still,
Shaken out dead from tree and hill:
I had walked on at the wind's will, —
I sat now, for the wind was still.

Between my knees my forehead was, —
My lips, drawn in, said not Alas!
My hair was over in the grass,
My naked ears heard the day pass.

My eyes, wide open, had the run
Of some ten weeds to fix upon;
Among those few, out of the sun,
The woodspurge flowered, three cups in one.

From perfect grief there need not be
Wisdom or even memory:
One thing then learnt remains to me, —
The woodspurge has a cup of three.

DANTE GABRIEL ROSSETTI
(1828–1882)

Dante Gabriel Rossetti was born in London to Italian parents and was the older brother to poet Christina Rossetti. Like William Blake, Rossetti possessed a rare double gift for both writing and painting and is considered a master artist. The woodspurge, a plant of the genus *Euphorbia,* has large, cup-shaped flowers. This poem was composed in 1856 and first published in 1870 in a volume simply titled *Poems.*

Preface to a Twenty Volume Suicide Note
(for Kellie Jones, Born 16 May 1959)

Lately, I've become accustomed to the way
The ground opens up and envelops me
Each time I go out to walk the dog.
Or the broad-edged silly music the wind
Makes when I run for a bus . . .

Things have come to that.

And now, each night I count the stars,
And each night I get the same number.
And when they will not come to be counted,
I count the holes they leave.

Nobody sings anymore.

And then last night, I tiptoed up
To my daughter's room and heard her
Talking to someone, and when I opened
The door, there was no one there . . .
Only she on her knees, peeking into

Her own clasped hands.

IMAMU AMIRI BARAKA
(1934–)

Imamu Amiri Baraka was born Everett LeRoi Jones in Newark, New Jersey. He received his B.A. from Howard University, an M.A. in philosophy from Columbia University, and an M.A. in German literature from the New School for Social Research. He served in the U.S. Air Force from 1954 until 1957 as a weather-gunner. In 1965, after the assassination of Malcolm X, he changed his name from LeRoi Jones to Amiri Baraka and in 1969 he adopted the title Imamu, which means "spiritual leader." He lives with his wife Amina Baraka in Newark, New Jersey, where he co-directs Kimako's Blues People, a community art space. In 2002 he was appointed Poet Laureate of New Jersey. This is the title poem from his first book, published in 1961.

Look into Thought

Look into thought and say what dost thou see,
   Dive, be not fearful, how dark the waves flow,
Sink through the surge, and bring pearls up to me,
   Deeper, ay, deeper; the fairest lie low.

I have dived, I have sought them, but none have I found,
   In the gloom that closed o'er me no form floated by,
As I sunk through the void depths so black and profound
   How dim died the sun and how far hung the sky!

What had I given to hear the soft sweep
   Of a breeze bearing life through that vast realm of death!
Thoughts were untroubled and dreams were asleep,
   The spirit lay dreadless and hopeless beneath.

CHARLOTTE BRONTË
(1816–1855)

Older sister to Emily and Anne Brontë, Charlotte Brontë was born in Yorkshire, England. At the age of twenty, she wrote to English Poet Laureate Robert Southey, asking him his advice about her writing. He replied "Literature cannot be the business of a woman's life: & it ought not to be. The more she is engaged in her proper duties, the less leisure she will have for it, even as an accomplishment and a recreation. To those duties you have not yet been called & when you are you will be less eager for celebrity." Brontë marked the letter "Southey's Advice / To be kept forever," though she obviously disregarded his remarks. Though she wrote and published poems under the pseudonym Currer Bell, she eventually gave up poetry after she became well known for her novel *Jane Eyre*, published in 1847. Charlotte Brontë died in childbirth at the age of thirty-nine.

He or She That's Got the Limb,
That Holds Me Out on It

The girls are drifting in their ponytails
and their pig iron boat. So much for Sunday.
The dodo birds are making a racket
to beat the band. You could have come too.

The girls wave and throw their garters
from their pig iron boat. Why is this charming?
Where they were nailed on their knees
the garters all rip. You were expected.

The youngest sees a Fury in a Sentra
in a cloud. This is her imitation and she balks.
The boat begins rocking from the scourge
of the sunset. The youngest starts the song.

SUSAN WHEELER
(1955–)

Susan Wheeler was born in Pittsburgh, Pennsylvania. She is a member of the faculty of the graduate creative writing program at the New School and also teaches at Princeton University.

Untitled

Disheveled, drunk, and cup in hand, clothes torn
and fragrant with the scent of wine, a song
upon her lips, eyes bright and quarrelsome,
love came to sit beside my bed last night.
She bowed her head down close to mine,
and whispered sadly in my ear, "Ah, love,
old love, why are you sleeping still?" A lover
whom they give a draught like this to greet
the morning sun, would be a renegade
to Love, should he not worship wine.
Ascetic! Hypocrite! Be still! Don't scold
us if we drain the cup. The day we pledged
our souls this was our only gift. Whether
it's from paradise or comes from earthly vines,
we drink the measure He poured out for us.
Ah, Hafez! How many fine resolutions
have, like yours, been shattered by a softly
twining tress and the laughter of the grape!

HAFEZ
(1326–1389)
translated by J. W. Clinton

Sufi master and Persian poet Khwaja Shams sd-Din Mohammad of Shiraz is better
known by the name Hafez (or Hafiz), which literally means "memorizer of the
Koran." Writing in the fourteenth century, Hafez experienced wide popularity for
his *ghazals* and ecstatic poems on the subject of love. Ralph Waldo Emerson, who
first read Hafez in a German translation and later translated him into English, refers
to Hafez frequently in his journals and notebooks, once writing that "Hafiz defies
you to show him or put him in a condition inopportune and ignoble. Take all you
will, and leave him but a corner of Nature, a lane, a den, a cowshed, out of cities,
far from letters and taste and culture; he promises to win to that scorned spot, the
light of moon and stars, the love of men, the smile of beauty, the homage of art."

To Mistress Margaret Hussey

Mirry Margaret,
As midsomer flowre,
Jentill as faucoun
Or hawke of the towre;
    With solace and gladnes,
Moche mirthe and no madnes,
all good and no badnes,
So joyously,
So maidenly,
So womanly
Her demening
In every thinge,
Far, far passinge
That I can endight,
Or suffice to wright
Of mirry Margarete,
As midsomer flowre,
Jentill as facoun
Or hawke of the towre;
    As pacient and as still,
And as full of good will,
As faire Ysaphill;
Coliaunder,
Swete pomaunder,
Good Cassaunder;
Steadfast of thought,
Wele made, wele wrought;
Far may be sought
Erst that ye can finde

So corteise, so kinde
As mirry Margarete,
This midsomer flowre,
Jentill as faucoun
Or hawke of the towre.

JOHN SKELTON
(1460–1529)

English poet John Skelton was fluent in French, Latin, and Greek. Educated at
Oxford and Cambridge, he was employed as the tutor to Prince Henry, later King
Henry VIII. Though not officially appointed by the monarch, Skelton frequently
referred to himself as "poet laureate" and was in fact honored as such by both Oxford
and Cambridge. His rhymed, short-lined style became so popular and was so widely
imitated that his signature form is now known as Skeltonics. The addressee of this
poem, Margaret Hussey, though she has not been identified with certainty, is thought
to perhaps be a stand-in for the daughter of Simon Blount of Mangotsfield and the
wife of John Hussey. "Margaret" is another word for daisy, a "midsummer flower."

July 31

Siren

I have a fish's tail, so I'm not qualified to love you.
But I do. Pale as an August sky, pale as flour milled
a thousand times, pale as the icebergs I have never seen,
and twice as numb — my skin is such a contrast to the rough
rocks I lie on, that from far away it looks like I'm a baby
riding a dinosaur. The turn of centuries or the turn
of a page means the same to me, little or nothing.
I have teeth in places you'd never suspect. Come. Kiss me
and die soon. I slap my tail in the shallows — which is to say
I appreciate nature. You see my sisters and me perched
on rocks and tiny islands here and there for miles:
untangling our hair with our fingers, eating seaweed.

AMY GERSTLER
(1956–)

Amy Gerstler was born in San Diego, California, and writes fiction and art criticism in addition to poetry. Gerstler is on the graduate faculty in creative writing at Antioch University, Los Angeles, and is also a graduate adviser at Art Center College of Design in Pasadena.

August on Sourdough, A Visit from Dick Brewer

You hitched a thousand miles
    north from San Francisco
Hiked up the mountainside a mile in the air
The little cabin — one room —
    walled in glass
Meadows and snowfields hundreds of peaks.
We lay in our sleeping bags
    talking half the night;
Wind in the guy-cables summer mountain rain.
Next morning I went with you
    as far as the cliffs,
Loaned you my poncho — the rain across the shale —
You down the snowfield
    flapping in the wind
Waving a last goodbye half hidden in the clouds
To go on hitching
    clear to New York;
Me back to my mountain and far, far, west.

GARY SNYDER
(1930–)

Gary Snyder was born in San Francisco, California, and grew up on his family's small dairy farm ten miles north of Seattle. He earned his B.A. from Reed College in Portland, Oregon, where he roomed with poet Philip Whalen and majored in philosophy and literature. He went on to study Oriental languages at the University of California, Berkeley. A major figure in the San Francisco Renaissance, in 1955 Snyder took part in the reading at the Six Gallery at which Allen Ginsberg first read *Howl.* Snyder moved to Japan in 1956 on a scholarship from the First Zen Institute of America and began to practice Zen Buddhism, returning to the United States in 1968. He has been awarded the Pulitzer Prize among other honors. Snyder is a Professor of English at the University of California, Davis.

Summer

Ah, what a pleasure
    to cross a stream in summer —
sandals in hand.

YOSA BUSON
(1716–1784)
translated by Steven D. Carter

After Bashō, Yosa Buson is considered the second of the Four Great Masters of Haiku. Buson made his living as a painter and brought many of the images of Southern Chinese painting into Japanese art. These same visual images, painted in words, distinguished Buson's poetry from that of his contemporaries. A fervent admirer of Bashō, Buson wrote several pieces lamenting the loss of Bashō's wisdom and helped to revive interest in the deceased master's work. In addition to haiku and the occasional *renga*, Buson also wrote poetry in Chinese and experimented with other Japanese forms.

Meditation at Lagunitas

All the new thinking is about loss.
In this it resembles all the old thinking.
The idea, for example, that each particular erases
the luminous clarity of a general idea. That the clown-
faced woodpecker probing the dead sculpted trunk
of that black birch is, by his presence,
some tragic falling off from a first world
of undivided light. Or the other notion that,
because there is in this world no one thing
to which the bramble of *blackberry* corresponds,
a word is elegy to what it signifies.
We talked about it late last night and in the voice
of my friend, there was a thin wire of grief, a tone
almost querulous. After a while I understood that,
talking this way, everything dissolves: *justice,*
pine, hair, woman, you and *I.* There was a woman
I made love to and I remembered how, holding
her small shoulders in my hands sometimes,
I felt a violent wonder at her presence
like a thirst for salt, for my childhood river
with its island willows, silly music from the pleasure boat,
muddy places where we caught the little orange-silver fish
called *pumpkinseed.* It hardly had to do with her.
Longing, we say, because desire is full
of endless distances. I must have been the same to her.
But I remember so much, the way her hands dismantled bread,

the thing her father said that hurt her, what
she dreamed. There are moments when the body is as numinous
as words, days that are the good flesh continuing.
Such tenderness, those afternoons and evenings,
saying *blackberry, blackberry, blackberry.*

ROBERT HASS
(1941–)

Robert Hass was born in San Francisco, California. He earned his B.A. from St. Mary's College of California and his M.A. and Ph.D. from Stanford University. Stanley Kunitz selected Hass's first book, *Field Guide,* for the Yale Series of Younger Poets in 1973. Hass served as Poet Laureate of the United States from 1995 until 1997 and is currently a Chancellor of the Academy of American Poets. He teaches at the University of California, Berkeley.

Her Kind

I have gone out, a possessed witch,
haunting the black air, braver at night;
dreaming evil, I have done my hitch
over the plain houses, light by light:
lonely thing, twelve-fingered, out of mind.
A woman like that is not a woman, quite.
I have been her kind.

I have found the warm caves in the woods,
filled them with skillets, carvings, shelves,
closets, silks, innumerable goods;
fixed the suppers for the worms and the elves:
whining, rearranging the disaligned.
A woman like that is misunderstood.
I have been her kind.

I have ridden in your cart, driver,
waved my nude arms at villages going by,
learning the last bright routes, survivor
where your flames still bite my thigh
and my ribs crack where your wheels wind.
A woman like that is not ashamed to die.
I have been her kind.

ANNE SEXTON
(1928–1974)

Born in Newton, Massachusetts, Anne Sexton began writing poetry after a break-down, while being treated at Glenside Hospital. She later studied with Robert Lowell, and she went on to win the Pulitzer Prize in 1967 for her book *Live or Die*. "Her Kind" was included in her first book, *To Bedlam and Part Way Back*. She committed suicide in 1974.

August 5

Sonnet VII

At the round earths imagin'd corners, blow
Your trumpets, Angells, and arise, arise
From death, you numberlesse infinities
Of soules, and to your scattred bodies goe,
All whom the flood did, and fire shall o'erthrow,
All whom warre, dearth, age, agues, tyrannies,
Despaire, law, chance, hath slaine, and you whose eyes,
Shall behold God, and never tast deaths woe.
But let them sleepe, Lord, and mee mourne a space,
For, if above all these, my sinnes abound,
'Tis late to aske abundance of thy grace,
When wee are there; here on this lowly ground,
Teach mee how to repent; for that's as good
As if thou'hadst seal'd my pardon, with thy blood.

JOHN DONNE
(1572–1631)

"Sonnet VII" is one of John Donne's so-called "Holy Sonnets," a sequence of nine-teen poems, most of which have been dated to 1609, though a few were composed much later. The first line echoes *Revelations* 7:1: "I saw four angels standing in the four corners of the earth." "Sonnet VII" was first published in 1633.

Advice to a Prophet

When you come, as you soon must, to the streets of our city,
Mad-eyed from stating the obvious,
Not proclaiming our fall but begging us
In God's name to have self-pity,

Spare us all word of the weapons, their force and range,
The long numbers that rocket the mind;
Our slow, unreckoning hearts will be left behind,
Unable to fear what is too strange.

Nor shall you scare us with talk of the death of the race.
How should we dream of this place without us? —
The sun mere fire, the leaves untroubled about us,
A stone look on the stone's face?

Speak of the world's own change. Though we cannot conceive
Of an undreamt thing, we know to our cost
How the dreamt cloud crumbles, the vines are blackened by frost,
How the view alters. We could believe,

If you told us so, that the white-tailed deer will slip
Into perfect shade, grown perfectly shy,
The lark avoid the reaches of our eye,
The jack-pine lose its knuckled grip

On the cold ledge, and every torrent burn
As Xanthus once, its gliding trout
Stunned in a twinkling. What should we be without
The dolphin's arc, the dove's return,

These things in which we have seen ourselves and spoken?
Ask us, prophet, how we shall call
Our natures forth when that live tongue is all
Dispelled, that glass obscured or broken

In which we have said the rose of our love and the clean
Horse of our courage, in which beheld
The singing locust of the soul unshelled,
And all we mean or wish to mean.

Ask us, ask us whether with the worldless rose
Our hearts shall fail us; come demanding
Whether there shall be lofty or long standing
When the bronze annals of the oak-tree close.

RICHARD WILBUR
(1921–)

Richard Wilbur was born in New York City and grew up in North Caldwell, New Jersey. He published his first book, *The Beautiful Changes and Other Poems,* just months after his twenty-sixth birthday, shortly after serving as a sergeant of the Thirty-sixth Infantry in World War II. He went on to win two Pulitzers and a National Book Award, and he served as United States Poet Laureate from 1987 to 1988. Speaking to an interviewer, Wilbur once remarked, "You don't necessarily read a poem and pick up the telephone. But something you might call 'tonalizing' does occur, a preparation to feel in a certain way, and consequently to act in a certain way. That does occur, I think, when you read a poem which goes to the words that are bothering you. I suppose you can't expect, by means of a poem, to produce a perfect *volte face* in anybody; that would be very presumptuous; even a propagandist doesn't expect to do that; but you can help a man to see what he may be about to see."

from *The Descent of Alette*

"A woman came into" "a car I rode" "about thirty-seven" "maybe
forty" "Face" "a harsh response to" "what she did" "had to do"
"face rigid" "but she was beautiful" "Was," "we could see,"
"one of the ones who" "strip for coins" "on the subway —"

"They simply" "very quickly" ("illegally") "remove all their
clothes" "Stand, for a moment" "Turning to face" "each end"
"of the car" "Then dress quickly," "pass quickly" "the cup."
"But she — this one —" "face of hating to so much that" "as she

took off her blouse," "her face" "began to change" "Grew
feathers, a small beak" "& by the time she was naked," "she wore the
head" "of an eagle" "a crowned eagle" "a raptor" "herself —
"And as she stood" "& faced the car" "her body" "was changing"

"was becoming entirely" "that bird" "those wings," "she shrank to
become the bird" "but grew wings that" "were wider" "than she had been
tall" "Instantly," "instantly, a man caught her" "A cop came"
"As if ready" "as if they knew" "Her wings were clipped,"

"talons cut" "as if as quickly" "as possible" "She was released
then, to the car" "to the subway" "Perched" "on the bar the
straps hang from"

ALICE NOTLEY
(1945–)

Alice Notley was born in Bisbee, Arizona, and grew up in Needles, California. She
received a B.A. from Barnard College and an M.F.A. from the University of Iowa.
An important figure in the poetry scene of the Lower East Side of Manhattan,
Notley is associated with the second generation of the New York School poets. *The
Descent of Alette* was published in 1996 and, as Notley explains in a note in that
volume, the quotation marks are "there, mostly, to measure the poem. The phrases
they enclose are poetic feet. If I had simply left white spaces between the phrases, the
phrases would be rushed by the reader—read too fast for my musical intention."

The Minimal

I study the lives on a leaf: the little
Sleepers, numb nudgers in cold dimensions,
Beetles in caves, newts, stone-deaf fishes,
Lice tethered to long limp subterranean weeds,
Squirmers in bogs,
And bacterial creepers
Wriggling through wounds
Like elvers in ponds,
Their wan mouths kissing the warm sutures,
Cleaning and caressing,
Creeping and healing.

Theodore Roethke
(1908–1963)

While Roethke was still in grade school, he wrote an essay concerning America's responsibility to aid poorer nations which he entered in a contest sponsored by the Junior Red Cross. The essay proved so popular that it was eventually translated into twenty-six languages and distributed internationally, more widely than any of Roethke's later poems. Roethke published his first poems in the May–June 1930 issues of *The Harp*, during his first year at University of Michigan Law School. He dropped out of the law program soon afterward, transferred to the Graduate School in English, and then later transferred to Harvard to continue his studies. He dropped out again and suffered the first of several mental breakdowns in 1931. After his recovery at Mercywood, a private hospital in Ann Arbor, he finished his M.A. at Michigan and began applying for teaching jobs. At Bennington College in Vermont he told an interviewer, "I may look like a beer salesman, but I'm a poet."

Myra

I, with whose colours Myra dressed her head,
I, that ware posies of her own hand-making,
I, that mine own name in the chimneys read
By Myra finely wrought ere I was waking;
Must I look on, in hope time coming may
With change bring back my turn again to play?

I, that on Sunday at the church-stile found
A garland sweet, with true-love knots in flowers,
Which I to wear about mine arm was bound,
That each of us might know that all was ours;
Must I now lead an idle life in wishes,
And follow Cupid for his loaves and fishes?

I, that did wear the ring her mother left,
I, for whose love she gloried to be blamed,
I, with whose eyes her eyes committed theft,
I, who did make her blush when I was named;
Must I lose ring, flowers, blush, theft, and go naked,
Watching with sighs till dead love be awaked?

I, that, when drowsy Argus fell asleep,
Like jealousy o'erwatched with desire,
Was even warnéd modesty to keep,
While her breath, speaking, kindled Nature's fire;
Must I look on a-cold, while others warm them?
Do Vulcan's brothers in such fine nets arm them?

Was it for this that I might Myra see
Washing the water with her beauties white?
Yet would she never write her love to me.
Thinks wit of change, while thoughts are in delight?
Mad girls must safely love as they may leave;
No man can print a kiss: lines may deceive.

FULKE GREVILLE, LORD BROOKE
(1554–1628)

Fulke Greville was born into a family of wealthy landowners in Warwickshire, England. He and Philip Sidney became friends in grade school and remained close throughout their lives. Greville was knighted in 1597 and was a favorite of Queen Elizabeth. He was stabbed to death by a servant in his home in Warwick Castle, after the servant learned he would not be included in Greville's will. The servant then turned the knife on himself. "Myra" is also known as "Sonnet 22 from *Caelica*" and is from a cycle of more than one hundred sonnets addressed to three ladies named Caelica, Myra, and Cynthia, first published in 1633. Greville's own note on the sequence claims that the poems were written "in his youth and familiar exercise with Sir Philip Sidney" and so have been dated prior to Sidney's death in 1586. Line three refers to the period custom of writing the name of one's lover in the soot from a chimney.

My Mother Once Told Me

My mother once told me
Not to sleep with flowers in the room.
Since then I have not slept with flowers.
I sleep alone, without them.

There were many flowers.
But I've never had enough time.
And persons I love are already pushing themselves
Away from my life, like boats
Away from the shore.

My mother said
Not to sleep with flowers.
You won't sleep.
You won't sleep, mother of my childhood.

The bannister I clung to
When they dragged me off to school
Is long since burnt.
But my hands, clinging,
Remain
Clinging.

YEHUDA AMICHAI
(1924–2000)
translated by Assia Gutmann

Israeli poet Yehuda Amichai was born in Wurzburg, Germany, and emigrated with his
family to Palestine in 1936. He later became an Israeli citizen and master-sergeant in
the Israeli army. Though German was his native language, Amichai wrote his poetry
and fiction in Hebrew, which he had mastered at a young age. He received the Israel
Prize for Poetry in 1982 and his work has been translated into thirty-seven languages.

August II

Looking West from Laguna Beach at Night

I've always liked the view from my mother-in-law's house at night,
Oil rigs off Long Beach
Like floating lanterns out in the smog-dark Pacific,
Stars in the eucalyptus,
Lights of airplanes arriving from Asia, and town lights
Littered like broken glass around the bay and back up the hill.

In summer, dance music is borne up
On the sea winds from the hotel's beach deck far below,
"Twist and Shout," or "Begin the Beguine."
It's nice to think that somewhere someone is having a good time,
And pleasant to picture them down there
Turned out, tipsy and flushed, in their white shorts and their turquoise
    shirts.

Later, I like to sit and look up
At the mythic history of Western civilization,
Pinpricked and clued through the zodiac.
I'd like to be able to name them, say what's what and how who got where,
Curry the physics of metamorphosis and its endgame,
But I've spent my life knowing nothing.

CHARLES WRIGHT
(1935–)

Charles Wright was born in Pickwick Dam, Tennessee, in 1935 and educated at Davidson College and the University of Iowa. Among other honors, Wright has received the Pulitzer Prize for *Black Zodiac*. He is the Souder Family Professor of English at the University of Virginia in Charlottesville. He was elected to the American Academy of Arts and Sciences in 2002.

August 12

I Wake and Feel the Fell of Dark, Not Day

I wake and feel the fell of dark, not day.
What hours, O what black hours we have spent
This night! what sights you, heart, saw; ways you went!
And more must, in yet longer light's delay.

With witness I speak this. But where I say
Hours I mean years, mean life. And my lament
Is cries countless, cries like dead letters sent
To dearest him that lives alas! away.

I am gall, I am heartburn. God's most deep decree
Bitter would have me taste: my taste was me;
Bones built in me, flesh filled, blood brimmed the curse.

Selfyeast of spirit a dull dough sours. I see
The lost are like this, and their scourge to be
As I am mine, their sweating selves; but worse.

GERARD MANLEY HOPKINS
(1844–1889)

This sonnet was first published in 1918, in the collection of Hopkins's work edited by English Poet Laureate Robert Bridges, though its composition has been dated to 1885. The last line has particular resonance for a poem written so late in Hopkins's life; he died of typhoid fever in 1889 at the age of forty-five in Dublin, Ireland. His final words were "I am so happy, so happy."

August 13

Tea Mind

Even as a child I could
induce it at will.
I'd go to where the big rocks

stayed cold in the woods all summer,
and tea mind would come to me

like water over stones, pool to pool,
and in that way I taught myself to think.
Green teas are my favorites, especially

the basket-fired Japanese ones
that smell of baled hay.

Thank you, makers of this tea.
Because of you my mind is still tonight,
transparent, a leaf in air.

Now it rides a subtle current.
Now it can finally disappear.

CHASE TWICHELL
(1950–)

Chase Twichell was born in New Haven, Connecticut. She received a B.A. from Trinity College in Hartford, Connecticut, and an M.F.A. from the University of Iowa. She is the founder and publisher of Ausable Press. She lives in Keene, New York.

An easy way to become published!

The Tropics in New York

Bananas ripe and green, and ginger-root,
    Cocoa in pods and alligator pears,
And tangerines and mangoes and grape fruit,
    Fit for the highest prize at parish fairs,

Set in the window, bringing memories
    Of fruit-trees laden by low-singing rills,
And dewy dawns, and mystical blue skies
    In benediction over nun-like hills.

My eyes grew dim, and I could no more gaze;
    A wave of longing through my body swept,
And, hungry for the old, familiar ways,
    I turned aside and bowed my head and wept.

CLAUDE MCKAY
(1889–1948)

Festus Claudius McKay was born in Sunny Ville, Jamaica. He studied classic authors of English literature, Milton, Pope, and the Romantics, as well as the philosophy of Schopenhauer under his schoolteacher brother Uriah and an English neighbor named Walter Jekyll. In 1912 he published a collection of poems on black life in Jamaica called *Songs of Jamaica,* which brought him an award and stipend from the Jamaican Institute of Arts and Sciences. With this money he traveled to America, where he enrolled at the Tuskegee Institute in Alabama and then Kansas State College. He moved to New York in 1914 and became a prominent figure of the Harlem Renaissance.

"An archive of confessions, a genealogy of confessions"

Now the summer air exerts its syrupy drag on the half-dark
City under the strict surveillance of quotation marks.

The citizens with their cockades and free will drift off
From the magnet of work to the terrible magnet of love.

In the far suburbs crenellated of Cartesian yards and gin
The tribe of mothers calls the tribe of children in

Across the bluing evening. It's the hour things get
To be excellently pointless, like describing the alphabet.

Yikes. It's fine to be here with you watching the great events
Without taking part, clinking our ice as they advance

Yet remain distant. Like the baker always about to understand
Idly sweeping up that he is the recurrence of Napoleon

In a baker's life, always interrupted by the familiar notes
Of a childish song, "no more sleepy dreaming," we float

Casually on the surface of the day, staring at the bottom,
Jotting in our daybooks, how beautiful, the armies of autumn.

JOSHUA CLOVER
(1962–)

Joshua Clover was born in Berkeley, California. Clover has taught English and Creative Writing at the University of Iowa, St. Mary's College, Grinnell College, and Colorado State University. He is also a literary and music critic whose essays have appeared in the *Village Voice*, the *Voice Literary Supplement*, *Spin*, and elsewhere.

August 16

Alma in the Dark

She reaches over and puts a hand on his hipbone
and presses. He turns softly away and she makes
his shape against the back, her arm around
the waist covering his unguarded stomach.
He does not wake. Her heart in its nest
sings foolishly. It is awake and happy
and useless at this time. Saying dumb things
like *The stone house is firm*
or *The almond tree is blown around in the wind.*

LINDA GREGG
(1942–)

Linda Gregg was born in Suffern, New York. She received a B.A. and an M.A. from San
Francisco State University. She lived for many years in Greece and has taught at various
universities throughout the United States. She currently lives in New York City.

The Three Ravens

1

There were three ravens sat on a tree,
   Down a down, hay down, hay down
There were three ravens sat on a tree,
   With a down
There were three ravens sat on a tree,
They were as black as they might be.
   With a down derry, derry, derry, down, down.

2

The one of them said to his mate,
"Where shall we our breakfast take?"

3

"Down in yonder greene field,
There lies a knight slain under his shield.

4

"His hounds they lie down at his feet,
So well they can their master keep.

5

"His hawks they fly so eagerly,
There's no fowl dare him come nigh."

6

Down there comes a fallow doe,
As great with young as she might go.

7

She lift up his bloody head
And kissed his wounds that were so red.

8

She got him up upon her back
And carried him to earthen lake.

9

She buried him before the prime;
She was dead herself ere even-song time.

10

God send every gentleman
Such hawks, such hounds, and such a leman.

Anonymous

This ballad was first published in *Melismata: Musical Phansies Fitting the Court, Citie, and Country Humours,* a songbook edited by Thomas Ravenscroft in 1611, and variant versions were printed as late as the nineteenth century. The refrain "Down a down, hay down, hay down / With a down / With a down derry, derry, derry, down, down" is meant to alternate with the lines of stanzas 2 through 10 as it does in the first. "Leman" in the last line means "sweetheart."

The Visitor

In Spanish he whispers there is no time left.
It is the sound of scythes arcing in wheat,
the ache of some field song in Salvador.
The wind along the prison, cautious
as Francisco's hands on the inside, touching
the walls as he walks, it is his wife's breath
slipping into his cell each night while he
imagines his hand to be hers. It is a small country.

There is nothing one man will not do to another.

CAROLYN FORCHÉ
(1950–)

Carolyn Forché was born in Detroit, Michigan, and educated at Michigan State
University and Bowling Green State University. Her first book, *Gathering the Tribes,*
was selected by Stanley Kunitz for the 1976 Yale Series of Younger Poets. In 1977 she
traveled to El Salvador, where she worked as a journalist and human rights activist.
Forché was also a correspondent for National Public Radio's *All Things Considered*
in Beirut in 1983. She is currently an associate professor at George Mason University
in Fairfax, Virginia.

Before the Birth of One of Her Children

All things within this fading world hath end,
Adversity doth still our joyes attend;
No tyes so strong, no friends so clear and sweet,
But with deaths parting blow is sure to meet.
The sentence past is most irrevocable,
A common thing, yet oh inevitable;
How soon, my Dear, death may my steps attend,
How soon't may be thy Lot to lose thy friend,
We both are ignorant, yet love bids me
These farewell lines to recommend to thee,
That when that knot's unty'd that made us one,
I may seem thine, who in effect am none.
And if I see not half my dayes that's due,
What nature would, God grant to yours and you;
The many faults that well you know I have,
Let be interr'd in my oblivious grave;
If any worth or virtue were in me,
Let that live freshly in thy memory
And when thou feel'st no grief, as I no harms,
Yet love thy dead, who long lay in thine arms:
And when thy loss shall be repaid with gains
Look to my little babes my dear remains.
And if thou love thy self, or loved'st me
These O protect from step Dames injury.
And if chance to thine eyes shall bring this verse,
With some sad sighs honour my absent Herse;
And kiss this paper for thy loves dear sake,
Who with salt tears this last Farewel did take.

ANNE BRADSTREET
(1612–1672)

Anne Dudley, born in Northamptonshire, England, married Simon Bradstreet in 1628, at the age of sixteen. The couple emigrated from England to America with the Winthrop Puritan group in 1630, settling in Ipswich, Massachusetts. Anne Bradstreet was thus one of the first poets of the American colonies. Her brother-in-law took a collection of her poems with him back to England and had them published, without Anne's knowledge, as *The Tenth Muse, Lately Sprung Up in America* in 1650. Her first American book was published in 1678.

The Mill

The miller's wife had waited long,
  The tea was cold, the fire was dead;
And there might yet be nothing wrong
  In how he went and what he said:
"There are no millers any more,"
  Was all that she had heard him say;
And he had lingered at the door
  So long that it seemed yesterday.

Sick with a fear that had no form
  She knew that she was there at last;
And in the mill there was a warm
  And mealy fragrance of the past.
What else there was would only seem
  To say again what he had meant;
And what was hanging from a beam
  Would not have heeded where she went.

And if she thought it followed her,
  She may have reasoned in the dark
That one way of the few there were
  Would hide her and would leave no mark:
Black water, smooth above the weir
  Like starry velvet in the night,
Though ruffled once, would soon appear
  The same as ever to the sight.

EDWIN ARLINGTON ROBINSON
(1869–1935)

Edwin Arlington Robinson was born in Maine and lived for many years in Gardiner, which he renamed "Tilbury Town" in his poems. He was educated at Harvard and moved to New York City in 1897 where he worked as a subway inspector. President Theodore Roosevelt was a fan of Robinson's poetry and wrote an article in praise of his book *Captain Craig and Other Poems,* and he later secured Robinson a job in the U.S. Customs House in New York. Robinson won his first Pulitzer Prize in 1922 for his *Collected Poems* and then won the prize twice more in 1925 and 1927. He died of cancer in 1935.

Sandpiper

The roaring alongside he takes for granted,
and that every so often the world is bound to shake.
He runs, he runs to the south, finical, awkward,
in a state of controlled panic, a student of Blake.

The beach hisses like fat. On his left, a sheet
of interrupting water comes and goes
and glazes over his dark and brittle feet.
He runs, he runs straight through it, watching his toes.

— Watching, rather, the spaces of sand between them,
where (no detail too small) the Atlantic drains
rapidly backwards and downwards. As he runs,
he stares at the dragging grains.

The world is a mist. And then the world is
minute and vast and clear. The tide
is higher or lower. He couldn't tell you which.
His beak is focussed; he is preoccupied,

looking for something, something, something.
Poor bird, he is obsessed!
The millions of grains are black, white, tan, and gray,
mixed with quartz grains, rose and amethyst.

ELIZABETH BISHOP
(1911–1979)

Elizabeth Bishop was born in Worcester, Massachusetts. Practically orphaned after her father died and her mother was committed to a mental hospital, Bishop was raised by her grandparents in Nova Scotia. She was independently wealthy and did a great deal of traveling, her poems picking up souvenirs along the way. She lived in Florida for a time, and she spent several years in Brazil. "Sandpiper" is from Bishop's book *Questions of Travel*, first published in 1965. She wrote to Randall Jarrell in February 1965: "[T]he title is to be *Questions of Travel*, after one of the first descriptive Brazilian ones. I know I can't compete with you in the matter of good titles, but it seems alright to me — covers everything!"

August 22

#107

If ever anyone anywhere, Lesbia, is looking
                for what he knows will not happen
and then unexpectedly it happens —
the soul is astonished,
as we are now in each other,
                an event dearer than gold,
for you have restored yourself, Lesbia, desired
restored yourself, longed for, unlooked for,
                    brought yourself back
to me. White day in the calendar!
              Who happier than I?
What more can life offer
than the longed for unlooked for event when it happens?

CATULLUS
(CA. 84–54 B.C.)
translated by Peter Whigham

Most of the facts we have about the life of Gaius Valerius Catullus amount to edu-
cated guesses, based on information in his poems. He is supposed to have been born
in Verona circa 84 B.C. to a prominent family — his father was friendly with Julius
Caesar, for example. Though the epic mode was very much the fashion of the day,
Catullus chose instead to write poems from his personal experience in colloquial lan-
guage. All of his extant poems were discovered in a single manuscript in 1305, which
has since disappeared. Two copies of it were made, though one belonging to Petrarch
was also eventually lost. The remaining copy is kept in the Bodleian Library at
Oxford. Lesbia is a lover Catullus addressed in several of his poems.

Glow Worm

We are all worms but I am a glow worm.

WINSTON CHURCHILL

Lost in self, drowned; asphyxiated in ego,
blind to same: the dog-
after-a-gut-wagon drivenness, self-righteousness,
all (*the male is small, winged, the female*

larger, wingless) to fill
the memory hole
with matter or to extract
from the final bone its marrow.

In spite, the glow worm's inner fire
is chemical, cold, cold,
and therefore false
in drawing others to it for love.

THOMAS LUX
(1946–)

Thomas Lux was born in Northampton, Massachusetts, and grew up on a dairy farm, the son of a milkman. He was educated at Emerson College and the University of Iowa. He has been a member of the Graduate Writing Program faculty at Sarah Lawrence College in Bronxville, New York, since 1975.

August 24

from *As You Like It*
Act II, Scene i

Are not these woods
More free from peril than the envious court?
Here feel we but the penalty of Adam,
The seasons' difference; as, the icy fang
And churlish chiding of the winter's wind,
Which, when it bites and blows upon my body,
Even till I shrink with cold, I smile and say
"This is no flattery: these are counsellors
That feelingly persuade me what I am."
Sweet are the uses of adversity,
Which like the toad, ugly and venomous,
Wears yet a precious jewel in his head;
And this our life exempt from public haunt,
Finds tongues in trees, books in the running brooks,
Sermons in stones, and good in every thing.

WILLIAM SHAKESPEARE
(1564–1616)

In *As You Like It,* the character Duke Senior, who has been banished to the forest by his brother Frederick, speaks these lines to Amiens, one of his attending lords. Shakespeare, in effect, compliments himself on the beauty of this poem, when he has Amiens answer, "I would not change it. Happy is your Grace / That you can translate the stubbornness of fortune / Into so quiet and so sweet a style."

On the King and His Courage

He arose laden with doubt as to how he should begin. He looked back at the bed where the grindstone lay. He looked out at the world, the most famous experimental prison of its time. Beyond the torture stakes he could see, nothing. Yet he could see.

ANNE CARSON
(1950–)

Poet, essayist, translator, and classical scholar Anne Carson was born in Toronto, Ontario, Canada, and educated at the University of Toronto. She is the John MacNaughton Professor of Classics at McGill University in Montreal, Quebec, Canada.

August 26

To the Same Purpose

To the same purpose: he, not long before
   Brought home from nurse, going to the door
      To do some little thing
      He must not do within,
         With wonder cries,
         As in the skies
He saw the moon, "O yonder is the moon,
   Newly come after me to town,
That shined at Lugwardin but yesternight,
   Where I enjoyed the self-same sight."

As if it had ev'n twenty thousand faces,
   It shines at once in many places;
      To all the earth so wide
      God doth the stars divide,
         With so much art
         The moon impart,
They serve us all; serve wholly every one
   As if they servèd him alone.
While every single person hath such store,
   'Tis want of sense that makes us poor.

THOMAS TRAHERNE
(1637–1674)

Thomas Traherne was born near the Welsh border in England to a family of modest means. After receiving his education at Brasenose College, Oxford, he became a clergyman and eventually chaplain to Sir Orlando Bridgeman, Lord Keeper of the Great Seal. Traherne published only one book in his lifetime, a nonfiction account titled *Roman Forgeries: Or, A True Account of False Records Discovering the Impostures and Counterfeit Antiquities of the Church of Rome* (1673). It is something of a miracle that we know his poems today. His manuscripts were discovered by an antiquarian bookseller in London in 1896, after surviving more than two hundred years. A scholar named A. B. Grosart incorrectly attributed the poems to Henry Vaughan, but a later bookseller, Betram Dobell, correctly identified Traherne as the author and published the poems in 1903 and the prose in 1908. An additional selection of Traherne's poems was discovered in the archives of the British Museum and published by H. J. Bell in 1910.

Fawn's Foster Mother

The old woman sits on a bench before the door and quarrels
With her meager pale demoralized daughter.
Once when I passed I found her alone, laughing in the sun
And saying that when she was first married
She lived in the old farmhouse up Garapatas Canyon.
(It is empty now, the roof has fallen
But the log walls hang on the stone foundation; the redwoods
Have all been cut down, the oaks are standing;
The place is now more solitary than ever before.)
"When I was nursing my second baby
My husband found a day-old fawn hid in a fern-brake
And brought it; I put its mouth to the breast
Rather than let it starve, I had milk enough for three babies.
Hey, how it sucked, the little nuzzler,
Digging its little hoofs like quills into my stomach.
I had more joy from that than from the others."
Her face is deformed with age, furrowed like a bad road
With market-wagons, mean cares and decay.
She is thrown up to the surface of things, a cell of dry skin
Soon to be shed from the earth's old eyebrows,
I see that once in her spring she lived in the streaming arteries,
The stir of the world, the music of the mountain.

ROBINSON JEFFERS
(1887–1962)

James Dickey wrote of Robinson Jeffers in 1964, "Jeffers is cast in a large mold; he
fills a position in this country that would simply have been an empty gap without
him: that of the poet as prophet, as large-scale philosopher, as doctrine-giver. This is
a very real, very old and honorable function for poets, and carries with it a *tone* that
has, but for Jeffers, not been much heard among us, in our prevailing atmosphere of
ironic shrugs and never-too-much."

August 28

Heaven

O who will show me those delights on high?
             Echo.   I.
Thou Echo, thou art mortall, all men know.
             Echo.   No.
Wert thou not born among the trees and leaves?
             Echo.   Leaves.
And are there any leaves, that still abide?
             Echo.   Bide.
What leaves are they? impart the matter wholly.
             Echo.   Holy.
Are holy leaves the Echo then of blisse?
             Echo.   Yes.
Then tell me, what is that supreme delight?
             Echo.   Light.
Light to the minde: what shall the will enjoy?
             Echo.   Joy.
But are there cares and businesse with the pleasure?
             Echo.   Leisure.
Light, joy, and leisure; but shall they persever?
             Echo.   Ever.

GEORGE HERBERT
(1593–1633)

"Heaven" was included in George Herbert's book *The Temple: Sacred Poems and Private Ejaculations* in 1633, which was published shortly after his death. The poem is an example of a form called "echo verse" in which the final syllables of the lines are repeated in answer to a question. Echo verse can be traced back as early as the thirteenth century and often addresses the subject of unrequited love.

August 29

Haiku

1

Eastern guard tower
glints in sunset; convicts rest
like lizards on rocks.

2

The piano man
is stingy at 3 A.M.
his songs drop like plum.

3

Morning sun slants cell.
Drunks stagger like cripple flies
On jailhouse floor.

4

To write a blues song
is to regiment riots
and pluck gems from graves.

5

A bare pecan tree
slips a pencil shadow down
a moonlit snow slope.

6

The falling snow flakes
Cannot blunt the hard aches nor
Match the steel stillness.

7

Under moon shadows
A tall boy flashes knife and
Slices star bright ice.

8

In the August grass
Struck by the last rays of sun
The cracked teacup screams.

9

Making jazz swing in
Seventeen syllables AIN'T
No square poet's job.

ETHERIDGE KNIGHT
(1931–1991)

Etheridge Knight was born in Corinth, Mississippi, and dropped out of school at the age of sixteen to join the army. He served in Korea from 1947 to 1951 and returned to the United States with a shrapnel wound and burgeoning drug addiction. Knight was arrested for robbery in 1960 and sentenced to eight years in Indiana State Prison, where he first began to write poetry. His first book was published one year before the end of his sentence in 1968. After his release, he went on to publish other books and became a leading figure with the Black Arts Movement. In 1990 he graduated from Martin Center University in Indianapolis with a degree in American poetry and criminal justice. Knight credited poetry with saving his life and sanity while incarcerated, saying, "I died in 1960 from a prison sentence and poetry brought me back to life."

When I Heard the Learn'd Astronomer

When I heard the learn'd astronomer,
When the proofs, the figures, were ranged in columns before me,
When I was shown the charts and diagrams, to add, divide, and
    measure them,
When I sitting heard the astronomer where he lectured with much
    applause in the lecture-room,
How soon unaccountable I became tired and sick,
Till rising and gliding out I wander'd off by myself,
In the mystical moist night-air, and from time to time,
Look'd up in perfect silence at the stars.

WALT WHITMAN
(1819–1892)

"When I Heard the Learn'd Astronomer" was first published in 1865 and added to
Leaves of Grass for subsequent editions.

#510

It was not Death, for I stood up,
And all the Dead, lie down —
It was not Night, for all the Bells
Put out their Tongues, for Noon.

It was not Frost, for on my Flesh
I felt Siroccos — crawl —
Nor Fire — for just my Marble feet
Could keep a Chancel, cool —

And yet, it tasted, like them all,
The Figures I have seen
Set orderly, for Burial,
Reminded me, of mine —

As if my life were shaven,
And fitted to a frame,
And could not breathe without a key,
And 'twas like Midnight, some —

When everything that ticked — has stopped —
And Space stares all around —
Or Grisly frosts — first Autumn morns,
Repeal the Beating Ground —

But, most, like Chaos — Stopless — cool —
Without a Chance, or Spar —
Or even a Report of Land —
To justify — Despair.

EMILY DICKINSON
(1830–1886)

"510" has been dated to 1862, the same year Emily Dickinson first wrote to Thomas
Wentworth Higginson, though like most of her poems it was not published until
after her death. The "siroccos" of line six are moist, hot winds that blow from the
Libyan desert across the Mediterranean toward Italy.

Divan

I'm a slave of the moon. Speak only moon to me.
Speak of candles and of sweetness or don't speak at all.
Speak of gains not losses, and if
you don't know how, never mind. Say nothing.
I went crazy last night. Love saw me and said,
"I'm here. Don't shout! Don't tear your clothes! Be still!"
I said, "Oh, love. It's not that I fear. It's something more!"
"That something more *is* no more. Don't say a word!
I'm going to whisper secrets in your ear.
Just nod your head and say nothing.
A moon, a being made of soul, appeared on the path of love.
Ah, how delicious it is, a journey on the heart's path! Don't speak!"
I said, "Oh, my heart, what moon is this?" Love pointed and said,
"This one's not right for you. Pass by in silence!"
I said, "Could this be an angel's face? Could it be human?"
"It's neither human nor angel. Hush!"
I said, "What is it? Tell me! You've turned me upside down!"
"Stay upside down, and be silent!
You're seated in this house filled with images and illusions.
Get up! Don't say a word! Just pack your bags and leave!
I said, "Oh, my love. Be like a father to me.
Isn't this the face of God?"
"It is. But by your father's soul,
Hush! Be silent! Don't say a word!"

RUMI

(1207–1273)

translated by J. W. Clinton

The poems of Persian poet Jelalludin Rumi have become exceedingly popular in English translation, selling hundreds of thousands of books. In about 1244 Rumi met a man named Shams-I Tabriz and the two became inseparable friends. Rumi found in Shams-I Tabriz the image of the Divine Beloved and began to write his first poems. Shams-I Tabriz disappeared without a trace around 1247. "Divan" is a term used to denote a collection of Persian poetry, and the *Divan-I Shams-I Tabriz,* from which this poem is taken, means "a collection of poems of, or for, Shams-I Tabriz."

Talking to the Mule

In the evening there is a snail
passing through life across your lawn,
his trail official, a government seal.
The lawn is delicious, dry and cool,
the color of pepper.

Someone took a gun and shot that cone
off the pine tree.
He might have stopped to think
you heard for weeks the way the wind
blew through its sculptured sections.
It had skin soft as your ears.

The stars have started out the night.
They are something of importance
that clouds cover. They are too much
to be seen, but still they belong to us.

Rub your nose along the fence.
Tip back your head and bray,
for night is yours. It is never
against you. You are not its enemy.

LAURA JENSEN
(1948–)

Laura Jensen was born in Tacoma, Washington, and received her B.A. from the
University of Washington, Seattle. She earned her M.F.A. from the University of
Iowa. Jensen is the author of several collections, including *Bad Boats,* in which this
poem appeared.

The Afternoon Sun

This room, how well I know it.
Now they're renting it, and the one next to it,
as offices. The whole house has become
an office building for agents, merchants, companies.

This room, how familiar it is.

Here, near the door, was the couch,
a Turkish carpet in front of it.
Close by, the shelf with two yellow vases.
On the right — no, opposite — a wardrobe with a mirror.
In the middle of the table where he wrote,
and the three big wicker chairs.
Beside the window was the bed
where we made love so many times.

They must still be around somewhere, those old things.

Beside the window was the bed;
the afternoon sun fell across half of it.

. . . One afternoon at four o'clock we separated
for a week only . . . And then —
that week became forever.

C. P. CAVAFY
(1863–1933)
translated by Edmund Keeley and Philip Sherrard

Greek poet Constantine Cavafy was born Konstantínos Pétrou Kaváfis to Greek par-
ents in Alexandria, Egypt, and educated in England. After finishing his studies, he
returned with his mother to Greece and lived with her there until her death in 1899.
He then moved to Alexandria and briefly worked as a journalist and a stockbroker
before being appointed special clerk of the Irrigation Service of the Ministry of
Public Works. Eventually promoted to assistant director, Cavafy kept his job at the
Ministry of Public Works for thirty years. A rather solitary man, Cavafy privately
printed his poems and distributed them to his family and friends. Only about two-
thirds of his poems were printed in any form during his lifetime. Cavafy died in 1933
in Alexandria, from cancer of the larynx.

September 4

You, orange tree —

You, orange tree —
please answer me this question:
the Fifth Month has passed,
but might you still have the scent
of the sleeves he wore long ago?

LADY UKYŌ DAIBU
(1157–CA. 1232)
translated by Steven D. Carter

Lady Daibu was a lady-in-waiting to the Empress Tokudu from 1174 to 1178. As was customary at the time, she was not referred to by her birth name, but by a feudal appellation that designated which family she served: Kenreimon-in Ukyō no Daibu. She wrote this poem after her lover was killed in the Gempei Wars. In her journals, the following passage precedes this poem: "I went about my devotions most earnestly, praying only for the welfare in the next world of the one I loved. But it was no good; I could do nothing against my memories. So I got up and looked outside, where I saw snow lying thick on a wild orange tree, which made me think of the time — I don't recall exactly when — that he had come to me on a snowy morning at the palace, his robes wrinkled after guard duty, offering me a branch from a similar tree still covered with snow. 'Why,' I asked, 'did you take a sprig from *that* tree?' He responded by saying that he had developed an attachment for it because he so often stood near it. Now it all came back to me, making me more sad than I can say."

A Grave

Man looking into the sea,
taking the view from those who have as much right to it as you have to
    yourself,
it is human nature to stand in the middle of a thing,
but you cannot stand in the middle of this;
the sea has nothing to give but a well excavated grave.
The firs stand in a procession, each with an emerald turkey-foot at the
    top,
reserved as their contours, saying nothing;
repression, however, is not the most obvious characteristic of the sea;
the sea is a collector, quick to return a rapacious look.
There are others besides you who have worn that look —
whose expression is no longer a protest; the fish no longer investigate them
for their bones have not lasted:
men lower nets, unconscious of the fact that they are desecrating a grave,
and row quickly away — the blades of the oars
moving together like the feet of water-spiders as if there were no such
    thing as death.
The wrinkles progress among themselves in a phalanx — beautiful under
    networks of foam,
and fade breathlessly while the sea rustles in and out of the seaweed;
the birds swim through the air at top speed, emitting catcalls as
    heretofore —
the tortoise-shell scourges about the feet of the cliffs, in motion beneath
    them;

and the ocean, under the pulsation of lighthouses and noise of bell-buoys,
advances as usual, looking as if it were not that ocean in which
     dropped things are bound to sink —
in which if they turn and twist, it is neither with volition nor
     consciousness.

MARIANNE MOORE
(1887–1972)

Marianne Moore did not annotate "A Grave" as she did with so many of her other
poems. She wrote the first draft of the poem between 1916 and 1918 and titled the
original, unpublished version "A Graveyard in the Middle of the Sea." She revised it,
as she did with most of her poems, several times. A revised version was published in
The Dial in July 1921 under the title "A Graveyard." She eventually settled on this
version and the simplest title "A Grave" for her book *Observations* in 1924. In *The
Autobiography of William Carlos Williams,* Williams remembered Moore warmly,
writing, "Marianne was our saint — if we had one — in whom we all instinctively
felt our purpose come together to form a stream. Everyone loved her."

Mouse's Nest

I found a ball of grass among the hay
And progged it as I passed and went away;
And when I looked I fancied something stirred,
And turned agen and hoped to catch the bird —
When out an old mouse bolted in the wheats
With all her young ones hanging at her teats;
She looked so odd and so grotesque to me,
I ran and wondered what the thing could be,
And pushed the knapweed bunches where I stood;
Then the mouse hurried from the craking brood.
The young ones squeaked, and as I went away
She found her nest again among the hay.
The water o'er the pebbles scarce could run
And broad old cesspools glittered in the sun.

JOHN CLARE
(1793–1864)

John Clare wrote a whole series of "nest" poems, including "The Thrush's Nest," "The Pettichap's Nest," "The Robin's Nest," and "The Nightingale's Nest." English critic John Wareham has written that "[t]he melancholy landscape in the closing couplet of 'Mouse's Nest' presents, in Eliot's phrase, an 'objective correlative' for the speaker's recognition of man as trespasser, outsider, or marauder, and of nature as a network whose distant parts, like sun and cesspools, are linked to the near, like the pebbles and the nest and its contents. The correspondence between the running of man, mouse, and water is but one aspect of this interdependence. Clare shows nature's network to be strange indeed, fragile and unthinkingly harmed by man even as it survives against the odds."

Where does this tenderness come from?

Where does this tenderness come from?
These are not the — first curls I
have stroked slowly — and lips I
have known are — darker than yours

as stars rise often and go out again
(where does this tenderness come from?)
so many eyes have risen and died out
    in front of these eyes of mine.

and yet no such song have
I heard in the darkness of night before,
(where does this tenderness come from?):
    here, on the ribs of the singer.

Where does this tenderness come from?
And what shall I do with it, young
sly singer, just passing by?
Your lashes are — longer than anyone's.

MARINA TSVETAEVA
(1892–1941)
translated by Elaine Feinstein

Marina Ivanovna Tsvetaeva was born in Moscow, Russia, and educated at the Sorbonne in Paris. She published her first book of poems at the age of eighteen, at her own expense. The little book attracted the attention of established writers and Tsvetaeva found her entrée to literary circles. She was a prolific writer who wrote not just poetry, but also essays, plays, translations, and criticism. During the War Communism period, Tsvetaeva was forced to live apart from her soldier husband, and one of their younger daughters died from malnutrition. She and her surviving daughter left Russia in 1922, spending time in Berlin and Czechoslovakia before settling in Paris in 1925. In the 1930s Tsvetaeva's husband was discovered to be an agent for the Soviet Secret Police, though she herself refused to believe it. She returned to the Soviet Union from France at the insistence of her family, though she knew she would be stifled as a writer under the Stalinist regime. Her daughter and husband were arrested upon their return, and he was eventually executed. Most of her former friends were afraid to associate with her. In 1941, after the German invasion of Russia, Tsvetaeva relocated with her son to a small village called Elabulga. Tsvetaeva hanged herself in their rented room and was buried in an unmarked mass grave.

This Living Hand

This living hand, now warm and capable
Of earnest grasping, would, if it were cold
And in the icy silence of the tomb,
So haunt thy days and chill thy dreaming nights
That thou wouldst wish thine own heart dry of blood
So in my veins red life might stream again,
And thou be conscience-calmed — see here it is —
I hold it towards you.

JOHN KEATS
(1795–1821)

In an incredible burst of creative activity, most of Keats's major poems were written between January and September of 1819. "This Living Hand" is an unfinished poem, probably written in November of that same year. It was found on the back of one of the manuscript pages of *The Cap and Bells*, which Keats also left unfinished. Fifteen months later, Keats was gone, consumed by tuberculosis. He instructed that his headstone be inscribed, "Here lies one whose name was writ in water."

September 9

The Heart

When I saw my son's heart blown up in bland black and white on the
     sonogram screen,
an amoebic, jellylike mass barely contained by invisible layers of
     membrane, I felt faint.

Eight years old, Jed lay, apparently unafraid, wires strung from him into
     the clicking machine,
as the doctor showed us a pliable, silvery lid he explained was the valve,
     benignly prolapsed,

which to me looked like some lost lunar creature biting too avidly,
     urgently at an alien air,
the tiniest part of that essence I'd always allowed myself to believe could
     stand for the soul.

Revealed now in a nakedness nearly not to be looked upon as the muscular
     ghost of itself,
it majestically swelled and contracted, while I stood trembling before it,
     in love, in dread.

C. K. WILLIAMS
(1936–)

Charles Kenneth Williams was born in Newark, New Jersey. Among other honors, he has received the Pulitzer Prize for Poetry. He is a professor in the Council of the Humanities and Creative Writing at Princeton University. Williams recalls his experience of writing his first poem this way: "I just finished my last class [in my freshman year at the University of Pennsylvania], which was a required class in English, and I wrote a poem, and I just really liked the feeling. And I kept going. That was the first thing I felt that I really loved to do that could be a life." He lives in Paris for most of the year, and teaches at Princeton in the spring.

The Fish, the Man, and the Spirit

To a Fish

You strange, astonished-looking, angle-faced,
　　Dreary-mouthed, gaping wretches of the sea,
　　Gulping salt-water everlastingly,
Cold-blooded, though with red your blood be graced,
And mute, though dwellers in the roaring waste;
　　And you, all shapes beside, that fishy be, —
　　Some round, some flat, some long, all devilry,
Legless, unloving, infamously chaste: —

O scaly, slippery, wet, swift, staring wights,
　　What is't ye do? What life lead? eh, dull goggles?
How do ye vary your vile days and nights?
　　How pass your Sundays? Are ye still but joggles
In ceaseless wash? Still nought but gapes, and bites,
　　And drinks, and stares, diversified with boggles?

A Fish Answers

Amazing monster! that, for aught I know,
　　With the first sight of thee didst make our race
　　For ever stare! O flat and shocking face,
Grimly divided from the breast below!
Thou that on dry land horribly dost go
　　With a split body and most ridiculous pace,
　　Prong after prong, disgracer of all grace,
Long-useless-finned, haired, upright, unwet, slow!

O breather of unbreathable, sword-sharp air,
　　How canst exist? How bear thyself, thou dry
And dreary sloth? What particle canst share
　　Of the only blessed life, the watery?
I sometimes see of ye an actual *pair*
　　Go by! linked fin by fin! most odiously.

The Fish Turns into a Man, and Then
into a Spirit, and Again Speaks

Indulge thy smiling scorn, if smiling still,
    O man! and loathe, but with a sort of love;
    For difference must its use by difference prove,
And, in sweet clang, the spheres with music fill.
One of the spirits am I, that at his will
    Live in whate'er has life — fish, eagle, dove —
    No hate, no pride, beneath nought, nor above,
A visitor of the rounds of God's sweet skill.

Man's life is warm, glad, sad, 'twixt loves and graves,
    Boundless in hope, honoured with pangs austere,
Heaven-gazing; and his angel-wings he craves: —
    The fish is swift, small-needing, vague yet clear.
A cold, sweet, silver life, wrapped in round waves,
    Quickened with touches of transporting fear.

LEIGH HUNT
(1784–1859)

James Henry Leigh Hunt was born in England to American parents; his father had been forced to flee America at the beginning of the Revolutionary War to avoid being tarred and feathered as a Tory. A gifted child, Hunt published his first book of poems at the age of seventeen. In 1808 he became the editor of the *Examiner,* a newspaper founded by his brother John. In 1812 Hunt was convicted of slander for writing an editorial that described the Prince Regent as a "fat Adonis of fifty." Hunt was sentenced to three years in prison, though he received a comfortable room in the infirmary, continued to edit the *Examiner,* and was allowed to bring his family with him. Plagued by financial troubles most of his life, Hunt was the basis for Dickens's character Mr. Skimpole in *Bleak House.*

#280

I felt a Funeral, in my Brain,
And Mourners to and fro
Kept treading — treading — till it seemed
That Sense was breaking through —

And when they all were seated,
A Service, like a Drum —
Kept beating — beating — till I thought
My Mind was going numb —

And then I heard them lift a Box
And creak across my Soul
With those same Boots of Lead, again,
Then Space — began to toll,

As all the Heavens were a Bell,
And Being, but an Ear,

And I, and Silence, some strange Race
Wrecked, solitary, here —

And then a Plank in Reason, broke,
And I dropped down, and down —
And hit a World, at every plunge,
And Finished knowing — then —

EMILY DICKINSON
(1830–1886)

In the manuscript copy of this poem, Emily Dickinson included variations on the
last two lines. For "plunge" in line 19, she made a note that "Crash" could also fill
that space. For "Finished" in the final line, she contemplated the more colloquial
"got through." Since the poem was not published until ten years after her death, it
is hard to know what her final choices would have been, but the poem as we know
it is as she wrote it first, in her most decisive hand. For "Soul" in line 10, she initially
wrote "Brain," but scratched out that option completely.

September 12

Sleeping in the Forest

I thought the earth
remembered me, she
took me back so tenderly, arranging
her dark skirts, her pockets
full of lichens and seeds. I slept
as never before, a stone
on the riverbed, nothing
between me and the white fire of the stars
but my thoughts, and they floated
light as moths among the branches
of the perfect trees. All night
I heard the small kingdoms breathing
around me, the insects, and the birds
who do their work in the darkness. All night
I rose and fell, as if in water, grappling
with a luminous doom. By morning
I had vanished at least a dozen times
into something better.

MARY OLIVER
(1935–)

Mary Oliver was born in Maple Heights, Ohio, and educated at Ohio State University and Vassar College. She has won the Pulitzer Prize and the National Book Award for Poetry, among other honors. She holds the Catharine Osgood Foster Chair for Distinguished Teaching at Bennington College in Bennington, Vermont, and lives in Provincetown, Massachusetts. "I decided very early that I wanted to write," Oliver once told an interviewer. "But I didn't think of it as a career. I didn't even think of it as a profession. . . . It was the most exciting thing, the most powerful thing, the most wonderful thing to do with my life. And I didn't question if I should — I just kept sharpening the pencils!"

I Have Not Forgotten . . .

I have not forgotten the house I shared with you
In the suburbs, small and white, but quiet too.
A Venus and Pomona hid their bare
Worn stucco limbs in the scant shrubbery there;
And the sun at evening splendidly ablaze
Behind the panes that caught the glittering rays
As if he watched with open, curious eye
Our long and silent dinners, from the sky,
Like candle-gleams his lavish glories shed
On the hanging serge, the frugal cloth we spread.

CHARLES BAUDELAIRE
(1821–1867)
translated by Sir Eric Maclagan

Baudelaire's early poems caught the attention of Gustave Flaubert and Victor Hugo, both of whom wrote letters to Baudelaire in praise of his work. Each book he published reinforced his reputation as a scandalous, inheritance-squandering dandy and *poète maudit*, and one gets the idea that Baudelaire enjoyed the infamy. Credited with being the first poet to make significant innovations with the genre of the prose poem, Baudelaire was also an influential translator who introduced the French-speaking world to the works of Edgar Allen Poe. "I Have Not Forgotten . . ." is from the 1861 edition of Baudelaire's book *Les Fleurs du Mal (The Flowers of Evil)*, first published in 1857.

September 14

from "Voyages"

I

Above the fresh ruffles of the surf
Bright striped urchins flay each other with sand.
They have contrived a conquest for shell shucks,
And their fingers crumble fragments of baked weed
Gaily digging and scattering.

And in answer to their treble interjections
The sun beats lightning on the waves,
The waves fold thunder on the sand;
And could they hear me I would tell them:

O brilliant kids, frisk with your dog,
Fondle your shells and sticks, bleached
By time and the elements; but there is a line
You must not cross nor ever trust beyond it
Spry cordage of your bodies to caresses
Too lichen-faithful from too wide a breast.
The bottom of the sea is cruel.

HART CRANE
(1899–1932)

Harold Hart Crane was born in Garrettsville, Ohio, near Cleveland. Crane had an intense emotional affair with a sailor named Emil Opffer, whom he met in 1924, and the series of six "Voyages" poems explore their brief relationship, in which Crane acknowledges their failure and comes to terms with the lasting pain such failure caused him. Most of his poems were written between 1924 and 1926. He wrestled with his major work *The Bridge* for several years and took to drinking excessively, causing friends to worry about him. He published *The Bridge* in 1930, and the book was well received, but two years later Crane had had enough. He committed suicide by flinging himself overboard from the *S. S. Orizaba* near the coast of Florida in 1932.

Ashboughs

Not of all my eyes see, wándering on the world,
Is anything a milk to the mind so, só sighs déep
Poetry to it. As a tree whose boughs break the sky.
Say it is áshboughs: whether on a December day and furled
Fast or they in clammyish láshtender combs creep
Apart wide and new-nestle at heaven most high.
They touch heaven, tabour on it; how their talons sweep
The smouldering enormous winter welkin! May
Mells blue and snowwhite through them, a fringe and fray
Of greenery: it is old earth's groping towards the steep
                     Heaven whom she childs us by.

GERARD MANLEY HOPKINS
(1844–1889)

According to his friend and posthumous editor Robert Bridges, Hopkins's manuscripts contained two versions of this poem. From line 7, the variant reads as follows:

They touch, they tabour on it, hover on it; here, there hurled,
         With talons sweep
The smouldering enormous winter welkin. Eye,
         But more cheer is when May
Mells blue with snowwhite through their fringe and fray
Of greenery and old earth gropes for, grasps at steep
         Heaven with it whom she childs things by.

Miniature

The woman stood up in front of the table. Her sad hands
begin to cut thin slices of lemon for tea
like yellow wheels for a very small carriage
made for a child's fairy tale. The young officer sitting opposite
is buried in the old armchair. He doesn't look at her.
He lights up his cigarette. His hand holding the match trembles,
throwing light on his tender chin and the teacup's handle. The clock
holds its heartbeat for a moment. Something has been postponed.
The moment has gone. It's too late now. Let's drink our tea.
Is it possible, then, for death to come in that kind of carriage?
To pass by and go away? And only this carriage to remain,
with its little yellow wheels of lemon
parked for so many years on a side street with unlit lamps,
and then a small song, a little mist, and then nothing?

YANNIS RITSOS
(1909–1990)
translated by Edmund Keeley

Yannis Ritsos was born in Monemvasia, Greece, and suffered a troubled childhood. His father and sister were mentally ill, and his mother and brother died of tuberculosis. Ritsos was also consumptive and was plagued by ill health most of his life. He managed, despite everything, to turn out hundreds of poems, several plays, and numerous essays. He was twice nominated for the Nobel Prize, and he won the Lenin Peace Prize in 1977.

For That He Looked Not upon Her

You must not wonder, though you think it strange,
To see me hold my louring head so low,
And that mine eyes take no delight to range
About the gleams which on your face do grow.
The mouse which once hath broken out of trap
Is seldom 'ticèd with the trustless bait,
But lies aloof for fear of more mishap,
And feedeth still in doubt of deep deceit.
The scorchèd fly, which once hath 'scaped the flame,
Will hardly come to play again with fire,
Whereby I learn that grievous is the game
Which follows fancy dazzled by desire:
    So that I wink or else hold down my head,
    Because your blazing eyes my bale have bred.

GEORGE GASCOIGNE
(CA. 1535–1577)

George Gascoigne was an important pioneer of Elizabethan letters who is credited with composing the first Greek-style tragedy in English, the first essay on English prosody, the first prose comedy, the first English satire using Roman form and, some scholars argue, the first English novel. The facts of Gascoigne's early life are sketchy; his proposed birthdates range from 1525 to 1539. It is known that he was born into nobility in Cardington, Bedfordshire, England, and was eventually disinherited by his dying father. He may have attended Trinity College, Cambridge, but he did not take a degree. A restless soul, Gascoigne tried his hand at several occupations: lawyer, gentleman farmer, courtier, poet, playwright, soldier. Nothing seemed to hold his attention for long. Interestingly, Gascoigne chose to publish his first volume (publication being still something of a stigma in those days) under the ruse that it was a miscellany by several authors. He even added notes by a fictitious editor, represented by the initials G. T.

Going Blind

She sat just like the others at the table.
But on second glance, she seemed to hold her cup
a little differently as she picked it up.
She smiled once. It was almost painful.

And when they finished and it was time to stand
and slowly, as chance selected them, they left
and moved through many rooms (they talked and laughed),
I saw her. She was moving far behind

the others, absorbed, like someone who will soon
have to sing before a large assembly;
upon her eyes, which were radiant with joy,
light played as on the surface of a pool.

She followed slowly, taking a long time,
as though there were some obstacle in the way;
and yet: as though, once it was overcome,
she would be beyond all walking, and would fly.

RAINER MARIA RILKE
(1875–1926)
translated by Stephen Mitchell

Rainer Maria Rilke was born in Prague in 1875. He traveled widely most of his life, spending time in France, Russia, and Switzerland. He married the sculptor Clara Westhoff in 1901, but the couple did not live together long and Rilke had notable romances outside his marriage. He acted as secretary to Auguste Rodin in Paris in the early 1900s. "Going Blind" was first published in *New Poems* (1907 and 1908), written during this period. Rilke died of leukemia in Switzerland in 1926.

The Two Houses

When she returned, the house was occupied.

Who occupied the house?

The houses were adjoined; one, her family
lived in, and the other, her grandmother.

Which house was this?

Her brother would be sent to Russia and she
might never see him again. So she rode her
bicycle the whole way.

How old was her brother?

How far did she ride?

During the war, her father had a nervous
breakdown, and he never really recovered.

Define breakdown.

One teacher turned Hitler's portrait
to the wall. After a classmate reported him,
he disappeared.

What subject did he teach?

Was he a Jew?

Her father wore white driving gloves. He let
her mother change the tire.

Her brother pinched the tips off the asparagus
on their grandmother's plate.

She didn't know about the Jews. No one knew
about the Jews.

JODY GLADDING

(1955–)

Jody Gladding was born in York, Pennsylvania, and educated at Franklin and Marshall College and at Cornell University. She has been a Stegner Fellow at Stanford University, and her first book, *Stone Crop*, was selected by James Dickey for the 1993 Yale Series of Younger Poets. She lives in East Calais, Vermont.

Aspen Tree

Aspen tree your leaves glance white into the dark.
My mother's hair was never white.

Dandelion, so green is the Ukraine.
My yellow-haired mother did not come home.

Rain cloud, above the well do you hover?
My quiet mother weeps for everyone.

Round star, you wind the golden loop.
My mother's heart was ripped by lead.

Oaken door, who lifted you off your hinges?
My gentle mother cannot return.

PAUL CELAN
(1920–1970)
translated by Michael Hamburger

Paul Celan is the pseudonym of Paul Antschel, born in Czernovitz, Bukovina, Romania, to German-speaking Jewish parents. After the outbreak of World War II, his parents were imprisoned in Nazi concentration camps, where his father died of typhus and his mother was murdered with a shot to the neck. Antshcel was sentenced to a Romanian labour camp and managed to survive until it was dissolved in 1944. After the war, he settled in Budapest and chose to write under the name Celan, an anagram for the Romanian form of his surname, Ancel. "Aspen Tree" is from his second book, *Mohn und Gedächtnis (Poppy and Memory)*, published in 1952. Celan committed suicide by drowning in 1970 at the age of fifty.

The Old Men of Euripides, an Abject Throng

The old men of Euripides, an abject throng,
Shamble out like sheep.
I slither like a snake,
In my heart — dark injury.

But it will not be long
Before I shake off sadness,
Like a boy in the evening
Shaking sand from his sandals.

OSIP MANDELSTAM
(1891–1938)
translated by James Greene

Osip Mandelstam, with Anna Akhmatova and others, was a prominent member of a Russian literary movement called Acmeism, which rejected the vagueness of the Symbolists and called for lucidity and sensory vividness. In an essay called "The Morning of Acmeism" published in 1919, Mandelstam describes the goals of the group this way: "For the Acmeists the conscious sense of the word, the Logos, is just as splendid a form as is music for the Symbolists. And if for the Futurists the word as such is still creeping on all fours, in Acmeism it has for the first time assumed a more adequate vertical position and has entered upon the stone age of its existence. The sharp edge of Acmeism is not the stiletto nor the sting of Decadence. Acmeism is for those who, seized with the spirit of building, do not cravenly refuse to bear its heavy weight, but joyously accept it, in order to awaken and use the forces architecturally sleeping in it."

September 22

Waiting

When I am alone I am happy.
The air is cool. The sky is
flecked and splashed and wound
with color. The crimson phalloi
of the sassafras leaves
hang crowded before me
in shoals on the heavy branches.
When I reach my doorstep
I am greeted by
the happy shrieks of my children
and my heart sinks.
I am crushed.

Are not my children as dear to me
as falling leaves or
must one become stupid
to grow older?
It seems much as if Sorrow
had tripped up my heels.
Let us see, let us see!
What did I plan to say to her
when it should happen to me
as it has happened now?

WILLIAM CARLOS WILLIAMS
(1883–1963)

This poem is from Williams's early collection, *Sour Grapes* (1921). By this time
Williams was actively practicing as a pediatrician, often writing poems on prescrip-
tion pads and late at night.

The Grain-Tribute

There came an officer knocking by night at my door —
In a loud voice demanding grain-tribute.
My house-servants dared not wait till the morning,
But brought candles and set them on the barn-floor.
Passed through the sieve, clean-washed as pearls,
A whole cart-load, thirty bushels of grain.
But still they cry that it is not paid in full:
With whips and curses they goad my servants and boys.
Once, in error, I entered public life;
I am inwardly ashamed that my talents were not sufficient.
In succession I occupied four official posts;
For doing nothing, — ten years' salary!
Often have I heard that saying of ancient men
That "good and ill follow in an endless chain."
And to-day it ought to set my heart at rest
To return to others the corn in my great barn.

PO CHÜ-I
(772–846)
translated by Arthur Waley

Po Chü-I is also known by the name Hakurakuten. He was one of the most important poets of the T'ang Dynasty period, and a particularly strong influence on the work of Haiku masters Matsuo Basho and Yosa Buson. Born into a poor family, he eventually became a high government official. In 832 he went to live in an unoccupied part of the Hsiang-shan monastery, calling himself the Hermit of Hsiang-shan. The remaining years of his life were spent collecting and arranging his complete works.

Autumn Begins in Martins Ferry, Ohio

In the Shreve High football stadium,
I think of Polacks nursing long beers in Tiltonsville,
And gray faces of Negroes in the blast furnace at Benwood,
And the ruptured night watchman of Wheeling Steel,
Dreaming of heroes.

All the proud fathers are ashamed to go home.
Their women cluck like starved pullets,
Dying for love.

Therefore,
Their sons grow suicidally beautiful
At the beginning of October,
And gallop terribly against each other's bodies.

JAMES WRIGHT
(1927–1980)

James Wright was born in Martins Ferry, Ohio. After high school he joined the Army and spent time in Japan, after which he took advantage of the G.I. Bill to get his education at Kenyon College (where he studied with John Crowe Ransom) and the University of Washington. Wright lived a turbulent life, frequently sidetracked by alcoholism and nervous breakdowns, experiencing his first at sixteen. His long-time friend Donald Hall remembers that Wright loved football, and the two of them would often go to games together. Hall last saw Wright just three days before he died from cancer in Mount Sinai Hospital. "Jim couldn't talk because of his tracheotomy," Hall recalled in the preface to Wright's complete poems, *Above the River,* "but he scrawled questions and answers on a yellow pad. . . . Annie asked him if I could look at his new poems; he was still tinkering. So I first read *This Journey* as I sat beside Jim's bed in Mount Sinai, scarcely able to distinguish one word from another; I let my eyes scan across lines, down pages, and I murmured, 'Wonderful, Jim, wonderful.'" "Autumn Begins in Martins Ferry, Ohio" is from Wright's fourth book, *The Branch Will Not Break,* published in 1963.

A Corn Grinding Song of Tesuque

There towards the north,
There the fog is lying,
There the fog is lying.
In the middle stands Blue Corn
Happily, prettily, she is singing
Ha-we-ra-na na-a-se

There towards the west
There the fog is lying,
There the fog is lying,
In the middle stands Yellow Corn
Happily, prettily, she is singing
Ha-we-ra-na na-a-se

There towards the south
There the fog is lying,
There the fog is lying,
In the middle stands Red Corn
Happily, prettily, she is singing
Ha-we-ra-na na-a-se

There towards the east
There the fog is lying,
There the fog is lying,
In the middle stands White Corn
Happily, prettily, she is singing
Ha-we-ra-na na-a-se

TEWA SONG
translated by Herbert Joseph Spinden

Tesuque is an unincorporated town near Santa Fe, New Mexico. Tesuque Pueblo has stood in the foothills of the Sangre de Cristo Mountains near Camel Rock since 1200 A.D. About four hundred people still inhabit the pueblo, and many of them still speak the Tewa language in addition to English and Spanish. (For other Tewa songs, see March 31 and June 24.)

September 26

Widow's Walk

*When he visited Nantucket, Crevecoeur noted, "A singular
custom prevails here among the women. . . . They have
adopted these many years the Asiatic custom of taking a dose
of opium every morning; and so deeply rooted is it, that they
would be at a loss how to live without this indulgence."*

WALTER TELLER,
Cape Cod and the Offshore Islands

Captain: the weathervane's rusted.
Iron-red, its coxcomb leans into the easterly wind
as I do every afternoon swinging
a blind eye out to sea. The light
fails, day closes around me, a vast oceanic whirlpool . . .
I can still see your eyes, those monotonic palettes,
smell your whiskeyed kisses!
Still feel the eelgrass of embrace —
the ocean pounds outside the heart's door.
Dearest, the lamps are going on. I'm caught
in the smell of whales burning! Vaporous and drowsy,
I spiral down the staircase in my wrapper,
a shadow among many shadows in Nantucket Town.
Out in the yard, the chinaberry tree
turns amber. A hymn spreads through the deepening air —
the church steeple's praying for the people. Last night
I dreamed you waved farewell.
I stood upon the pier, the buoys tolling
a warning knell. Trussed in my whalebone,
I grew away from you, fluttering in the twilight,
a cutout, a fancy French silhouette.

ELIZABETH SPIRES
(1952–)

Elizabeth Spires was born in Lancaster, Ohio, and was educated at Vassar College
and The Johns Hopkins University. She currently holds the Goucher Chair for
Distinguished Achievement and is a Professor of English at Goucher College, where
she has taught since 1982.

The Bond

If I use my forbidden hand
To raise a bridge across the river,
All the work of the builders
Has been blown up by sunrise.

A boat comes up the river by night
With a woman standing in it,
Twin candles lit in her eyes
And two oars in her hands.

She unsheathes a pack of cards,
'Will you play forfeits?' she says.
We play and she beats me hands down,
And she puts three banns upon me:

Not to have two meals in one house,
Not to pass two nights under one roof,
Not to sleep twice with the same man
Until I find her. When I ask her address,

'If it were north I'd tell you south,
If it were east, west.' She hooks
Off in a flash of lightning, leaving me
Stranded on the bank,

My eyes full of candles,
And the two dead oars.

NUALA NÍ DHOMHNAILL
(1952–)
translated by Medbh McGuckian

Irish poet Nuala Ní Dhomhnaill (NOO-la Nee GO-nal) was born in Lancashire, England, to Irish parents and grew up in the Irish-speaking region of the Dingle Peninsula in West Kerry, Ireland. Though she wrote her first poems in English, she eventually chose to write in Irish, uncommon today even for the few people who speak it fluently. She has been awarded the American Ireland Fund Literary Award and has been widely acclaimed for her efforts to revitalize the Irish language in modern poetry. She lives in Dublin. This poem's Irish title is "Geasa."

The Evil Minute

When for me the wheatfields were habitations of stars and gods
and frost the frozen tears of a gazelle,
someone cast in plaster my breast and shadow,
betraying me.

That was the minute of stray bullets,
of the sea's kidnapping of men who wanted to be birds,
of the inopportune telegram and the finding of blood,
of the death of water that always looked at the sky.

RAFAEL ALBERTI

(1902–1999)

translated by Christopher Sawyer-Lauçanno

Rafael Alberti suffered from tuberculosis and frequently had to rest and recuperate, interrupting his writing. He was particularly productive in 1927, however, writing the bulk of two books. He also arranged to fulfill his lifelong dream of becoming a bullfighter, but abandoned the idea in terror the minute he saw the bull. His health gradually deteriorated and, by 1929, his physical and emotional turmoil had started to influence his work. "The Evil Minute (El Mal Minuto)" is from Alberti's book Concerning the Angels (Sobre los ángeles), first published in the summer of 1929. The book is considered Alberti's masterpiece, and marks a shift in direction from his earlier, more light-hearted work.

In a Station of the Metro

The apparition of these faces in the crowd;
Petals on a wet, black bough.

EZRA POUND
(1885–1972)

In 1914, Ezra Pound commented on this poem in *Forthnightly Review:* "Three years ago in Paris I got out of a 'metro' train at La Concorde, and saw suddenly a beautiful face, and then another and another, and then a beautiful child's face, and then another beautiful woman, and I tried all that day to find words for what this had meant to me, and I could not find any words that seemed to me worthy, or as lovely as that sudden emotion." Pound wrote a thirty-line poem, which he destroyed, and then six months later a poem half that length, which he again rejected. A year later he wrote the poem as it appears here. "I dare say it is meaningless unless one has drifted into a certain vein of thought," Pound continued. "In a poem of this sort one is trying to record the precise instant when a thing outward and objective transforms itself, or darts into a thing inward and subjective."

Sixteenth Canto

The sinking of the *Titanic* proceeds according to plan.
It is copyrighted.
It is 100% tax-deductible.
It is a lucky bag for poets.
It is further proof that the teachings of Vladimir I. Lenin are correct.
It will run next Sunday on Channel One as a spectator sport.
It is priceless.
It is inevitable.
It is better than nothing.
It closes down in July for holidays.
It is ecologically sound.
It shows the way to a better future.
It is Art.
It creates new jobs.
It is beginning to get on our nerves.
It has a solid working-class basis.
It arrives in the nick of time.
It works.
It is a breathtaking spectacle.
It ought to remind those in charge of their responsibility.
It isn't anymore what it used to be.

HANS MAGNUS ENZENSBERGER
(1929–)
translated by the author

German poet Hans Magnus Enzensberger was born in Bavaria and grew up in Nuremberg. He was educated at the University of Erlangen, the University of Hamburg, and the Sorbonne. He took his Ph.D. from the University of Freiburg. An essayist, playwright, journalist, and translator as well as a poet, Enzensberger is one of Germany's leading literary figures and his work has been widely translated. "Sixteenth Canto" is from Enzensberger's long poem *The Sinking of the Titanic*, first published in the United States by Houghton Mifflin in 1980.

I Chop Some Parsley While Listening to Art Blakey's Version of "Three Blind Mice"

And I start wondering how they came to be blind.
If it was congenital, they could be brothers and sisters,
and I think of the poor mother
brooding over her sightless young triplets.

Or was it a common accident, all three caught
in a searing explosion, a firework perhaps?
If not,
if each came to his or her blindness separately,

how did they ever manage to find one another?
Would it not be difficult for a blind mouse
to locate even one fellow mouse with vision
let alone two other blind ones?

And how, in their tiny darkness,
could they possibly have run after a farmer's wife
or anyone else's wife for that matter?
Not to mention why.

Just so she could cut off their tails
with a carving knife, is the cynic's answer,
but the thought of them without eyes
and now without tails to trail through the dewy grass

or slip around the corner of a baseboard
has the cynic who always lounges within me
up off his couch and at the window
trying to hide the rising softness that he feels.

By now I am on to dicing an onion
which might account for the wet stinging
in my own eyes, though Freddie Hubbard's
mournful trumpet on "Blue Moon,"

which happens to be the next cut,
cannot be said to be making matters any better.

BILLY COLLINS
(1941–)

Billy Collins was born in New York City. He is Writer-in-Residence at Sarah
Lawrence College and a Distinguished Professor of English at Lehman College, City
University of New York, where he has been teaching for thirty years. He was
appointed United States Poet Laureate in 2001, and he has introduced a program
called Poetry 180 to promote daily poetry readings in public high schools across the
country. Art Blakey (1919–1990) was a bandleader and drummer for the hard-bop
ensemble The Jazz Messengers.

Haiku

> Deep autumn —
> my neighbor,
> how does he live, I wonder?

BASHŌ
(1644–1694)
translated by Robert Hass

Japanese poet Matsuo Bashō is considered the foremost of the Four Great Masters of Haiku and, in fact, is often referred to as simply the Master. He made his living traveling the country, teaching people to write *renga,* an art that was widely practiced by the middle class in those days. In his own time, Bashō was much better known for his *renga* and *hakai-no-renga,* or humorous *renga,* than his haiku, which he considered mere starting points for the longer poems.

October 3

Neither Out Far nor In Deep

The people along the sand
All turn and look one way.
They turn their back on the land.
They look at the sea all day.

As long as it takes to pass
A ship keeps raising its hull;
The wetter ground like glass
Reflects a standing gull.

The land may vary more;
But wherever the truth may be —
The water comes ashore,
And the people look at the sea.

They cannot look out far.
They cannot look in deep.
But when was that ever a bar
To any watch they keep?

ROBERT FROST
(1874–1963)

"Neither Out Far nor In Deep" is from Frost's sixth book *Further Range,* from the section titled "Taken Singly." Frost wrote against the abstraction of the modern poem in the foreword to his *Complete Poems,* saying, "No tears in the writer, no tears in the reader. No surprise for the writer, no surprise for the reader. For me the initial delight is the surprise of remembering something I didn't know I knew. I am in a place, in a situation, as if I had materialized from cloud or risen out of the ground. There is a glad recognition of the long lost and the rest follows. Step by step the wonder of the unexpected supply keeps growing."

The Seekers of Lice

When the child's forehead, full of red torments,
Implores the white swarm of indistinct dreams,
There come near his bed two tall charming sisters
With slim fingers that have silvery nails.

They seat the child in front of a wide open
Window where the blue air bathes a mass of flowers,
And in his heavy hair where the dew falls,
Move their delicate, fearful and enticing fingers.

He listens to the singing of their apprehensive breath
Which smells of long rosy plant honey,
And which at times a hiss interrupts, saliva
Caught on the lip or desire for kisses.

He hears their black eyelashes beating in the perfumed
Silence; and their gentle electric fingers
Make in his half-drunken indolence the death of the little lice
Crackle under their royal nails.

Then the wine of Sloth rises in him,
The sigh of an harmonica which could bring on delirium;
The child feels, according to the slowness of the caresses,
Surging in him and dying continuously a desire to cry.

ARTHUR RIMBAUD
(1854–1891)
translated by Wallace Fowlie

Jean Nicolas Arthur Rimbaud was born in Charleville, France. The outbreak of the Franco-Prussian war in 1870 forced the closing of his school, and he received no further education. After running away several times, he eventually landed in Paris, where he lived with the poet Paul Verlaine. An intense romantic relationship consumed the two poets and destroyed Verlaine's marriage. When Rimbaud eventually tried to end the affair, Verlaine shot him in the wrist in an attempt to keep him from leaving and was sentenced to two years of hard labor in a Belgian prison. During this time Rimbaud wrote some of the most influential French poetry of all time. He advocated a deliberate deranging of the senses as the key to poetic vision. By 1875, at the age of only twenty-one, Rimbaud abandoned poetry. He traveled widely, briefly joined the Dutch army but deserted in Sumatra, and went on to Egypt, Java, Cypress, and Ethiopia, apparently writing no verse at all. Diagnosed with a tumor on his knee in 1891, Rimbaud died of cancer at the age of thirty-seven.

This Morning

Enter without knocking, hard-working ant.
I'm just just sitting here mulling over
What to do this dark, overcast day.
It was a night of the radio turned low,
Fitful sleep, vague, troubling dreams.
I woke up lovesick and confused.
I thought I heard Estella in the garden singing
And some bird answering her,
But it was the rain. Dark treetops swaying
And whispering. "Come to me, my desire,"
I said. And she came to me by and by,
Her breath smelling of mint, her tongue
Wetting my cheek, and then she vanished.
Slowly day came, a gray streak of daylight
To bathe my hands and face in.
Hours passed, and then you crawled
Under the door, and stopped before me.
You visit the same tailors the mourners do,
Mr. Ant. I like the silence between us,
The quiet — that holy state even the rain
Knows about. Listen to her begin to fall,
As if with eyes closed,
Muting each drop in her wild-beating heart.

CHARLES SIMIC
(1938–)

Charles Simic was born in Belgrade, Yugoslavia, and immigrated to the United States in 1954. He earned his bachelor's degree at New York University and became an American citizen in 1971. Simic has been awarded the Pulitzer Prize, among other honors. He was elected a Chancellor of the Academy of American Poets in 2000. He teaches at the University of New Hampshire, Durham. In addition to his own poetry, Simic has translated French, Serbian, Croatian, Macedonian, and Slovenian poetry into English. (For example, see also: May 5 and August 10.)

Rules and Lessons

When first thy Eies unveil, give thy Soul leave
To do the like; our Bodies but forerun
The spirits duty; True hearts spread, and heave
Unto their God, as flow'rs do to the Sun.
    Give him thy first thoughts then; so shalt thou keep
    Him company all day, and in him sleep. . . .

Walk with thy fellow-creatures: note the *hush*
And *whispers* amongst them. There's not a *Spring*,
Or *Leafe* but hath his *Morning-hymn;* Each *Bush*
And *Oak* doth know *I AM;* canst thou not sing?
    O leave thy Cares, and follies! go this way
    And thou art sure to prosper all the day. . . .

Spend not an hour so, as to weep another,
For tears are not thine own; If thou giv'st words
Dash not thy *friend,* nor *Heav'n;* O smother
A vip'rous thought; some *Syllables* are *Swords.*
    Unbitted tongues are in their penance double,
    They shame their *owners,* and the *hearers* trouble. . . .

When Seasons change, then lay before thine Eys
His wondrous *Method;* mark the various *Scenes*
In heavn'n; *Hail, Thunder, Rain-bows, Snow,* and *Ice,*
Calmes, Tempests, Light, and *darknes* by his means;
    Thou canst not misse his Praise; Each *tree, herb, flowre*
    Are shadows of his *wisedome,* and his Pow'r.

HENRY VAUGHAN
(1622–1695)

Fiercely proud of his Welsh heritage, Henry Vaughan gave himself the title "Silurist" and appended it after his name to all of his writings. The Silures, to whom this title refers, were an ancient Celtic tribe from southeastern Wales (near Caerwent, Gwent) who resisted the Roman invasion of Britain. "Rules and Lessons" is from *Silex Scintallans (The Firey Flint),* published in 1650 and in an expanded edition in 1655.

Solitary Living in Early Winter

This innermost room, with little to do,
is adequate to commit my plain life to.
Drink a bit, and I forget my clothes are thin,
an idea, and I let my brush run aslant.
Wind at the eaves, and the maple sheds its leaves,
on the wet stones chrysanthemums fade.
All day with no guests visiting me,
I've perused books, delighted to learn.

EMA SAIKŌ
(1787–1861)
translated by Hiroaki Sato

Japanese painter and poet Ema Saikō took the name Saikō, which means roughly "breeze through bamboo," from a line by Tu Fu: "When the wind blows the bamboo is delicately fragrant." She became well known in the Tokugawa period for her beautiful *kanshi*, when almost all practitioners of the art were men. She never married or had children, though some suggest she may have been romantically involved with her poetry teacher Rai San'yo. She did not publish her poems during her lifetime, but left behind more than fifteen hundred pieces, which were sorted and selected by her family members and published as *Shomu Iko* in 1870.

October 8

Sonnet — To Science

Science! true daughter of Old Time thou art!
  Who alterest all things with thy peering eyes.
Why preyest thou thus upon the poet's heart,
  Vulture, whose wings are dull realities?
How should he love thee? Or how deem thee wise,
  Who wouldst not leave him in his wandering
To seek for treasure in the jewelled skies,
  Albeit he soared with an undaunted wing?
Hast thou not dragged Diana from her car?
  And driven the Hamadryad from the wood
To seek a shelter in some happier star?
  Hast thou not torn the Naiad from her flood,
The Elfin from the green grass, and from me
The summer dream beneath the tamarind tree?

EDGAR ALLAN POE
(1809–1849)

Edgar Poe was born in Boston, Massachusetts, the son of actor parents. He and his sister were orphaned after their parents died of illness in 1811. Edgar was raised by Mr. and Mrs. John Allan in Richmond, Virginia, and was baptized Edgar Allan Poe in 1813. In 1827, Poe abandoned his studies at the University of Virginia at Charlottesville after one year due to gambling problems. He then enlisted in the army under the name Edgar A. Perry, but he was soon expelled for disobeying orders. In 1836 he married his fourteen-year-old cousin Virginia Clemm, who died eleven years later in 1847. Though Poe's reputation as a writer had been made after the publication of *Tales* and *The Raven and Other Poems* in 1845, in the two years after Virginia's death Poe's battles with alcoholism and opium addiction got the better of him. He was found half-conscious in the streets of Baltimore, Maryland, in October of 1849. Because there was no known reason for Poe to have been in Baltimore, and because he was found wearing another man's clothes, one theory holds that he was drugged and used as a repeat voter in an election-fixing scheme. He died a few days later of "acute congestion of the brain."

Medusa

I had come to the house, in a cave of trees,
Facing a sheer sky.
Everything moved, — a bell hung ready to strike,
Sun and reflection wheeled by.

When the bare eyes were before me
And the hissing hair,
Held up at a window, seen through a door.
The stiff bald eyes, the serpents on the forehead
Formed in the air.

This is a dead scene forever now.
Nothing will ever stir.
The end will never brighten it more than this,
Nor the rain blur.

The water will always fall, and will not fall,
And the tipped bell make no sound.
The grass will always be growing for hay
Deep on the ground.

And I shall stand here like a shadow
Under the great balanced day,
My eyes on the yellow dust, that was lifting in the wind,
And does not drift away.

LOUISE BOGAN
(1897–1970)

Louise Bogan was born in Livermore, Maine, and attended Boston University, though she left without taking a degree. Bogan was poetry editor of *The New Yorker* from 1931 to 1969. While at the *New Yorker* she continued to publish her own poems and criticism and to enjoy her increasing status as a writer, winning several major awards. She died of a heart attack in 1970. "Medusa" is from Bogan's book *Body of this Death: Poems*, published in 1923. The poem first appeared in 1921 in the December issue of the *New Republic* magazine.

On the Beach at Night

On the beach at night,
Stands a child with her father,
Watching the east, the autumn sky.

Up through the darkness,
While ravening clouds, the burial clouds, in black masses spreading,
Lower sullen and fast athwart and down the sky,
Amid a transparent clear belt of ether yet left in the east,
Ascends large and calm the lord-star Jupiter,
And nigh at hand, only a very little above,
Swim the delicate sisters the Pleiades.

From the beach the child holding the hand of her father,
Those burial clouds that lower victorious soon to devour all,
Watching, silently weeps.

Weep not, child,
Weep not, my darling,
With these kisses let me remove your tears,
The ravening clouds shall not long be victorious,
They shall not long possess the sky, they devour the stars only in
    apparition,
Jupiter shall emerge, be patient, watch again another night, the
    Pleiades shall emerge,
They are immortal, all those stars both silvery and golden shall
    shine out again,
The great stars and the little ones shall shine out again, they endure,
The vast immortal suns and the long-enduring pensive moons shall
    again shine.

Then dearest child mournest thou only for Jupiter?
Considerest thou alone the burial of the stars?

Something there is,
(With my lips soothing thee, adding I whisper,
I give thee the first suggestion, the problem and indirection,)
Something there is more immortal even than the stars,
(Many the burials, many the days and nights, passing away,)
Something that shall endure longer even than lustrous Jupiter
Longer than sun or any revolving satellite,
Or the radiant sisters the Pleiades.

WALT WHITMAN
(1819–1892)

Whitman wrote "On the Beach at Night" in 1871 and first published it in the seventh edition of *Leaves of Grass* in 1881. The Pleiades, according to Roman mythology, were the seven daughters of Atlas who were pursued by Orion and transformed into pigeons, then into stars in the constellation Taurus, by Jupiter after pleading for his help. "On the Beach at Night" recalls an earlier poem by Whitman, originally published as "Clef Poem" in 1956, but which he later retitled "On the Beach at Night Alone." That poem begins: "On the beach at night alone, / As the old mother sways to and fro singing her husky song, / As I watch the bright stars shining, I think a thought of the clef of the universes and of the future."

A Supermarket in California

What thoughts I have of you tonight, Walt Whitman, for I walked down the sidestreets under the trees with a headache self-conscious looking at the full moon.

In my hungry fatigue, and shopping for images, I went into the neon fruit supermarket, dreaming of your enumerations!

What peaches and what penumbras! Whole families shopping at night! Aisles full of husbands! Wives in the avocados, babies in the tomatoes! — and you, García Lorca, what were you doing down by the watermelons?

I saw you, Walt Whitman, childless, lonely old grubber, poking among the meats in the refrigerator and eyeing the grocery boys.

I heard you asking questions of each: Who killed the porkchops? What price bananas? Are you my Angel?

I wandered in and out of the brilliant stacks of cans following you, and followed in my imagination by the store detective.

We strode down the open corridors together in our solitary fancy tasting artichokes, possessing every frozen delicacy, and never passing the cashier.

Where are we going, Walt Whitman? The doors close in an hour. Which way does your beard point tonight?

(I touch your book and dream of our odyssey in the supermarket and feel absurd.)

Will we walk all night through solitary streets? The trees add shade to shade, lights out in the houses, we'll both be lonely.

Will we stroll dreaming of the lost America of love past blue automobiles in driveways, home to our silent cottage?

Ah, dear father, graybeard, lonely old courage-teacher, what America did you have when Charon quit poling his ferry and you got out on a smoking bank and stood watching the boat disappear on the black waters of Lethe?

ALLEN GINSBERG
(1926–1997)

Allen Ginsberg was born in Newark, New Jersey, and educated at Columbia University, where he met William S. Burroughs, Neal Cassady, and Jack Kerouac. The four friends later went on to become the leading figures of the Beat movement. Ginsberg's major work *Howl and Other Poems* was published in 1956 by Lawrence Ferlinghetti's City Lights Press. The San Francisco Police Department declared the book obscene and arrested Ferlinghetti. The ensuing trial captured national attention and, in the end, *Howl* became one of the most widely read poems of the twentieth century, translated into more than twenty languages. Ginsberg frequently invoked Walt Whitman, as he does here, as his poetic father and greatest influence. He died of a heart attack, while also sick with liver cancer, in 1997.

The Pleasures of the Door

Kings do not touch doors.

They know nothing of this pleasure: pushing before one gently or brusquely one of those large familiar panels, then turning back to replace it — holding a door in one's arms.

. . . The pleasure of grabbing the midriff of one of these tall obstacles to a room by its porcelain node; that short clinch during which movement stops, the eye widens, and the whole body adjusts to its new surrounding.

With a friendly hand one still holds on to it, before closing it decisively and shutting oneself in — which the click of the tight but well-oiled spring pleasantly confirms.

FRANCIS PONGE
(1899–1988)
translated by Beth Archer

As in "The Pleasures of the Door," Francis Ponge often treated a single object to a close-up view in his poems, including pieces such as "The Candle" and the long prose poem "Introduction to the Pebble." An appreciative article written by Jean-Paul Sartre in the early 1940s helped bring attention to Ponge's work. James Merrill was also a fan. In a review published in *The New York Review of Books* in 1972, Merrill wrote that "Ponge may be the first poet ever to expose so openly the machinery of a poem, to present his revisions, blind alleys, critical asides, and accidental felicities as part of a text perfected, as it were, without 'finish.'. . . One meets a mind desiring and deferring, both, according to the laws of baroque music, solution and resolution, the final breaking of an enchantment that may already have lasted weeks, years. . . ." (See also: June 30.)

October 13

Mediocrity in Love Rejected

Give me more love, or more disdain;
    The torrid or the frozen zone
Bring equal ease unto my pain;
    The temperate affords me none:
Either extreme, of love or hate,
Is sweeter than a calm estate.

Give me a storm; if it be love,
    Like Danae in that golden shower,
I swim in pleasure; if it prove
Disdain, that torrent will devour
My vulture hopes; and he's possessed
Of heaven that's but from hell released.
    Then crown my joys, or cure my pain;
    Give me more love, or more disdain.

THOMAS CAREW
(1595–1640)

As with several of his contemporaries, there is some debate over the exact year of Thomas Carew's birth, though most sources agree it is either 1594 or 1595. Carew was born in West Wickham, Kent, England, to Matthew and Alice Carew. He entered Merton College at age thirteen, took his B.A. in 1611, and went on to Middle Temple to continue his studies. A financial setback for his family forced him to leave Middle Temple to work as a secretary for Sir Dudley Carleton, English Ambassador to Venice. On his travels with Carleton, Carew began reading Italian literature and studying European languages. After his service to Carleton ended, he became Gentleman of the Privy Chamber Extraordinary and later cup-bearer to Charles I. Carew died in 1640 after suffering from syphilis and the effects of the harsh winter in Scotland where he'd accompanied Charles I to the wars. "Mediocrity in Love Rejected" was first published posthumously in his only collection, *Poems*.

The Moon Rising

When the moon rises,
the bells hang silent,
and impenetrable footpaths
appear.

When the moon rises,
the sea covers the land,
and the heart feels
like an island in infinity.

Nobody eats oranges
under the full moon.
One must eat fruit
that is green and cold.

When the moon rises,
moon of a hundred equal faces,
the silver coinage
sobs in the pocket.

FEDERICO GARCÍA LORCA
(1898–1936)
translated by Lysander Kemp

Federico García Lorca was born in Fuentevaqueros, Granada, Spain. He studied law at Sacred Heart University and the University of Madrid, and he published his first book, a travelogue titled *Impresiones y Viajes (Impressions and Views)*, at the age of twenty. As a student in Madrid, he met Luis Buñuel and Salvador Dali, both major figures of Spanish Surrealism. He visited New York City for eight months in 1929 and 1930, and his book *Poet in New York* would come from this experience, which he later credited with changing his life and art. García Lorca was prolific and well known, the author of several volumes of poems, dozens of plays — he even illustrated work by Pablo Neruda and others — though many of his works on homosexual themes remained unpublished in his lifetime. He was executed by Francisco Franco's soldiers in July 1936 and his body was never found.

October 15

After Love

Afterwards, the compromise.
Bodies resume their boundaries.

These legs, for instance, mine.
Your arms take you back in.

Spoons of our fingers, lips
admit their ownership.

The bedding yawns, a door
blows aimlessly ajar

and overhead, a plane
singsongs coming down.

Nothing is changed, except
there was a moment when

the wolf, the mongering wolf
who stands outside the self

lay lightly down, and slept.

MAXINE KUMIN
(1925–)

Maxine Kumin was born and raised in Philadelphia, Pennsylvania. In addition to
almost a dozen volumes of poetry, she has also written novels, short stories, essays,
and children's books. She has received many major awards for her work, including
the Pulitzer Prize in 1972, and has been Poet Laureate of New Hampshire, as well as
the United States Poet Laureate from 1981 to 1982. She is a former Chancellor of the
Academy of American Poets and lives with her husband in New Hampshire. Despite
the fact that she's comfortable working in various genres, she once told an inter-
viewer "If the muse came down and said 'choose,' I would choose poetry."

October 16

Dulce et Decorum Est

Bent double, like old beggars under sacks,
Knock-kneed, coughing like hags, we cursed through sludge,
Till on the haunting flares we turned our backs
And towards our distant rest began to trudge.
Men marched asleep. Many had lost their boots
But limped on, blood-shod. All went lame; all blind;
Drunk with fatigue; deaf even to the hoots
Of tired, outstripped Five-Nines that dropped behind.

Gas! GAS! Quick, boys! — An ecstasy of fumbling,
Fitting the clumsy helmets just in time;
But someone still was yelling out and stumbling,
And flound'ring like a man in fire or lime . . .
Dim, through the misty panes and thick green light,
As under a green sea, I saw him drowning.

In all my dreams, before my helpless sight,
He plunges at me, guttering, choking, drowning.

If in some smothering dreams you too could pace
Behind the wagon that we flung him in,
And watch the white eyes writhing in his face,
His hanging face, like a devil's sick of sin;
If you could here, at every jolt, the blood
Come gargling from the froth-corrupted lungs,
Obscene as cancer, bitter as the cud
Of vile, incurable sores on innocent tongues, —
My friend, you would not tell with such high zest
To children ardent for some desperate glory,
The old Lie: Dulce et decorum est
Pro patria mori.

WILFRED OWEN
(1893–1918)

Wilfred Owen was born in Oswestry, Shropshire, England. He enlisted in the English army in 1915 and was sent to the front in France that same year. In 1917 he was hospitalized for shellshock in Crailockhart War Hospital. Shortly after his release, he was killed in battle in 1918, one week before the signing of the armistice. *Poems by Wilfred Owen* was published later that year, with an introduction by Siegfried Sassoon.

October 17

Sonnet XIV

Batter my heart, three-personed God; for you
As yet but knock, breathe, shine, and seek to mend;
That I may rise, and stand, o'erthrow me, and bend
Your force, to break, blow, burn, and make me new.
I, like an usurped town to another due,
Labour to admit you, but oh, to no end:
Reason your viceroy in me, me should defend,
But is captived, and proves weak or untrue;
Yet dearly I love you, and would be loved fain,
But am betrothed unto your enemy:
Divorce me, untie, or break that knot again,
Take me to you, imprison me, for I
Except you enthral me, never shall be free,
Nor ever chaste, except you ravish me.

JOHN DONNE
(1572–1631)

John Donne was born in London, England, in 1572. Along with Andrew Marvell, George Herbert, Richard Crawshaw, Thomas Traherne, Henry Vaughan, and John Cleveland, Donne was dubbed a "Metaphysical Poet" by Samuel Johnson in 1744. "Sonnet XIV" is another one of Donne's so-called Holy Sonnets, and was first published in 1633. (See also: August 5.)

The Abduction

The bells, the cannons, the houses black with crepe,
all for the great Harrison! The citizenry of Washington
clotted the avenue — I among them, Solomon Northrup
from Saratoga Springs, free papers in my pocket, violin
under arm, my new friends Brown and Hamilton by my side.

Why should I have doubted them? The wages were good.
While Brown's tall hat collected pennies at the tent flap,
Hamilton's feet did a jig on a tightrope,
pigs squealed invisibly from the bleachers and I fiddled.

I remember how the windows rattled with each report.
Then the wine, like a pink lake, tipped.
I was lifted — the sky swivelled, clicked into place.

I floated on water I could not drink. Though the pillow
was stone, I climbed no ladders in that sleep.

I woke and found myself alone, in darkness and in chains.

RITA DOVE
(1952–)

The speaker of Dove's poem "The Abduction" is Solomon Northrup, who was born
a free man in Minerva, New York, in 1808. In 1841, Northrup was kidnapped from
Saratoga Springs and sold into slavery in the South, leaving behind a wife and three
children. His freedom was restored in 1853, thanks in part to the efforts of Samuel
Bass, a Canadian advocate. After his release, Northrup published an autobiography
titled *Twelve Years a Slave*.

A Kind of Loss

Used together: seasons, books, a piece of music.
The keys, teacups, bread basket, sheets and a bed.
A hope chest of words, of gestures, brought back, used, used up.
A household order maintained. Said. Done. And always a hand was there.

I've fallen in love with winter, with a Viennese septet, with summer.
With village maps, a mountain nest, a beach and a bed.
Kept a calendar cult, declared promises irrevocable,
bowed before something, was pious to a nothing

(— to a folded newspaper, cold ashes, the scribbled piece of paper),
fearless in religion, for our bed was the church.

From my lake view arose my inexhaustible painting.
From my balcony I greeted entire peoples, my neighbors.
By the chimney fire, in safety, my hair took on its deepest hue.
The ringing at the door was the alarm for my joy.

It's not you I've lost,
but the world.

INGEBORG BACHMANN
(1926–1973)
translated by Mark Anderson

As Ruth Franklin wrote in *The New Republic* in July 2000, "Bachmann wrestled with the problem of how to make sense of the crimes that Nazi Germany committed during the Holocaust — crimes so new and so shocking that they seemed to poison the German language itself, the essence of the German nation. Eventually Bachmann would come to see the legacy of the Holocaust as a brand of fascism that survived in the private sphere, in the relationships between men and women. At the same time, she would dream of a utopian language that could fill in the gaps, a language that could express the things about which one cannot speak and thus redeem the nearly universal silence of Germans in the face of, and even after, the Holocaust." (See also: May 11.)

Sonnet 73

That time of year thou mayst in me behold
When yellow leaves, or none, or few, do hang
Upon those boughs which shake against the cold,
Bare ruined choirs, where late the sweet birds sang.
In me thou see'st the twilight of such day
As after sunset fadeth in the west,
Which by and by black night doth take away,
Death's second self that seals up all in rest.
In me thou see'st the glowing of such fire,
That on the ashes of his youth doth lie,
As the death-bed, whereon it must expire
Consumed with that which it was nourished by.
This thou perceiv'st, which makes thy love more strong
To love that well, which thou must leave ere long.

WILLIAM SHAKESPEARE
(1564–1616)

Shakespeare's *Sonnets* was first published in 1609 with the following dedication: "To the Only Beggetter of / These Ensuing Sonnets / Mr. W. H. All Happiness / and That Eternity / Promised / By / Our Ever-Living Poet / Wisheth / the Well-Wishing / Adventurer in Setting Forth / T.T." T.T. has been identified as Thomas Thorpe, Shakespeare's publisher, but the identity of W. H. has long been a subject of debate. (See also: February 19.) Poet John Berryman, who wrote an entire book's worth of essays on Shakespeare's work, chose "Sonnet 73" as one of his favorites and pronounced it "one of the best poems in English."

The Wild Swans at Coole

The trees are in their autumn beauty,
The woodland paths are dry,
Under the October twilight the water
Mirrors a still sky;
Upon the brimming water among the stones
Are nine-and-fifty swans.

The nineteenth autumn has come upon me
Since I first made my count;
I saw, before I had well finished,
All suddenly mount
And scatter wheeling in great broken rings
Upon their clamorous wings.

I have looked upon those brilliant creatures,
And now my heart is sore.
All's changed since I, hearing at twilight,
The first time on this shore,
The bell-beat of their wings above my head,
Trod with a lighter tread.

Unwearied still, lover by lover,
They paddle in the cold
Companionable streams or climb the air;
Their hearts have not grown old;
Passion or conquest, wander where they will,
Attend upon them still.

But now they drift on the still water,
Mysterious, beautiful;
Among what rushes will they build,
By what lake's edge or pool
Delight men's eyes when I awake some day
To find they have flown away?

WILLIAM BUTLER YEATS
(1865–1939)

William Butler Yeats was born in Dublin, Ireland. His father was a painter who encouraged "Willie" to write poems and sent him to school at the Dublin Metropolitan School of Art instead of university. Yeats was keenly interested in mysticism and Irish history and folklore, and he also founded the Irish Literary Theatre in Dublin, which eventually became the famous Abbey. He met the love of his life, the radical Irish nationalist Maude Gonne, in 1889 when she visited him to say that his poem "The Wanderings of Oisin" had brought her to tears. Though Yeats and Gonne both married others, Yeats continued to write poems for her for many years. "The Wild Swans at Coole" refers to Coole Park, the estate in western Ireland owned by Lady Augusta Gregory. Yeats often visited Gregory at Coole Park and wrote many of his poems there. This poem was composed in 1916.

Death of a Pair of Shoes

They're dying on me! They've lived
Faithfully, Christian
Servants honored
And happy helping

And pleasing their master,
A tired traveler
Reading to quit
For peace of soul and foot.

These soles know. They know
Step by step long rambles
And wet days, floundering
Among slop and cobbles.

Even the color drains
From the sad skins
Which, plain as they were, livened
Some forgotten festival.

All this announces a ruin
I don't grasp. The affliction
Of living corrodes honor.
They're running. Specters! Shoes!

JORGE GUILLÉN
(1893–1984)
translated by Philip Levine

Jorge Guillén was born in Valladolid, Old Castle, Spain, in 1893 and educated in Spain, Switzerland, and Germany. He began writing poetry seriously in 1919 and was associated with the other poets of the "Generation of 1927," including Rafael Alberti, Pedro Celinas, Federico Garcia Lorca, and others. Guillén fled from Spain in 1938, after Francisco Franco installed himself as dictator. He lived in the United States for more than twenty years, teaching poetry at Wellesley College until his retirement in 1957. He received the Award of Merit from the American Academy of Arts and Letters, the San Luca Prize, the Alfonso Reyes Prize, and the Cervantes Prize, among other honors. He returned to Spain two years after Francisco Franco's death and died in 1984 in Malaga.

Dream Song #14

Life, friends, is boring. We must not say so.
After all, the sky flashes, the great sea yearns,
we ourselves flash and yearn,
and moreover my mother told me as a boy
(repeatingly) 'Ever to confess you're bored
means you have no

Inner Resources.' I conclude now I have no
inner resources, because I am heavy bored.
Peoples bore me,
literature bores me, especially great literature,
Henry bores me, with his plights & gripes
as bad as achilles,

who loves people and valiant art, which bores me.
And the tranquil hills, & grin, look like a drag
and somehow a dog
has taken itself & its tail considerably away
into mountains or sea or sky, leaving
behind: me, wag.

JOHN BERRYMAN
(1914–1972)

John Berryman was born John Allyn Smith in MacAlaster, Oklahoma, the son of a small-town banker and a schoolteacher. His father shot himself to death when John was not quite twelve, and John would never fully recover from this tragedy. His mother remarried and John took his stepfather's last name, Berryman. John Berryman went to Columbia University, where he met Dylan Thomas and W. B. Yeats and impressed his teachers with his brilliance. An alcoholic with a theatrical personality, Berryman cultivated writerly affectations, dressing in tweeds and putting on his own version of a British accent. He taught at the University of Minnesota for many years and by most accounts was a fascinating, if sometimes frustrating, lecturer. He was hospitalized several times for emotional exhaustion and complications from his alcohol abuse, and finally committed suicide in 1972 by leaping from a bridge in Minneapolis. "Dream Song #14" is from Berryman's major work *Dream Songs,* a long sequence of interconnected poems first published as *77 Dream Songs* in 1964. That book won him the Pulitzer Prize, and he continued to add to the sequence, which eventually contained almost four hundred poems.

October 24

All Hushed and Still within the House

All hushed and still within the house;
Without — all wind and driving rain;
But something whispers to my mind,
Through rain and through the wailing wind,
    Never again.
Never again? Why not again?
Memory has power as real as thine.

EMILY BRONTË
(1818–1848)

Emily Brontë, best known as the author of *Wuthering Heights,* was given drawing lessons as a girl when her father hired a tutor for her brother Branwell, allowing Branwell's sisters to participate as well. In the few drawings by her that remain, she portrays herself only from the back, face turned away from the viewer.

Poem (I Can't Speak for the Wind)

I don't know about the cold.
I am sad without hands.
I can't speak for the wind
which chips away at me.
When pulling a potato, I see only the blue haze.
When riding an escalator, I expect something orthopedic to happen.
Sinking in quicksand, I'm a wild appaloosa.
I fly into a rage at the sight of a double-decker bus,
I want to eat my way through the Congo,
I'm a double-agent who tortures himself
and still will not speak.
I don't know about the cold,
But I know what I like I like a tropical madness,
I like to shake the coconuts
and fingerprint the pythons, —
fevers which make the children dance.
I am sad without hands,
I'm very sad without sleeves or pockets.
Winter is coming to this city,
I can't speak for the wind
which chips away at me.

JAMES TATE
(1943–)

James Tate was born in Kansas City, Missouri. He is the author of numerous books of poetry and has also published a novel and short stories. He has received the National Book Award and the Pulitzer Prize, and he is a Chancellor of the Academy of American Poets. He teaches poetry at the University of Massachusetts in Amherst.

Brueghel's Two Monkeys

This is what I see in my dreams about final exams:
two monkeys, chained to the floor, sit on the windowsill,
the sky behind them flutters,
the sea is taking its bath.

The exam is History of Mankind.
I stammer and hedge.

One monkey stares and listens with mocking disdain,
the other seems to be dreaming away —
but when it's clear I don't know what to say
he prompts me with a gentle
clinking of his chain.

WISLAWA SZYMBORSKA

(1923–)

translated by Stanislav Baránczak and Clare Cavanagh

Polish poet Wislawa Szymborska was born in Bnin (now a part of Kórnik) in western
Poland in 1923. She studied Polish literature and sociology at Jagiellonian University
in Krakow, where she has lived since 1931. She received the Nobel Prize for Literature
in 1996. "Brueghel's Two Monkeys" is from her book *Calling Out to Yeti,* published
in 1957. The title refers to Pieter Brueghel, the Flemish painter, and his painting "Two
Monkeys" (1562), which is housed in the Dahlem Museum in Berlin.

from *The Tempest*
  Act III, Scene ii

Be not afeard: the isle is full of noises,
Sounds and sweet airs, that give delight, and hurt not.
Sometimes a thousand twangling instruments
Will hum about mine ears; and sometime voices,
That, if I then had wak'd after long sleep,
Will make me sleep again: and then, in dreaming,
The clouds methought would open and show riches
Ready to drop upon me; that, when I wak'd
I cried to dream again.

WILLIAM SHAKESPEARE
(1564–1616)

In *The Tempest,* the character Caliban, the "savage and deformed slave" of Prospero,
speaks this poem to Stephano and Trinculo, with whom he is drinking. Caliban has
asked Stephano and Trinculo to free him from Prospero's service and help him take
revenge. Ariel, unseen, stands listening to their plot and frightens the drunkards by
playing a song on pipe and tabor, the "sweet airs" to which Caliban refers to in line 2.
(See also: May 19.)

October 28

Guitar

I have always loved the word *guitar.*

I have no memories of my father on the patio
At dusk, strumming a Spanish tune,
Or my mother draped in that fawn wicker chair
Polishing her flute;
I have no memories of your song, distant Sister
Heart, of those steel strings sliding
All night through the speaker of the car radio
Between Tucumcari and Oklahoma City, Oklahoma.
Though I've never believed those stories
Of gypsy cascades, stolen horses, castanets,
And stars, of Airstream trailers and good fortune,
Though I never met Charlie Christian, though
I've danced the floors of cold longshoremen's halls,
Though I've waited with the overcoats at the rear
Of concerts for lute, mandolin, and two guitars —
More than the music I love scaling its woven
Stairways, more than the swirling chocolate of wood

I have always loved the word *guitar.*

DAVID ST. JOHN
(1949–)

David St. John was born in Fresno, California. He received a B.A. from California State University, Fresno, and an M.F.A. from the University of Iowa. He is a professor in the English department of the University of Southern California, Los Angeles. "Poems are living things," St. John once told an interviewer, "breathing quite literally with the breaths and the rhythms of their poets, singing with the melodies of their makers, and following the course or courses of a mind in movement across an experience, a memory, a desire."

Talking in Bed

Talking in bed ought to be easiest,
Lying together there goes back so far,
An emblem of two people being honest.

Yet more and more time passes silently.
Outside, the wind's incomplete unrest
Builds and disperses clouds about the sky,

And dark towns heap up on the horizon.
None of this cares for us. Nothing shows why
At this unique distance from isolation

It becomes still more difficult to find
Words at once true and kind,
Or not untrue and not unkind.

PHILIP LARKIN
(1922–1985)

English poet Philip Larkin was born in Coventry and educated at St. John's College, Oxford. Larkin was a leading figure of a group of English poets called simply "The Movement," which included Kingsley Amis, Thom Gunn, Donald Davie, and John Wain. The group's members valued clarity and wit over what they considered the grand poetic gestures of poets such as Yeats and Dylan Thomas. Larkin, though he was one of the most popular poets in England, was a reclusive, somewhat antisocial man who never married and lived a quiet life as a librarian at the University of Hull. He refused the title of English Poet Laureate when it was offered to him in 1984, unable to stand the thought of the media attention and high public profile. He died of cancer in 1985. "Talking in Bed" is from Larkin's book *The Whitsun Wedding*, for which he won the Queen's Gold Medal in Poetry, published in 1964.

October 30

Notes on the 1860s

George Boole's book on the laws of thought appeared in 1844;
that's three years before Baudelaire's *Les Fleurs du Mal.*

In Boole's book the seed of the computer is to be found,
the ticking relays, the vacuum tubes of the future.

With charming innocence this algebra teaches us
that every set has something in common with the "empty set."

The empty set. In a dream I meet Baudelaire,
small, transparent, dark shadows under his eyes,

and I insist that he comment on Boole.
He accepts this request as being altogether natural

and starts with a quotation from the Marquis de Sade:

"Nothing floods us with fear and lust so much
as knowledge of the ticking relays, the vacuum tubes,

murmurs that come from the hotter mineshafts of the future."

All of a sudden he checks himself, as if he'd said too much.

"Sir, we walk on ice polished by the wind. You understand?

We live in a time when the wind is rising."

LARS GUSTAFSSON
(1936–)
translated by Christopher Middleton

Lars Gustafsson was born in Vesteraas, Sweden, and received his doctorate in philosophy from the University of Uppsala. He is the former editor-in-chief of *Bonniers,* a Stockholm-based literary magazine. He has been teaching in the Department of Germanic Studies at the University of Texas since 1981 and is currently the Hayden W. Head Regents Professor in the Plan II Honors Program there. In addition to poetry, Gustafsson is also the author of highly acclaimed short stories and novels, works of philosophy, plays, and translations of Rainer Maria Rilke and Christopher Middleton, among other poets.

October 31

Halloween
(from "19 Hadley Street")

The children's room glows radiantly by
The light of the pumpkins on the windowsill
That fiercely grin on sleeping boy and girl.
She stirs and mutters in her sleep, Goodbye,

Who scared herself a little in a sheet
And walked the streets with devils and dinosaurs
And bleeping green men flown from distant stars.
We sit up late, and smoke, and talk about

Our awkward, loving Frankenstein in bed
Who told his sister that it isn't true,
That real men in real boxes never do
Haunt houses. But the King of the Dead

Has taken off his mask tonight, and twirled
His cape and vanished, and we are his
Who know beyond all doubt how real he is:
Out of his bag of sweets he plucks the world.

GJERTRUD SCHNACKENBERG
(1953–)

Gjertrud Schnackenberg was born in Tacoma, Washington, and educated at Mount
Holyoke College. "19 Hadley Street" is a sequence of sixteen poems that involve the
history of New England and range backward in time from the present to 1725.
Schnackenberg wrote "19 Hadley Street" in 1975 and the poem was included in her
1982 volume *Portraits and Elegies*.

November 1

Five Dawn Skies in November

1

At the roots of clouds a cutworm hollowing
The night, its eyes moonblind.

2

On the sheen of a lake the moment before wind,
Before rain, a loon floating asleep.

3

As smoothly blurred as (seen through water) a marten
Rippling among marshgrass.

4

Deepening into winter, a bear at her burrow
At first light on the first light snow.

5

A salmon stranded on stones, its mouth still opening
And closing toward the river.

DAVID WAGONER
(1926–)

David Wagoner was born in Masillon, Ohio, and has published ten novels in addition to more than a dozen collections of poems. He was editor of *Poetry Northwest* for several decades and is a former Chancellor of the Academy of American Poets. He is currently Professor Emeritus of English and Creative Writing at the University of Washington.

Poem

Lana Turner has collapsed!
I was trotting along and suddenly
it started raining and snowing
and you said it was hailing
but hailing hits you on the head
hard so it was really snowing and
raining and I was in such a hurry
to meet you but the traffic
was acting exactly like the sky
and suddenly I see a headline
LANA TURNER HAS COLLAPSED!
there is no snow in Hollywood
there is no rain in California
I have been to lots of parties
and acted perfectly disgraceful
but I never actually collapsed
oh Lana Turner we love you get up

FRANK O'HARA
(1926–1966)

As with his poem "The Day Lady Died," in "Poem" Frank O'Hara is responding to a newspaper story (see the poem for July 17). On February 9, 1962, the tabloids ran a story reporting that the actress Lana Turner had fainted at a recent party. O'Hara wrote the poem on the fly, as he so often did, on his way to give a poetry reading with Robert Lowell at Wagner College on Staten Island, New York City. He read it later that night to the appreciative audience.

November 3

The Voice of the Rain

And who art thou? said I to the soft-falling shower,
Which, strange to tell, gave me an answer, as here translated:
I am the Poem of Earth, said the voice of the rain,
Eternal I rise impalpable out of the land and the bottomless sea,
Upward to heaven, whence, vaguely form'd, altogether changed,
    and yet the same,
I descend to lave the drouths, atomies, dust-layers of the globe,
And all that in them without me were seeds only, latent, unborn;
And forever, by day and night, I give back life to my own origin
    and make pure and beautify it;

(For song, issuing from its birth-place, after fulfilment, wandering,
Reck'd or unreck'd, duly with love returns.)

WALT WHITMAN
(1819–1892)

"The Voice of the Rain" is from the "First Annex: Sands of Seventy" of the later editions of *Leaves of Grass*. The entire annex originally appeared with the poems from the section now known as "A Backward Glance O'er Travel'd Roads" in a collection titled *November Boughs* in 1888. In that same year, Whitman's young friend Horace Traubel began taking shorthand transcriptions of his daily conversations with the poet. Traubel served as something of a secretary to Whitman, buying his pens, ordering his stationery, having his clothes specially tailored. In the evenings, the two would sit around the stove at Whitman's home at Mickle Street in Camden, New Jersey, where Whitman would promise some day to tell him a great secret. Or he would ask about the outside world, a world he saw less and less of as his health deteriorated. "Horace, this telephone thing," he once asked, "can you really hear the fellow on the other end?" Traubel continued to take down Whitman's words right up until the poet's death in 1892. His last word was "shift," as he was asking to be turned on his waterbed.

November 4

#168

The Autumn day its course has run — the Autumn evening falls
Already risen the Autumn moon gleams quiet on these walls
And Twilight to my lonely house a silent guest is come
In mask of gloom through every room she passes dusk and dumb
Her veil is spread, her shadow shed o'er stair and chamber void
And now I feel her presence steal even to my lone fireside
Sit silent Nun — sit there and be
Comrade and Confidant to me

CHARLOTTE BRONTË
(1816–1855)

Although Charlotte Brontë died at the age of thirty-nine, she had outlived all of her sisters and her brother. She is best known, of course, for her novel, *Jane Eyre*. (See also: July 27.)

O Taste and See

The world is
not with us enough.
O taste and see

the subway Bible poster said,
meaning The Lord, meaning
if anything all that lives
to the imagination's tongue,

grief, mercy, language,
tangerine, weather, to
breathe them, bite,
savor, chew, swallow, transform

into our flesh our
deaths, crossing the street, plum, quince,
living in the orchard and being

hungry, and plucking
the fruit.

DENISE LEVERTOV
(1923–1997)

Denise Levertov was born in Ilford, Essex, England, and at the age of twelve sent some of her poems in a letter to T. S. Eliot. The older poet replied with two pages of advice and encouraged Levertov to keep writing. She published her first poems in *Poetry Quarterly* at the age of seventeen. During World War II, she served as a civilian nurse in London, and she published her first book at the age of twenty-three in 1946. In 1947 she married American writer Mitchell Goodman and the couple settled in New York City the following year. She became a United States citizen in 1956. Denise Levertov published more than twenty volumes of poetry, served as an editor of *Mother Jones* magazine, and won several major awards. She died from complications of lymphoma in 1997. "O Taste and See" is the title poem of her 1964 collection of new poems. The first stanza is a comment on William Wordsworth's poem "The World Is Too Much with Us," which begins "The world is too much with us; late and soon, / Getting and spending, we lay waste our powers."

A Birthday

My heart is like a singing bird
    Whose nest is in a watered shoot;
My heart is like an apple-tree
    Whose boughs are bent with thickset fruit;
My heart is like a rainbow shell
    That paddles in a halcyon sea;
My heart is gladder than all these
    Because my love is come to me.

Raise me a dais of silk and down;
    Hang it with vair and purple dyes;
Carve it in doves and pomegranates,
    And peacocks with a hundred eyes;
Work it in gold and silver grapes,
    In leaves and silver fleurs-de-lys;
Because the birthday of my life
    Is come, my love is come to me.

CHRISTINA ROSSETTI
(1830–1894)

Sister to poet and painter Dante Gabriel Rossetti, Christina Rossetti was born in London to Italian parents. She published her first poems privately via her grandfather's printing press and also published early work under the pseudonym Ellen Alleyne in *The Germ,* a magazine founded by her brother William Michael and others. Rossetti suffered from Graves' disease and was often restricted to bed rest, though she continued to write her poems and children's verses, in addition to prose works on religious topics. She died of cancer in 1894. "A Birthday" was first published in *Macmillan's Magazine* in 1861.

Black Stone on a White Stone

I'll die in Paris on a rainy day,
a day which I can already remember.
I'll die in Paris — and I won't skip town —
maybe on Thursday, like today, in autumn.

It must be Thursday, since today Thursday, as
I set these lines down, I've put my shoulder bones
on wrong, and never like today have I turned,
with all my road, to see myself alone.

César Vallejo is dead. Everyone beat him
although he didn't do a thing to them;
they beat him hard with a big stick and hard

also with a gross rope; witnesses are
the Thursdays and the crooked shoulder bones,
the lonely solitude, the rain, the roads.

CÉSAR VALLEJO
(1892–1938)
translated by Willis Barnstone

César Vallejo was born in Santiago de Chuco, Peru, an isolated village in the northern region of the country. He attended classes at Trujillo University, but had to drop out due to financial circumstances. He continued his education in this stop-and-start manner until 1915, when he finally achieved his master's degree in Spanish literature, and he continued to study law until 1917. He worked as a school principal in Lima until he was forced to resign because of a scandalous romantic affair. After being fired from a second teaching job, Vallejo was arrested and briefly imprisoned for being an "intellectual instigator" in a feud in his hometown. He returned to Lima after he was paroled. He left Peru permanently in 1923 and settled in Paris, where he began studying Marxism and became interested in Communism, until he was forced by police to leave the country. He traveled to Madrid, Spain, where he remained until he could obtain a permit to return to Paris. He did receive one, but it forbade him from engaging in political activity of any kind. He nevertheless became intensely involved with the loyalist cause in the Spanish Civil War, even visiting the front at one point. He died of a mysterious fever in Paris in 1938, saying, "I am going to Spain! I want to go to Spain!"

To Marguerite

Yes! in the sea of life enisled,
With echoing straits between us thrown,
Dotting the shoreless watery wild,
We mortal millions live alone.
The islands feel the enclasping flow,
And then their endless bounds they know.

But when the moon their hollows lights,
And they are swept by balms of spring,
And in their glens, on starry nights,
The nightingales divinely sing;
And lovely notes, from shore to shore,
Across the sounds and channels pour —

Oh! then a longing like despair
Is to their farthest caverns sent;
For surely once, they feel, we were
Parts of a single continent!
Now round us spreads the watery plain —
Oh might our marges meet again!

Who ordered, that their longing's fire
Should be, as soon as kindled, cooled?
Who renders vain their deep desire? —
A God, a God their severance ruled!
And bade betwixt their shores to be
The unplumbed, salt, estranging sea.

MATTHEW ARNOLD
(1822–1888)

Matthew Arnold was born in Laeland-on-Thames, England. He received his education at Balliol College, Oxford, and then became an inspector of schools, a job he held for thirty-five years. He wrote most of his major poetry between 1845 and 1867, after which he focused his writing on education and literary criticism, convinced that he could not successfully convey the joy he meant to express in his poems. "To Marguerite" was first published under the title "To Marguerite, in Returning a Volume of Letters of Ortis." In later editions of Arnold's work, he combined this poem with one called "Isolation: To Marguerite" as a single piece. The identity of Marguerite remains a matter of debate among scholars.

November 9

#92

Do you remember

How a golden
broom grows on
the sea beaches

SAPPHO
(CA. 610–580 B.C.)
translated by Mary Barnard

Since our knowledge of the facts of Sappho's life is so fragmentary, it is difficult to separate fact from fiction in stories about the early Greek poet. According to legend, she fell in love with a beautiful youth named Phaon, and when he did not return her love, she committed suicide by flinging herself off a cliff in Leucadia and drowned in the sea. Byron refers to this story in the second canto of his long poem "Childe Harold": "Childe Harold sailed and passed the barren spot / Where sad Penelope o'erlooked the wave, / And onward viewed the mount, not yet forgot, / The lover's refuge and the Lesbian's grave. / Dark Sappho! could not verse immortal save / That breast imbued with such immortal fire?" This story gave rise to the idea of the "lover's leap." (See also: January 20.)

Song: To Celia (I)

Come, my Celia, let us prove,
While we can, the sports of love;
Time will not be ours forever;
He at length our good will sever.
Spend not then his gifts in vain.
Suns that set may rise again;
But if once we lose this light,
'Tis with us perpetual night.
Why should we defer our joys?
Fame and rumor are but toys.
Cannot we delude the eyes
Of a few poor household spies,
Or his easier ears beguile,
So removèd by our wile?
'Tis no sin love's fruit to steal;
But the sweet thefts to reveal,
To be taken, to be seen,
These have crimes accounted been.

BEN JONSON
(1572–1637)

Benjamin Jonson was born in London and educated at Westminster School. He served in the military in the Low Countries and then returned to England to pursue a career in the theater. In 1598 he killed a fellow actor in a duel. To escape a sentence, all he had to do was prove he could read a verse from the Bible, a legal maneuver known then as "the benefit of clergy." As a playwright, Jonson was both censored and imprisoned for what authorities considered lewd material, but he eventually earned the favor of King James I of Scotland and received a substantial royal pension. Unlike his contemporary William Shakespeare, Jonson cultivated a public persona as an author and drew disciples, sometimes called the "tribes of Ben," around him. This poem is from his play *Volpone,* and is one of two songs addressed to Celia by the lusty protagonist.

November 11

Facing It

My black face fades,
hiding inside the black granite.
I said I wouldn't,
dammit: No tears.
I'm stone. I'm flesh.
My clouded reflection eyes me
like a bird of prey, the profile of night
slanted against morning. I turn
this way — the stone lets me go.
I turn that way — I'm inside
the Vietnam Veterans Memorial
again, depending on the light
to make a difference.
I go down the 58,022 names,
half-expecting to find
my own in letters like smoke.
I touch the name Andrew Johnson;
I see the booby trap's white flash.
Names shimmer on a woman's blouse
but when she walks away
the names stay on the wall.
Brushstrokes flash, a red bird's
wings cutting across my stare.
The sky. A plane in the sky.
A white vet's image floats
closer to me, then his pale eyes
look through mine. I'm a window.
He's lost his right arm
inside the stone. In the black mirror
a woman's trying to erase names:
No, she's brushing a boy's hair.

YUSEF KOMUNYAKAA
(1947–)

"Facing It" explores Yusef Komunyakaa's experiences as a soldier and war correspondent
in Vietnam. The polished black granite surface of the Vietnam Veterans Memorial lists
chronologically all the American soldiers killed in the war.

My Young Mother

My young mother, her face narrow
and dark with unresolved wishes
under a hatbrim of the twenties,
stood by my middleaged bed.

Still as a child pretending sleep
to a grownup watchful or calling,
I lay in a corner of my dream
staring at the mole above her lip.

Familiar mole! but that girlish look
as if I had nothing to give her —
Eyes blue — brim dark —
calling me from sleep after decades.

JANE COOPER
(1924–)

Jane Cooper was born in Atlantic City, New Jersey, and grew up in Jacksonville, Florida, and Princeton, New Jersey. She received her B.A. from the University of Wisconsin and earned her M.A. from the University of Iowa, where she studied with Robert Lowell and John Berryman. She taught for many years at Sarah Lawrence College. In 1996 she was named New York State Poet. She lives in Manhattan. "My Young Mother" is from her first book, *From the Weather of Six Mornings,* which appeared in 1969. Cooper remarked in her New York State Poet acceptance speech that "poetry — like any art — exists to give everyone more life, and a people deprived of the arts will not know its own worth."

"Everything Is Plundered . . ."

Everything is plundered, betrayed, sold,
Death's great black wing scrapes the air,
Misery gnaws to the bone.
Why then do we not despair?

By day, from the surrounding woods,
cherries blow summer into town;
at night the deep transparent skies
glitter with new galaxies.

And the miraculous comes so close
to the ruined, dirty houses —
something not known to anyone at all,
but wild in our breast for centuries.

ANNA AKHMATOVA
(1889–1966)
translated by Stanley Kunitz with Max Hayward

Anna Andreyevna Akhmatova was born Anna Gorenko in Odessa, the Ukraine. Her father forced her to take a pseudonym when she was a young girl, apparently afraid she would become known as a "decadent poetess" and bring shame on the family. The name chosen, Akhmatova, was the last name of her maternal grandmother. A contemporary of Osip Mandelstam, Boris Pasternak, and Marina Tsvetaeva, Akhmatova lived through both World Wars and the Russian Revolution and suffered the execution of her ex-husband and an unofficial ban on her work from 1925 to 1940. A formal decree banning her poetry was issued during World War II, and she was expelled from the Writer's Union. Still, the Russian people loved her work, and Akhmatova was well respected for choosing to remain in her country during these difficult years. Ironically, she was eventually elected president of the very Writer's Union that once refused her. She died at the age of seventy-six in Leningrad.

Break, Break, Break

Break, break, break,
 On thy cold gray stones, O Sea!
And I would that my tongue could utter
 The thoughts that arise in me.

O, well for the fisherman's boy,
 That he shouts with his sister at play!
O, well for the sailor lad,
 That he sings in his boat on the bay!

And the stately ships go on
 To their haven under the hill;
But O, for the touch of a vanished hand,
 And the sound of a voice that is still!

Break, break, break,
 At the foot of thy crags, O Sea!
But the tender grace of a day that is dead
 Will never come back to me.

ALFRED, LORD TENNYSON
(1809–1892)

Alfred, Lord Tennyson was born in Somersby, Lincolnshire, England, and educated at Trinity College, Cambridge. According to Tennyson's own note, "Break, Break, Break" was "[m]ade in a Lincolnshire lane at five o'clock in the morning, between blossoming hedges." The poem was written in memory of Arthur Hallam, a friend of Tennyson's who died in 1833. Hallam was also the subject of Tennyson's long elegy *In Memoriam*, published in 1850. It took Tennyson seventeen years to finish his tribute, which he started within days of Hallam's death.

Leda and the Swan

A sudden blow: the great wings beating still
Above the staggering girl, her thighs caressed
By the dark webs, her nape caught in his bill,
He holds her helpless breast upon his breast.

How can those terrified vague fingers push
The feathered glory from her loosening thighs?
And how can body, laid in that white rush,
But feel the strange heart beating where it lies?

A shudder in the loins engenders there
The broken wall, the burning roof and tower
And Agamemnon dead.
                           Being so caught up,
So mastered by the brute blood of the air,
Did she put on his knowledge with his power
Before the indifferent beak could let her drop?

WILLIAM BUTLER YEATS
(1865–1939)

In his Nobel Prize acceptance speech in 1923, Yeats remarked, "Thirty years ago a number of Irish writers met together in societies and began a remorseless criticism of the literature of their country. It was their dream that by freeing it from provincialism they might win for it European recognition. I owe much to those men, still more to those who joined our movement a few years later, and when I return to Ireland these men and women, now growing old like myself, will see in this great honor a fulfillment of that dream. I in my heart know how little I might have deserved it if they had never existed." In Greek mythology, Leda was seduced by Zeus, in the form of a swan, and later gave birth to Helen of Troy and the twins Castor and Pollux.

We Wear the Mask

We wear the mask that grins and lies,
It hides our cheeks and shades our eyes, —
This debt we pay to human guile;
With torn and bleeding hearts we smile,
And mouth with myriad subtleties.

Why should the world be overwise,
In counting all our tears and sighs?
Nay, let them only see us, while
   We wear the mask.

We smile, but, O great Christ, our cries
To thee from tortured souls arise.
We sing, but oh the clay is vile
Beneath our feet, and long the mile;
But let the world dream otherwise,
   We wear the mask!

PAUL LAURENCE DUNBAR
(1872–1906)

One of the first African-American poets to achieve national recognition, Paul Laurence Dunbar was born the son of freed slaves in Dayton, Ohio. By the time he was fourteen, he had had poems published in the local newspaper, the *Dayton Herald.* Unable to afford college, Dunbar took a job as an elevator operator. When he self-published his first book in 1893, he sold it to elevator passengers for a dollar a copy. By 1895, Dunbar had moved to Chicago and met Frederick Douglass, and his poems had started to appear in national newspapers and magazines. He published *Majors and Minors,* which contained "major" poems in standard English and "minor" poems in dialect, to rave reviews in 1895. Dunbar's literary career was brief but bright, and he wrote several more collections of poems, plus short stories and novels, before he died at the age of thirty-three from tuberculosis.

November 17

#241

I like a look of Agony,
Because I know it's true —
Men do not sham Convulsion,
Nor simulate, a Throe —

The Eyes glaze once — and that is Death —
Impossible to feign
The Beads upon the Forehead
By homely Anguish strung.

EMILY DICKINSON
(1830–1886)

Dickinson's letters are often as oddly stunning as her poems. In one she wrote, "I always ran home to Awe when a child, if anything befell me. He was an awful Mother, but I liked him better than none."

Bright Star

Bright star, would I were steadfast as thou art —
   Not in lone splendor hung aloft the night
And watching, with eternal lids apart,
   Like nature's patient, sleepless Eremite,
The moving waters at their priestlike task
   Of pure ablution round earth's human shores,
Or gazing on the new soft fallen mask
   Of snow upon the mountains and the moors —
No — yet still steadfast, still unchangeable,
   Pillowed upon my fair love's ripening breast,
To feel forever its soft fall and swell,
   Awake forever in a sweet unrest,
Still, still to hear her tender-taken breath,
And so live ever — or else swoon to death.

JOHN KEATS
(1795–1821)

"Bright Star" was thought for a time to be Keats's last poem, but has now been dated no later than 1819. An earlier draft of the poem exhibits several minor variations, but the last two lines have a completely different tone and meaning from the later version: "To hear, to feel her tender-taken breath, / Half passionless, and so swoon on to death." In a letter to Fanny Brawne dated July 25, 1819, Keats reveals a similar wish: "I have two luxuries to brood over in my walks, your Loveliness and the hour of my death. Oh that I could have possession of them both in the same minute. . . . I will imagine you Venus tonight and pray, pray, pray to your star like a He[a]then."

Methought I Saw

Methought I saw my late espoused saint
    Brought to me like Alcestis from the grave,
    Whom Jove's great son to her glad husband gave,
    Rescued from Death by force, though pale and faint.
Mine, as whom washed from spot of child-bed taint
    Purification in the Old Law did save,
    And such, as yet once more I trust to have
    Full sight of her in heaven without restraint,
Came vested all in white, pure as her mind.
    Her face was veiled; yet to my fancied sight
    Love, sweetness, goodness, in her person shined
So clear as in no face with more delight.
    But O, as to embrace me she inclined,
    I waked, she fled, and day brought back my night.

JOHN MILTON
(1608–1674)

The "late espoused saint" in this poem is Katharine Woodcock, John Milton's second wife. The couple was married in 1656, after Milton had already lost his eyesight completely, thus he wishes here to glimpse "full sight of her in Heaven." She bore him one daughter in 1657, but the child did not survive, and Katherine died in childbirth in 1658. This poem was written shortly thereafter.

Sonata Pathétique

Let it be some sheets of music,
molding lamplight into the shapes
of music, and a fly, a last
survivor in this bleak November,
cross-legged on the page, humming
to itself like one of the black
notes come alive.
                    I listen
as though to overhear the strains
of a great green air it once
belonged to, archaic chord. Yet
flicking shabby wings that sparkle
in the haloing light, it sings
no plaintive tune.
                    Ah, fly,
about your composition what can
I say? But moments there are
undoubtedly so self-willed, self-
fulfilling, that the day of their
emerging glitters, little more
than grit upon their wings.
                                Then
they, outlandish, zither about
until they find some setting —
sheets of music in a lamplight —
they can be moderately at home in.
But one there was, old weather-
beat, much noted

for his feats,
like you a lone survivor, and what-
ever the measures meted out
to him, a dapper dancer, by his
clever footwork never too far
from his true estate . . . a scurry,
and you are purring in our cat.

THEODORE WEISS
(1916–2003)

Theodore Weiss was born in Reading, Pennsylvania, and educated at Muhlenberg College and Columbia University. He and his wife Renée edited and published the *Quarterly Review of Literature* for over fifty years. He was Paton Foundation Professor of Ancient and Modern Literature, Emeritus, at Princeton University.

Ah Sun-flower

Ah Sun-flower! weary of time,
Who countest the steps of the Sun,
Seeking after that sweet golden clime
Where the traveller's journey is done;

Where the Youth pined away with desire,
And the pale Virgin shrouded in snow,
Arise from their graves and aspire,
Where my Sun-flower wishes to go.

WILLIAM BLAKE
(1757–1827)

William Blake first included this poem in his book *Songs of Experience* in 1794. The poem has been set to music by dozens of composers, and it also served to inspire Allen Ginsberg's poem "Sunflower Sutra," in which he wrote, "Unholy battered old thing you were, my sunflower. O my soul, I loved you then!"

November 22

The Waltzer in the House

A sweet, a delicate white mouse,
A little blossom of a beast,
Is waltzing in the house
Among the crackers and the yeast.

O the swaying of his legs!
O the bobbing of his head!
The lady, beautiful and kind,
The blue-eyed mistress, lately wed,
Has almost laughed away her wits
To see the pretty mouse that sits
On his tiny pink behind
And swaying, bobbing, begs.

She feeds him tarts and curds,
Seed packaged for the birds,
And figs, and nuts, and cheese;
Polite as Pompadour to please
The dainty waltzer of her house,
The sweet, the delicate, the innocent white mouse.

As in a dream, as in a trance,
She loves his rhythmic elegance,
She laughs to see his bobbing dance.

STANLEY KUNITZ
(1905–)

Stanley Kunitz was born in Worcester, Massachusetts, and educated at Harvard. Among other honors, he has won the National Book Award and the Pulitzer Prize and has been the State Poet of New York. He has served two terms as the United States Poet Laureate and is a Chancellor Emeritus of the Academy of American Poets. Kunitz also founded Poets House in New York City and the Fine Arts Work Center in Provincetown, Massachusetts. He taught for many years in the graduate writing program at Columbia University.

Corridor

all those beer-bottle caps
where were they taken down busy streets
that year I cut class, in movie houses
inside the endless corridor of screens
I suddenly found myself enlarged
that moment was a wheelchair
and the days to come pushed me through distant travels —

the world's agents of freedom
entered me into their giant computer:
an alien voice sneaking into the dictionary
a dissident
perhaps a form of distance from the world

where the corridor ends, various words smolder
and a window robbed of its glass
looks out on the bureaucratic winter

BEI DAO
(1949–)
translated by David Hinton

Born Zhao Zhenkai in Bejing, China, Bei Dao is better known by his pseudonym and is one of the most prominent poets of modern China. Some of his verses were used as chants during the Tiananmen Square uprising in 1989. A former member of the Red Guard, Bei Dao had a change of heart in his teenage years and spent seven years sentenced to hard labor as a result of his denouncement of the Great Proletarian Cultural Revolution. During that time he began to write poetry and stories, though for many years he had to distribute his work informally among underground circles, unable to publish openly. He now lives in exile in Davis, California.

On a Girdle

That which her slender waist confined
Shall now my joyful temples bind;
No monarch but would give his crown,
His arms might do what this has done.

It was my heaven's extremest sphere,
The pale which held that lovely deer.
My joy, my grief, my hope, my love,
Did all within this circle move.

A narrow compass, and yet there
Dwelt all that's good and all that's fair;
Give me but what this riband bound;
Take all the rest the sun goes round!

EDMUND WALLER
(1606–1687)

Edmund Waller was born in Hertfordshire, England, and educated at Eton and King's College, Cambridge. He became a member of Parliament at the age of sixteen and had soon earned a reputation as a talented and persuasive speaker. Several years later he changed his politics and joined the Royalists in a plot to secure London for the king in 1643. He pleaded for his life so eloquently, however, that he managed to escape the death sentence that befell his co-conspirators. Exiled instead, he traveled through France, Italy, and Switzerland, eventually returning to England during the time of Oliver Cromwell. Apparently rethinking his politics yet again, Waller regained his seat in Parliament after the Restoration. "On a Girdle" was first published in 1645 in Waller's *Poems.*

To a Poor Old Woman

munching a plum on
the street a paper bag
of them in her hand

They taste good to her
They taste good
to her. They taste
good to her

You can see it by
the way she gives herself
to the one half
sucked out in her hand

Comforted
a solace of ripe plums
seeming to fill the air
They taste good to her

WILLIAM CARLOS WILLIAMS
(1883–1963)

Fellow poet Wallace Stevens once wrote that "Williams is a writer to whom writing is a grinding of glass, the polishing of a lens by means of which he hopes to be able to see clearly. His delineations are trials. They are rubbings of reality."

The Winter's Come

Sweet chestnuts brown, like soling leather, turn,
    The larch-trees, like the colour of the sun,
That paled sky in the autumn seem'd to burn.
    What a strange scene before us now does run —
Red, brown, and yellow, russet, black, and dun,
    Whitethorn, wild cherry, and the poplar bare;
The sycamore all withered in the sun.
    No leaves are now upon the birch-tree there:
All now is stript to the cold wintry air.

See, not one tree but what has lost its leaves —
    And yet the landscape wears a pleasing hue.
The winter chill on his cold bed receives
    Foliage which once hung o'er the waters blue.
Naked and bare the leafless trees repose,
    Blue-headed titmouse now seeks maggots rare,
Sluggish and dull the leaf-strewn river flows;
    That is not green, which was so through the year —
Dark chill November draweth to a close.

'Tis winter and I love to read indoors,
    When the moon hangs her crescent up on high;
While on the window shutters the wind roars,
    And storms like furies pass remorseless by,
How pleasant on a feather-bed to lie,
    Or sitting by the fire, in fancy soar
With Dante or with Milton to regions high,
    Or read fresh volumes we've not seen before,
    Or o'er old Burton's *Melancholy* pore.

JOHN CLARE
(1793–1864)

When his first book *Poems Descriptive of Rural Life and Seenery* [sic] was published in 1820, John Clare was considered something of a novelty. A reviewer in *The Monthly Magazine* wrote that, "considered as the productions of a common labourer, [the poems] are certainly remarkable, and deserving of encouragement and commendation; but, to maintain that they have the smallest pretensions to comparative excellence with the writings of others out of his own sphere, would be ridiculous and unjust, and would be trying them by a poetical law from which they ought to be exempt. We do not therefore require that they should possess the correctness and elegance of more classic bards."

The Sonogram

Only a few weeks ago, the sonogram of Jean's womb
resembled nothing so much
as a satellite-map of Ireland:

now the image
is so well-defined we can make out not only a hand
but a thumb;

on the road to Spiddal, a woman hitching a ride;
a gladiator in his net, passing judgement on the crowd.

PAUL MULDOON
(1951–)

Paul Muldoon was born in Portadown, County Armagh, in Northern Ireland. He was raised in a small village called The Moy, which is featured in many of his poems. He met fellow poets Seamus Heaney, Michael Longley, and others of the so-called Belfast Group at Queen's University. Muldoon moved to the United States in the mid-1980s. He is currently the Howard G. B. Clark '21 Professor in the Humanities at Princeton University and Professor of Poetry at Oxford University.

November 28

from *Dīwān over the Prince of Emgión*

In my dreams I heard a voice:
— Habīb, would you like this onion
Or just a slice of it?
At this I fell into great disquiet
This enigmatic question
Was the question of my life!
Did I prefer the part to the whole
Or the whole to the part
No, I wanted both
The part of the whole as well as the whole
And that this choice would involve no contradiction.

GUNNAR EKELÖF
(1907–1968)
translated by W. H. Auden and Leif Sjöberg

Swedish poet Gunnar Ekelöf was born in Stockholm and studied Oriental languages in London, England, and Uppsala, Sweden. He also studied art for a time in Paris in the 1920s. In 1932 he published his first book *Sent pa jorden (Late Arrival on Earth)*, and in 1933 he cofounded the short-lived surrealist journal *Karavan*. As a poet, Ekelöf's methods can best be described as experimental, and he often repositioned himself and his work, claiming for instance that several of his collections were not poetry at all, but more like verbal communications stripped to their essence. In 1960 he published a book called *En Moelga-Elegi (A Mölna Elegy)* in which he attempted to examine every thought, every movement of his mind in a single moment in time. In the mid-1960s, Ekelöf's project was his so-called Byzantine trilogy, which was set in the Middle Ages and based on Arabic verse forms. *Dīwān over the Prince of Emgión* is part of this trilogy, and this excerpt is taken from that larger work.

Bitter Fruit of the Tree

They said to my grandmother: "Please do not be bitter,"
When they sold her first-born and let the second die,
When they drove her husband till he took to the swamplands,
And brought him home bloody and beaten at last.
They told her, "It is better you should not be bitter,
Some must work and suffer so that we, who must, can live,
Forgiving is noble, you must not be heathen bitter;
These are your orders: you *are* not to be bitter."
And they left her shack for their porticoed house.

They said to my father: "Please do not be bitter,"
When he ploughed and planted a crop not his,
When he weatherstripped a house that he could not enter,
And stored away a harvest he could not enjoy.
They answered his questions: "It does not concern you,
It is not for you to know, it is past your understanding,
All you need know is: you must not be bitter."

STERLING A. BROWN
(1901–1989)

Sterling A. Brown was born in Washington, D.C., and educated at Williams College and Harvard University. He taught English at Howard University for forty years. Brown published his first book, *Southern Road,* in 1932, but the Great Depression made it difficult for him to find a publisher for his second collection, even though he had become a prominent figure of the Harlem Renaissance. His second collection of poems was finally published in 1975, and *The Collected Poems of Sterling A. Brown* was published in 1980. In addition to his career as a critic and professor, Brown also served as an Editor of Negro Affairs for the Federal Writers Project and a staff member of the Carnegie-Myrdal Study of the Negro, playing an important role in the preservation and promotion of African-American culture. Brown was named poet laureate of the District of Columbia in 1984. He died of leukemia in 1989.

Nightsong: City

Sleep well, my love, sleep well:
the harbour lights glaze over restless docks,
police cars cockroach through the tunnel streets

from the shanties creaking iron-sheets
violence like a bug-infested rag is tossed
and fear is immanent as sound in the wind-swung bell;

the long day's anger pants from sand and rocks;
but for this breathing night at least,
my land, my love, sleep well.

DENNIS BRUTUS
(1924–)

Poet and political activist Dennis Brutus was born in Salisbury, Southern Rhodesia (now Harare, Zimbabwe), and moved to the United States in 1971, where he was granted political asylum. A former political prisoner, Brutus has been chairman or board member of several institutions that work to abolish racism and ensure human rights in various countries, including the National Coalition to Abolish the Death Penalty and the World Campaign for the Release of South African Political Prisoners. Brutus has also been a representative to the United Nations for the International Defense and Aid Fund.

December 1
December 1

Pattern Poem with an Elusive Intruder

REINHARD DÖHL

(1934–)

Reinhard Döhl was born in Germany in 1934 and has been closely associated with the poets, writers, and artists of the Stuttgart Group. He taught at the University of Stuttgart until 1998. In addition to poetry, Döhl has also written essays, plays, radio plays, and experimental fiction and has created hypertext experiments and word art. "Pattern Poem with an Elusive Intruder" was written in 1965.

December 2

The Eel

The eel, the siren
of cold seas,
who leaves the Baltic for our seas,
our estuaries, rivers, rising
deep beneath the downstream flood,
from branch to branch, from twig to smaller twig,
ever more inward,
bent on the heart of rock,
infiltrating
muddy passages, until one day
light glancing off the chestnuts strikes
her slithering in stagnant pools,
in the ravines cascading down
from the Appennine escarpments to Romagna;
eel, torch, whiplash
arrow of Love on earth,
whom only our gullies
or dried-up Pyrenaean brooks draw back
to Edens of generation;
green spirit that finds life
where only drought and desolation sting;
spark that says that everything
begins when everything
seems charcoal, buried stump;
brief rainbow, iris,

twin to the one your lashes frame
that you set shining virginal among
the sons of men, sunk in your mire —
can you fail to see her as a sister?

EUGENIO MONTALE
(1896–1981)
translated by Jonathan Galassi

Eugenio Montale was born in Genoa, Italy, in 1896. He originally trained to be an opera singer, but after the death of his voice coach he turned to writing. His first book, *Cuttlefish Bones,* was published in 1925 and gained him a reputation as a unique poet with an experimental style. He served for ten years as the Director of the Gabinetto Vieusseux Research Library in Florence, but he was fired for refusing to join the Fascist party in 1938. After publishing two more collections of poetry, Montale became known as the founder of the hermeneutic school of Italian poetry. He won the Nobel Prize for Literature in 1975. After a long break from writing poetry, Montale experienced an intense creative outpouring that enabled him to publish four collections in the last decade of his life. He died in Milan in 1981.

Musée des Beaux Arts

About suffering they were never wrong,
The Old Masters: how well they understood
Its human position; how it takes place
While someone else is eating or opening a window or just walking
    dully along;
How, when the aged are reverently, passionately waiting
For the miraculous birth, there always must be

Children who did not specially want it to happen, skating
On a pond at the edge of the wood:
They never forgot
That even the dreadful martyrdom must run its course
Anyhow in a corner, some untidy spot
Where the dogs go on with their doggy life and the torturer's horse
Scratches its innocent behind on a tree.

In Breughel's *Icarus,* for instance: how everything turns away
Quite leisurely from the disaster; the ploughman may
Have heard the splash, the forsaken cry,
But for him it was not an important failure; the sun shone
As it had to on the white legs disappearing into the green
Water; and the expensive delicate ship that must have seen
Something amazing, a boy falling out of the sky,
Had somewhere to get to and sailed calmly on.

W. H. Auden
(1907–1973)

Born in York, England, Wystan Hugh Auden was educated at Christ Church, Oxford, where he met Christopher Isherwood and Stephen Spender, fellow writers who would become his lifelong friends. At the age of only twenty-one, Auden published his first book, which won him a reputation as the leading literary figure of the younger generation. Auden traveled widely and he eventually moved to the United States and became an American citizen. In March of 1939 in New York, he met Chester Kallman, who would become his longtime lover. Auden and Kallman lived for many years in Ischia on the Bay of Naples in Italy, then bought a house in Kirchstetten, near Vienna in Austria, though they still spent half their time in New York. Auden died of heart failure in a hotel room in Vienna in 1973. Kallman found him the next morning. This poem takes as its subject Pieter Breughel's painting "The Fall of Icarus," which hangs in the Musée des Beaux Arts in Brussels.

December 4

Eclipse of the Sun

Nothing will surprise me any more, nor be too wonderful
for belief, now that the lord upon Olympus, father Zeus,
dimmed the daylight and made darkness come upon us in the noon
and the sunshine. So limp terror has descended on mankind.
After this, men can believe in anything. They can expect
anything. Be not astonished any more, although you see
beasts of the dry land exchange with dolphins, and assume their place
in the watery pastures of the sea, and beasts who loved the hills
find the ocean's crashing waters sweeter than the bulk of land.

ARCHILOCHUS
(CA. SEVENTH CENTURY B.C.)
translated by Richmond Lattimore

The solar eclipse mentioned in this fragment by Greek poet Archilochus is one of
the items that has helped scholars date his poetry. April 6, 648, has been proposed
as the likeliest date on which Archilochus could have seen this eclipse. Other pos-
sible dates include June 27, 660, and March 14, 711. (See also: July 9.)

December 5

About an Excavation

About an excavation
a flock of bright red lanterns
has settled.

CHARLES REZNIKOFF
(1894–1976)

Charles Reznikoff was born in Brooklyn, New York, to Russian Jewish immigrant parents who had fled the pogroms after the assassination of Alexander II. Reznikoff was a precocious student, finishing grammar school at age eleven and heading off to the University of Missouri at sixteen. He earned his law degree at New York University in 1915 and was admitted to the bar, but he did not practice law for long, preferring to write. The terminology and methods of lawyering stayed with him, however, and two of his major works, *Testimony* and *Holocaust*, make use of trial transcripts and courtroom accounts. With Louis Zukofsky, Carl Rakosi, and George Oppen, Reznikoff established the Objectivist Press in the 1930s and the group worked collectively for almost fifty years. The members of this circle intentionally kept the term "objectivism" flexible and are now seen as a sort of link between Imagism and Vorticism (both Ezra Pound's creations) in the history of modern poetry. "About an Excavation" was written in 1934.

Follow Thy Fair Sun, Unhappy Shadow

Follow thy fair sun, unhappy shadow,
Though thou be black as night,
And she made all of light,
Yet follow thy fair sun, unhappy shadow.

Follow her whose light thy light depriveth,
Though here thou liv'st disgraced,
And she in heaven is placed,
Yet follow her whose light the world reviveth.

Follow those pure beams whose beauty burneth,
That so have scorchèd thee,
As thou still black must be,
Till her kind beams thy black to brightness turneth.

Follow her while yet her glory shineth:
There comes a luckless night,
That will dim all her light;
And this the black unhappy shade divineth.

Follow still since so thy fates ordainèd;
The sun must have his shade,
Till both at once do fade,
The sun still proud, the shadow still disdainèd.

THOMAS CAMPION
(1567–1620)

Thomas Campion was born in London and educated at Cambridge, Gray's Inn, and the University of Caen, from which he took a medical degree in 1605. He began practicing medicine in London in 1606, while also writing plays and poetry and composing music. "Follow Thy Fair Sun, Unhappy Shadow" was first published in 1601 in *A booke of ayres,* a collection of pieces for lute and voice. Campion never married. He died in 1620 in London, probably as a result of the plague.

In the Middle of the Road

In the middle of the road there was a stone
there was a stone in the middle of the road
there was a stone
in the middle of the road there was a stone.

I will never forget the occasion
never as long as my tired eyes stay open.
I will never forget that in the middle of the road
there was a stone
there was a stone in the middle of the road
in the middle of the road there was a stone.

CARLOS DRUMMOND DE ANDRADE
(1902–1987)
translated by Virginia de Araújo

Carlos Drummond de Andrade, born in Itabiera, Brazil, remains one of the most prominent poets of the Portuguese language. According to one critic, "[Drummond de] Andrade's lyrics are wry, tender, and teasing, the brunt of the poet's emotions held back in the belief that laughter is better than despondency. Yet for all their circumspection, [Drummond de] Andrade's lyrics do reach the very core of human experience."

That Winter

Cold ground and colder stone
Unearthed in ruined passageways,
The parodies of buildings in the snow —
Snow tossed and raging through a world
It imitates, that drives forever north
To what is rumored to be Spring.

To see the faces you had thought were put away
Forever, swept like leaves among the crowd,
Is to be drawn like them, on winter afternoons,
To avenues you saw demolished years before.
The houses still remain like monuments,
Their windows cracked, For Sale signs on the lawns.

Then grass upon those lawns again! — and dogs
In fashion twenty years ago, the streets mysterious
Through summer shade, the marvelous worlds
Within the world, each opening like a hand
And promising a constant course. — You see yourself,
A fool with smiles, one you thought dead.

And snow is raging, raging, in a darker world.

WELDON KEES
(1914–1955)

Poet, journalist, painter, and photographer, Weldon Kees also wrote fiction, played piano, and studied jazz. He published his first book of poems, *The Last Man,* in 1943, and his second, *The Fall of Magicians,* in 1947. In the mid-1950s Kees suffered from severe depression. During this period, his wife's troubles with alcoholism and paranoia increased and he eventually divorced her, after trying several times to get her to see a psychiatrist. Within a year of the publication of his final book of poems, *Poems 1947–1954,* Kees disappeared, leaving hardly a trace. His car was found abandoned near the Golden Gate Bridge in San Francisco. He had remarked to a friend that he had considered traveling to Mexico, but he had admitted to others that he had also contemplated suicide. Kees was never found and was presumed dead in 1955.

December 9

Night Feeding

Deeper than sleep but not so deep as death
I lay there sleeping and my magic head
remembered and forgot.   On first cry I
remembered and forgot and did believe.
I knew love and I knew evil:
woke to the burning song and the tree burning blind,
despair of our days had the calm milk-giver who
knows sleep, knows growth, the sex of fire and grass,
and the black snake with gold bones.

Black sleeps, gold burns;   on second cry I woke
fully and gave to feed and fed on feeding.
Gold seed, green pain, my wizards in the earth
walked through the house, black in the morning dark.
Shadows grew in my veins, my bright belief,
my head of dreams deeper than night and sleep.
Voices of all black animals crying to drink,
cries of all birth arise, simple as we,
found in the leaves, in clouds and dark, in dream,
deep as this hour, ready again to sleep.

MURIEL RUKEYSER
(1913–1980)

Born and raised in New York City, Muriel Rukeyser was educated at Vassar and Columbia, and she attended the Roosevelt Aviation School as well. Her first book, *Theory of Flight,* was chosen by Stephen Vincent Benét for the Yale Series of Younger Poets when she was twenty-two. Rukeyser was also a political activist, working for the International Labor Defense and serving as the president of PEN's American Center. As a journalist for the *Daily Worker,* she was sent to Madrid to cover the anti-fascist People's Olympiad in 1936, which was organized as an alternative to the official games in Berlin. She was evacuated when the Spanish Civil War broke out. Anne Sexton, who claimed Rukeyser as a major influence, wrote to her in 1967, "I just want to tell you again, beautiful Muriel, mother of everyone, how I cherish your words as much as the memory of your good face."

#754

My Life had stood — a Loaded Gun —
In Corners — till a Day
The Owner passed — identified —
And carried Me away —

And now We roam in Sovereign Woods —
And now We hunt the Doe —
And every time I speak for Him —
The mountains straight reply —

And do I smile, such cordial light
Upon the Valley glow —
It is as a Vesuvian face
Had let its pleasure through —

And when at Night — Our good Day done —
I guard My Master's Head —
'Tis better than the Eider-Duck's
Deep Pillow — to have shared —

To foe of His — I'm deadly foe —
None stir the second time —
On whom I lay a Yellow Eye —
Or an emphatic Thumb —

Though I than He — may longer live
He longer must — then I —
For I have but the power to kill,
Without — the power to die —

EMILY DICKINSON
(1830–1886)

R.W. Franklin dates this poem as having been written in 1864. Dickinson is thought to have written 98 poems that year. It is believed that in the previous year she wrote 295 poems.

December 11

Poor North

It is cold, the snow is deep,
the wind beats around in its cage of trees,
clouds have the look of rags torn and soiled with use,
and starlings peck at the ice.
It is north, poor north. Nothing goes right.

The man of the house has gone to work,
selling chairs and sofas in a failing store.
His wife stays home and stares from the window into the trees,
trying to recall the life she lost, though it wasn't much.
White flowers of frost build up on the glass.

It is late in the day. Brants and Canada geese are asleep
on the waters of St. Margaret's Bay.
The man and his wife are out for a walk; see how they lean
into the wind; they turn up their collars
and the small puffs of their breath are carried away.

MARK STRAND
(1934–)

Mark Strand was born in Summerside, Prince Edward Island, Canada, to American parents. He first studied painting and earned his M.F.A. from Yale, but he then went on to study poetry at the University of Iowa with Donald Justice. In addition to his own poetry, Strand has translated the work of Rafael Alberti, Carlos Drummond de Andrade, and others. He has been awarded the Pulitzer Prize, among other honors. He is a former Chancellor of the Academy of American Poets and served as United States Poet Laureate from 1990 to 1991. He currently teaches in the Committee on Social Thought at the University of Chicago.

A Farmer's Calendar

The twelfth moon for potato growing,
the first for beans, the second for eggplant.
In the third, we break the land
to plant rice in the fourth while the rains are strong.
The man ploughs, the woman plants,
and in the fifth: the harvest, and the gods are good —
an acre yields five full baskets this year.
I grind and pound the paddy, strew husks to cover the manure,
and feed the hogs with bran.
Next year, if the land is extravagant,
I shall pay the taxes for you.
In plenty or in want, there will still be you and me,
always the two of us.
Isn't that better than always prospering, alone?

VIETNAMESE FOLK POEM
translated by Nguyen Ngoc Bich

According to John Balaban, "Alongside and beneath the *nôm* [written poetry of Vietnam] and Chinese poetries, an even older poetry known as *ca dao* runs like a vast river or aquifer. This oral poetry, still sung in the countryside, originated perhaps thousands of years ago in the prayers and songs of the Mon-Khmer wet-rice cultures to which the Vietnamese are tied. The word-stock of *ca dao* is native, bearing few loan words from Chinese. It is a lyric poetry — not narrative — and its power lies in its allusive imagery and brief music. Its references are to nature, not to books; to delta fish and fowl, to creatures of the field and forest, to wind and moon, to village life. It belongs to the farmers of Viêt Nam, which is to say that it belongs to most Vietnamese because eighty percent live, as ever, in the countryside." "A Farmer's Calendar" is an example of this kind of folk poetry, sung by peasants and minstrels at rural festivals, and handed down through oral traditions.

Madam and Her Madam

I worked for a woman,
She wasn't mean —
But she had a twelve-room
House to clean.

Had to get breakfast,
Dinner, and supper, too —
Then take care of her children
When I got through.

Wash, iron, and scrub,
Walk the dog around —
It was too much,
Nearly broke me down.

I said, Madam,
Can it be
You trying to make a
Pack-horse out of me?

She opened her mouth.
She cried, Oh, no!
You know, Alberta,
I love you so!

I said, Madam,
That may be true —
But I'll be dogged
If I love you!

LANGSTON HUGHES
(1902–1967)

While at Yaddo during the summer of 1943, Langston Hughes began a series of poems featuring a character named Madam Alberta K. Johnson who lives in Harlem. In "Madam and Her Madam" Alberta confronts her employer, and in other poems such as "Madam's Calling Cards," "Madam and the Phone Company," and "Madam and the Rent Man," she takes on a host of other folks who threaten to oppress or take advantage of her in various ways. In "Madam's Calling Cards," she says to a printer who wants to know if he should print her name in Roman or in Old English typestyle, "There's nothing foreign / to my pedigree: / Alberta K. Johnson — / American that's me."

The Voice

A voice, a voice from so far away
It no longer makes the ears tingle.
A voice like a muffled drum
Still reaches us clearly.

Though it seems to come from the grave
It speaks only of summer and spring.
It floods the body with joy.
It lights the lips with a smile.

I listen. It is simply a human voice
Which passes over the noise of life and its battles
The crash of thunder and the murmur of gossip.

And you? Don't you hear it?
It says "The pain will soon be over"
It says "The happy season is near."

Don't you hear it?

ROBERT DESNOS
(1900–1945)
translated by William Kulik with Carole Frankel

Robert Desnos was born in Paris, France. As a member of the French surrealist movement, Desnos was associated with André Breton, Louis Aragon, and Paul Éluard until he gradually moved away from the group in the 1930s. He worked as a journalist and published several essays (under pseudonyms) in which he mocked the Nazis, who had by that time invaded France. He was also a member of the French Resistance. Desnos was arrested by the Gestapo and sent to Buchenwald in 1944. He died in a concentration camp in Terezine, Czechoslovakia, in 1945.

from "Auguries of Innocence"

The wild deer wandring here & there
Keeps the Human Soul from Care
The Beggers Dog & Widows Cat
Feed them & thou wilt grow fat
He who shall hurt the little Wren
Shall never be beloved by Men
He who the Ox to wrath has movd
Shall never be by Woman lovd
He who torments the Chafers sprite
Weaves a Bower in endless Night
The wanton Boy that kills the Fly
Shall feel the Spiders enmity
The Catterpiller on the Leaf
Repeats to thee thy Mothers grief
Kill not the Moth nor Butterfly
For the Last Judgment draweth nigh
The Bat that flits at close of Eve
Has left the Brain that wont Believe
The Owl that calls upon the Night
Speaks the Unbelievers fright
The Gnat that sings his Summers song
Poison gets from Slanders tongue
The poison of the Snake & Newt
Is the sweat of Envys Foot

The Poison of the Honey Bee
Is the Artists Jealousy
A Riddle or the Crickets Cry
Is to Doubt a fit Reply
The Emmets Inch & Eagles Mile
Make Lame Philosophy to smile
He who Doubts from what he sees
Will neer Believe do what you Please
If the Sun & Moon should doubt
Theyd immediately Go out

WILLIAM BLAKE
(1757–1827)

Though it has been dated to 1800–1803, William Blake's long poem "Auguries of Innocence" was first published in 1863 in a volume called *Life of William Blake.* The poem, left unfinished and in manuscript at the time of Blake's death, was edited for that volume by Dante Gabriel Rossetti. Another copy was discovered and edited by Mr. B. J. Pickering, who published his version in 1866. This excerpt represents about a quarter of the poem, which opens with the well-known lines: "To see a World in a Grain of Sand / And a Heaven in a Wild Flower / Hold Infinity in the palm of your hand / And Eternity in an hour."

On Time

Fly envious Time, till thou run out thy race,
Call on the lazy leaden-stepping hours,
Whose speed is but the heavy plummet's pace;
And glut thy self with what thy womb devours,
Which is no more than what is false and vain,
And merely mortal dross;
So little is our loss,
So little is thy gain.

For when as each thing bad thou has entombed,
And last of all, thy greedy self consumed,
Then long Eternity shall greet our bliss
With an individual kiss;
And Joy shall overtake us as a flood,
When every thing that is sincerely good
And perfectly divine,
With Truth, and Peace, and Love shall ever shine
About the supreme Throne
Of him, t' whose happy-making sight alone,
When once our heav'nly-guided soul shall climb,
Then all this earthy grossness quit,
Attired with stars, we shall for ever sit,
Triumphing over Death, and Chance, and thee, O Time.

JOHN MILTON
(1608–1674)

In the Trinity manuscript copy of "On Time" a subtitle reading "To be set on a clock case" is crossed out. The composition of the poem has been dated to the early 1630s. Plummets are the weights in a clock that cause it to tick.

The Pool

Are you alive?
I touch you.
You quiver like a sea-fish.
I cover you with my net.
What are you — banded one?

H. D.
(1886–1961)

"The Pool" was first published in *Poetry* magazine in 1915, probably at the suggestion of Ezra Pound, who sent H. D.'s poems to the editor, Harriet Monroe. Amy Lowell also included it in her influential anthology *Some Imagist Poets* in that same year.

Buy: 11/2 x 11/2
3 Photograph Albums

$600,000

Checking for
to us..."

"They came
(and)
opening
"alone, as never
before" ending"

Lucifer in Starlight

On a starred night Prince Lucifer uprose.
Tired of his dark dominion swung the fiend
Above the rolling ball in cloud part screened,
Where sinners hugged their specter of repose.
Poor prey to his hot fit of pride were those.
And now upon his western wing he leaned,
Now his huge bulk o'er Afric's sands careened,
Now the black planet shadowed Arctic snows.
Soaring through wider zones that pricked his scars
With memory of the old revolt from Awe,
He reached a middle height, and at the stars,
Which are the brain of heaven, he looked, and sank.
Around the ancient track marched, rank on rank,
The army of unalterable law.

GEORGE MEREDITH
(1828–1909)

George Meredith was born in Portsmith, Hampshire, England, and educated in Germany. He was apprenticed to a lawyer in 1845, but after five years he found that the legal profession did not suit him. Meredith began writing poetry in his early twenties, and though he became better known as a novelist, he always preferred his verses and considered novel-writing a solution to his financial troubles. He worked in publishing and as a literary critic and journalist, and he continued to contribute to various periodicals until shortly before his death in 1909. "Lucifer in Starlight" is from *Poems and Lyrics of the Joy of Earth,* first published in 1883.

December 19

Stains on the Wall

Before the night falls completely over us

Let's study the stains on the wall:
Some appear to be plants
Others look like mythological animals.

Hippogriphs,
     dragons,
          salamanders.

But the most extraordinary of all
Are those that seem to be atomic explosions.

In the cinematography of the wall
The soul sees what the body does not:

Kneeling men
Mothers with creatures in their arms
Statues on horseback
Priests lifting the host
Genitalia coming together.

But the most mysterious of all
Beyond a doubt
Are those that seem to be atomic explosions.

NICANOR PARRA
(1914–)
translated by Miller Williams

Poet and scientist Nicanor Parra was born in Chilla, Chile, and studied mathematics and physics at the University of Chile, going on to graduate study at Brown University and Oxford, where he studied cosmology. He taught theoretical physics at the University of Chile for many years, and he has been called an "antipoet" for his refusal to consider poetry an art of the elite. Mark Strand has written of his work, "Parra's poems are hallucinatory and violent, and at the same time factual. The well-timed disclosure of events — personal or political — gives his poems a cumulative, mounting energy and power that we have come to expect from only the best fiction."

Sea Grapes

That sail which leans on light,
tired of islands,
a schooner beating up the Caribbean

for home, could be Odysseus,
home-bound on the Aegean;
that father and husband's

longing, under gnarled sour grapes, is
like the adulterer hearing Nausicaa's name
in every gull's outcry.

This brings nobody peace. The ancient war
between obsession and responsibility
will never finish and has been the same

for the sea-wanderer or the one on shore
now wriggling on his sandals to walk home,
since Troy sighed its last flame,

and the blind giant's boulder heaved the trough
from whose ground-swell the great hexameters come
to the conclusions of exhausted surf.

The classics can console. But not enough.

DEREK WALCOTT
(1930–)

Derek Walcott was born in Castries, St. Lucia, in the West Indies. He received his B.A. and D.Litt. from the University of the West Indies. In 1992 he won the Nobel Prize for literature, and he has won the Obie award for Best Foreign Play, among other honors. He teaches Creative Writing at Boston University each fall and spends the rest of his time in St. Lucia. "Sea Grapes" is from his 1976 collection of the same name.

Jewish Immigrant, Michigan, 1885

The boy, alone in a new landscape on the Sabbath,
loafs along a dirt road when he spots,
amidst mustardy pink grasses, tall
and undulating, a glint, a maverick light,
and stoops for its source among the stalks: a knife,
wood handle smooth against his palm,
grain oiled by long handling, blade
tarnished but true.

        Though he knows, *Carry nothing
on the Sabbath,* he wants the way he'll want only
a few times in his life; hurting with want
for some improbable, immanent change, something
his, as he turns the knife in his hands and turns it;
warms it until his own heat comes back.

He knows what his father would say — *Throw it back* —
so he flings it away, watches it twirl as it falls,
like a star arcing over the stirring grasses.
And yet he cannot leave it at that: he must run
to find it.
        When next he throws the knife, he throws it
straight, blade burying in the rutted road.
Again, he'll pick it up, again hurl it,
seeking and finding the object of desire, following
what he's found until it takes him home.

SANDY SOLOMON
(1948–)

Sandy Solomon was born in Baltimore, Maryland, and worked in Washington, D.C., as an advocate for minority and low-income residents in urban areas before becoming a freelance writer. She lives in Princeton, New Jersey.

Danse Macabre

The dresses of my childhood
dance around me
without heads
without legs
without arms —
just exuberant, transparent
Scarlatti and Mozart fabrics,
just jabberwockies,
Klee and Miro designs . . .
My dresses dance
decapitated
amputated.

NINA CASSIAN
(1924–)

Nina Cassian was born Renée Annie Stefanescu in Galati, Romania. She has published more than fifty books, including fiction and works for children. She is also a classical composer and has worked as a translator, film critic, and journalist. In 1985 Cassian came to the United States to teach creative writing at New York University. This visit turned into a permanent stay when she found out that a friend in Romania had been tortured to death after the police found his diary, which contained some of her poems. The United States granted her request for political asylum and she lives on Roosevelt Island in New York City.

Sheep in Fog

The hills step off into whiteness.
People or stars
Regard me sadly, I disappoint them.

The train leaves a line of breath.
O slow
Horse the color of rust,

Hooves, dolorous bells ——
All morning the
Morning has been blackening,

A flower left out.
My bones hold a stillness, the far
Fields melt my heart.

They threaten
To let me through to a heaven
Starless and fatherless, a dark water.

SYLVIA PLATH
(1932–1963)

Born in Boston, Massachusetts, Sylvia Plath committed suicide in London in 1963. She was married to the British poet, Ted Hughes, and during her short life completed two collections of poems and one novel. "Sheep in Fog" is from her posthumously published book, *Ariel.*

The Oxen

Christmas Eve, and twelve of the clock.
  "Now they are all on their knees,"
An elder said as we sat in a flock
  By the embers in hearthside ease.

We pictured the meek mild creatures where
  They dwelt in their strawy pen,
Nor did it occur to one of us there
  To doubt they were kneeling then.

So fair a fancy few would weave
  In these years! Yet, I feel,
If someone said on Christmas Eve,
  "Come; see the oxen kneel,

"In the lonely barton by yonder coomb
  Our childhood used to know,"
I should go with him in the gloom,
  Hoping it might be so.

THOMAS HARDY
(1840–1928)

Thomas Hardy's first book of poetry appeared when he was already fifty-eight years old. He wrote nearly one thousand poems from 1898 until his death in 1928, hitting what some consider his poetic prime in his seventies. At the time of his burial, his ashes were set before mourners George Bernard Shaw, Rudyard Kipling, and British Prime Minister Stanley Baldwin, while crowds of admirers stood outside Westminster Abbey in the rain. He was interred in Poet's Corner, except for his heart, which had been removed to a tin and buried separately at Stinsford, near Hardy's birthplace in the Dorset countryside.

The Burning Babe

As I in hoary winter's night stood shivering in the snow,
Surprised I was with sudden heat, which made my heart to glow;
And lifting up a fearful eye to view what fire was near,
A pretty Babe all burning bright, did in the air appear,
Who scorchèd with excessive heat, such floods of tears did shed,
As though His floods should quench His flames which with His
    tears were fed;
Alas! quoth He, but newly born, in fiery heats I fry,
Yet none approach to warm their hearts or feel my fire but I!
My faultless breast the furnace is, the fuel wounding thorns,
Love is the fire, and sighs the smoke, the ashes shame and scorns;
The fuel Justice layeth on, and Mercy blows the coals,
The metal in this furnace wrought are men's defiled souls,
For which, as now on fire I am to work them to their good,
So will I melt into a bath to wash them in My blood:
With this He vanished out of sight, and swiftly shrunk away,
And straight I callèd unto mind that it was Christmas-day.

ROBERT SOUTHWELL
(1561–1595)

Robert Southwell was born in Harsham, Norwich, England. He took Jesuit orders
in Rome in 1585 and returned to England in 1586 despite a law that forbade him, as
an English-born Catholic priest, to remain in the country more than forty days, on
pain of death. In 1592 Southwell was arrested while saying mass and was sent to the
Tower. He was then executed, as the law required, at the age of thirty-four. He was
beatified by the Catholic Church in 1929 and canonized in 1970. Ben Jonson report-
edly remarked that he would be willing to destroy many of his own poems if he only
could have been the author of "The Burning Babe."

The Pigeon

Grain-fed belly, come down over here,
Saintly gray pigeon belly . . .

The way a storm rains, walks on broad talons,
Floats over, takes over the lawn,
Where first you rebounded
With the charming cooings of the thunder.

Show us soon your rainbow throat . . .

Then fly away obliquely, in a great flapping of wings
that pull, pleat, or rent the silken cover of the clouds.

FRANCIS PONGE
(1899–1988)
translated by Beth Archer

Poet and Ponge translator Robert Bly has remarked that "Ponge doesn't try to be
cool, distant, or objective, nor does he 'let the object speak for itself.' His poems are
funny, his vocabulary immense, his personality full of quirks, and yet the poem
remains somewhere in the place where the senses join the object."

December 27

The Snow-Storm

Announced by all the trumpets of the sky,
Arrives the snow, and, driving o'er the fields,
Seems nowhere to alight: the whited air
Hides hills and woods, the river, and the heaven,
And veils the farm-house at the garden's end.
The sled and traveller stopped, the courier's feet
Delayed, all friends shut out, the housemates sit
Around the radiant fireplace, enclosed
In a tumultuous privacy of storm.

  Come see the north wind's masonry.
Out of an unseen quarry evermore
Furnished with tile, the fierce artificer
Curves his white bastions with projected roof
Round every windward stake, or tree, or door.
Speeding, the myriad-handed, his wild work
So fanciful, so savage, nought cares he
For number or proportion. Mockingly,
On coop or kennel he hangs Parian wreaths;
A swan-like form invests the hidden thorn;
fills up the farmer's lane from wall to wall,
Maugre the farmer's sighs; and at the gate
A tapering turret overtops the work.
And when his hours are numbered, and the world
Is all his own, retiring, as he were not,

Leaves, when the sun appears, astonished Art
To mimic in slow structures, stone by stone,
Built in an age, the mad wind's night-work,
The frolic architecture of the snow.

RALPH WALDO EMERSON
(1803–1882)

Born in Boston, Massachusetts, Ralph Waldo Emerson achieved the rank of class poet at Harvard, but only after the title had been turned down by six other candidates. After suffering the loss of his first wife in 1831, Emerson remarried in 1834, but tragedy struck again when he lost his five-year-old son, Waldo. Emerson remained dissatisfied with many of his attempts at verse, lamenting, "though days go smoothly enough they do not bring me in their fine timely wallets the alms I incessantly beg of them. Where are their melodies, where the unattainable words." Nevertheless, as a poet, essayist, and lecturer he was held in such esteem that when he divulged his favorite books in a speech in Washington, D.C., bookstores all the way to Boston sold every last copy.

The Magi

Now as at all times I can see in the mind's eye,
In their stiff, painted clothes, the pale unsatisfied ones
appear and disappear in the blue depth of the sky
With all their ancient faces like rain-beaten stones,
And all their helms of silver hovering side by side,
And all their eyes still fixed, hoping to find once more,
Being by Calvary's turbulence unsatisfied,
The uncontrollable mystery on the bestial floor.

WILLIAM BUTLER YEATS
(1865–1935)

"The Magi" is from W. B. Yeats's book *Responsibilities,* published in 1914. In its "Introductory Rhymes," which were included as a sort of preface or epigraph, he apologizes for his "boyish lips" and indulgent fancy: "Pardon that for a barren passion's sake, / Although I have come close on forty-nine, / I have no child, I have nothing but a book, / Nothing but that to prove your blood and mine." Yeats also included a "Closing Rhyme" in which he compared his poems to the "post the passing dogs defile."

December 29

Cities & Eyes (3)

After a seven days' march through woodland, the traveler directed toward Baucis cannot see the city and yet he has arrived. The slender stilts that rise from the ground at a great distance from one another and are lost above the clouds support the city. You climb them with ladders. On the ground the inhabitants rarely show themselves: having already everything they need up there, they prefer not to come down. Nothing of the city touches the earth except those long flamingo legs on which it rests and, when the days are sunny, a pierced, angular shadow that falls on the foliage.

There are three hypotheses about the inhabitants of Baucis: that they hate the earth; that they respect it so much they avoid all contact; that they love it as it was before they existed and with spyglasses and telescopes aimed downward they never tire of examining it, leaf by leaf, stone by stone, ant by ant, contemplating with fascination their own absence.

ITALO CALVINO
(1923–1985)
translated by William Weaver

Italo Calvino was born in Santiago de Las Vegas, Cuba, and grew up in San Remo, Italy. He was elected to the prominent avant-garde group Oulipo (a French acronym for the Workshop of Potential Literature) in 1973. "Cities and Eyes (3)" comes from *Invisible Cities*, a work of fiction — or some would say prose poems — that tells of an imaginary conversation between Marco Polo and Kublai Khan in which Polo describes fifty-five cities in Kublai Khan's kingdoms in fantastic detail. Calvino died after a series of strokes in September 1985.

December 30

She Tells Her Love While Half Asleep

She tells her love while half asleep,
    In the dark hours,
        With half-words whispered low:
As Earth stirs in her winter sleep
    And puts out grass and flowers
        Despite the snow,
        Despite the falling snow.

ROBERT GRAVES
(1895–1985)

English poet Robert Graves was born in Wimbledon, near London, and educated at St. John's College, Oxford, on a scholarship. He left Oxford after one year, however, to enlist in the Royal Welsh Fusiliers. By the time Graves ended his military career, he had been wounded several times, but he had also managed to publish his first three volumes of poetry. He met Laura Riding in 1926 and separated from his wife the following year. His relationship with Riding had a profound effect on his writing, as it did on hers. They moved to Majorca, Spain, and founded their own press, collaboratively editing their own magazine, reading each other's poems, and sounding out their theories of poetics. They fled Spain at the onset of the Civil War. After coming to the United States they separated, and Graves soon met Beryl Hodge, who would remain his companion until his death in 1985. By then he had published more than 140 books and W. H. Auden had already dubbed him England's greatest living poet.

Mirabeau Bridge

Under the Mirabeau Bridge there flows the Seine
    Must I recall
  Our loves recall how then
After each sorrow joy came back again

      Let night come on bells end the day
      The days go by me still I stay

Hands joined and face to face let's stay just so
    While underneath
  The bridge of our arms shall go
Weary of endless looks the river's flow

      Let night come on bells end the day
      The days go by me still I stay

All love goes by as water to the sea
    All love goes by
  How slow life seems to me
How violent the hope of love can be

      Let night come on bells end the day
      The days go by me still I stay

The days the weeks pass by beyond our ken
    Neither time past
  Nor love comes back again
Under the Mirabeau Bridge there flows the Seine

      Let night come on bells end the day
      The days go by me still I stay

GUILLAUME APOLLINAIRE
(1880–1918)
translated by Richard Wilbur

A major figure of French Surrealism, Guillaume Apollinaire was born Wilhelm Apollinaris de Krostrowitzky in Rome. He grew up in Monte Carlo and was educated in Nice, Cannes, and Germany. He published several books considered scandalous at the time for their explicit sexual content. He had a reputation as a thief and was once detained as a suspect in the theft of the Mona Lisa. During World War I he enlisted in the French army and suffered a serious head wound that resulted in a permanent hole in his skull. He died in 1918 in the Parisian influenza epidemic.

Acknowledgments

Special thanks to Shanna Compton for her skillful work on the notes. This book would not be what it is without her. Thanks, too, to Michael Moore who first approached me with the idea. Chip, Robin, Kris, and Mary at Steerforth provided invaluable support and expertise. And finally, thanks to Jim Peck who, as always, helped in the best of ways when help was needed.

Every effort has been made to trace the ownership of all copywrited material and to secure the necessary permissions to reprint these selections. In the event of any question arising as to the use of any material, the editor and the publisher, while expressing regret for any inadvertent error, will be happy to make the necessary correction in future printings. Thanks are due to the following for permission to reprint the copywrited material listed below:

Julie Agoos, "Overnight" was originally published in *The New Yorker*. Reprinted by permission of Julie Agoos.

Bella Akhmadulina, "Silence," translated by David Halpern. Reprinted with permission from *The New York Review of Books*. Copyright © 1973 NYREV, Inc.

Yehuda Amichai, "My Mother Once Told Me" from *The Selected Poetry of Yehuda Amichai*, translated and edited by Chana Bloch and Stephen Mitchell. Copyright © 1996 by The Regents of the University of California.

A. R. Ammons, "The City Limits" from *The Selected Poems, Expanded Edition* by A. R. Ammons. Copyright © 1971 by A. R. Ammons. Used by permission of W. W. Norton & Company, Inc.

Guillaume Apollinaire, "Mirabeau Bridge," translated by Richard Wilbur, from *Random House Book of Twentieth-Century French Poetry* by Paul Auster, copyright 1943 by Editions Gallimard. Used by permission of Random House, Inc.

Archilochus of Paros, "Eclipse of the Sun," translated by Richmond Lattimore from *Greek Lyrics*, R. Lattimore, ed. Copyright © 1949, 1955, 1960 by Richard Lattimore. Reprinted by permission of The University of Chicago Press.

W. H. Auden, "Musée des Beaux Arts," copyright © 1940 and renewed 1968 by W. H. Auden, from *W. H. Auden: The Collected Poems*, by W. H. Auden. Used by permission of Random House, Inc.

Mary Jo Bang, "The Star's Whole Secret," originally published in *The New Yorker* on June 1, 1998. Reprinted by permission of Mary Jo Bang.

Imamu Amiri Baraka, "Preface to a Twenty Volume Suicide Note." Reprinted by permission of Sterling Lord Literistic, Inc. Copyright by Amiri Baraka.

Index of the Poems